ADLERIAN COUNSELING AND PSYCHOTHERAPY

ADLERIAN COUNSELING AND PSYCHOTHERAPY

DON C. DINKMEYER

Communication and Motivation Training Institute
Coral Springs, Florida

W. L. PEW

DON C. DINKMEYER, JR.

Brooks/Cole Publishing Company
Monterey, California
A Division of Wadsworth Publishing Company, Inc.

Printed in the United States of America

10 9 8 7 6 5 4 3 2

Library of Congress Cataloging in Publication Data

Dinkmeyer, Don C.
    Adlerian counseling and psychotherapy.

    Includes bibliographical references and index.
    1. Psychotherapy.   2. Counseling.   3. Adler,
Alfred, 1870–1937.   4. Dreikurs, Rudolf, 1897–
1972.   I. Pew, W. L., joint author.   II. Dink-
meyer, Don, joint author.   III. Title.
RC4805.D56   616.8'914   78-17399
ISBN 0-8185-0264-9

Acquisition Editor: *Claire Verduin*
Production Editor: *Fiorella Ljunggren*
Interior Design: *Jamie S. Brooks*
Cover Design: *Katherine Minerva*
Typesetting: *David R. Sullivan Company, Dallas, Texas*

To Rudolf and Tee Dreikurs,
our teachers and friends,
who have fostered and stimulated
the growth of Adlerian psychology
throughout the world;
and
to our wives and mothers.

PREFACE

Although it is now more than 40 years since the death of Alfred Adler and 7 years since the death of his most influential disciple, Rudolf Dreikurs, their ideas continue to dramatically influence the fields of psychology, psychotherapy, and counseling. The North American Society of Adlerian Psychology steadily grows in membership. Adlerian institutes, societies, and family-education centers are increasing in number and in the kinds of services they provide throughout the United States and Canada. There is a resurgence of interest in Adlerian psychology in Europe as well as in other parts of the world.

This book, by giving the reader an understanding of Adlerian theory and practice, is meant to satisfy this growing interest. It is designed for use in counselor-education programs and in the training of psychologists, social workers, and psychiatrists interested in the basics of Adlerian counseling and psychotherapy.

We begin with a brief review of the history and current status of Adlerian counseling and psychotherapy. After presenting the basic structure of Adlerian theory, in Chapter 3 we discuss the development of personality and the life style—a unique Adlerian concept that finds practical application in the therapeutic process. Chapter 4 deals with the Adlerian understanding of psychopathology. Chapters 5, 6, and 7 are designed to acquaint the reader with the actual process and techniques of Adlerian counseling and psychotherapy. Ensuing chapters review the application of Adlerian psychology to child and adolescent counseling, to group procedures, to parent and teacher education and consultation, and to family and marriage counseling.

The writing of a book often occurs over a period of years. This text was conceived while the senior author was working with Rudolf Dreikurs and was begun with Dreikurs' encouragement and support. Sharing Dreikurs' wisdom and techniques with the readers is a personally rewarding experience. W. L. Pew, M.D., a student of Rudolf Dreikurs, and Don Dinkmeyer, Jr., have collaborated in this effort to bring the ideas of Adler and Dreikurs to the attention of the counseling profession. The book also incorporates the thinking of contemporary Adlerians such as Bernard Shulman, Harold Mosak, Kurt Adler, Heinz and Rowena Ansbacher, and Walter O'Connell. Also reflected in the content is the senior author's intensive training at the Alfred Adler Institute of Chicago with Rudolf Dreikurs, Bernard Shulman, Harold Mosak, Bernice Grunwald, Bina Rosenberg, and Raymond Corsini. It is virtually impossible to list all the inspiring colleagues and teachers who have contributed to this book through their constructive criticism and encouragement and to express our appreciation to all of them.

We are particularly indebted to Edmund Allen of the University of South Florida, Bill Hillman of the University of Arizona, Raymond Lowe of the University of Oregon, Ken Matheny of Georgia State University, Thomas McSweeney of the University of San Francisco, Marvin Moore of Colorado State University, Peter Rocheotes of East Texas State University, Jimmy Walker of the University of Texas at El Paso, and Mel Witmer of Ohio University, who reviewed the manuscript and offered many helpful suggestions. Special thanks to Terry Hendrix and Claire Verduin of Brooks/Cole for their encouragement and support during the book's germination. Our appreciation to Fiorella Ljunggren, also of Brooks/Cole, for her excellent editorial work.

Just before this book was published, we were saddened by the death of our colleague, coauthor, and friend, Bill Pew. We rejoice that his latest thinking on Adlerian psychotherapy, marriage and family counseling, and psychopathology is permanently preserved for the professional community.

Don C. Dinkmeyer
Don C. Dinkmeyer, Jr.

CONTENTS

CHAPTER 13
FAMILY THERAPY   220

CHAPTER 14
MARRIAGE COUNSELING   232

CHAPTER 1

INTRODUCTION TO ADLERIAN COUNSELING AND PSYCHOTHERAPY

Alfred Adler's Individual Psychology is one of the oldest, and still most relevant, schools of psychological thought. It emerged during Adler's nine-year association with Freud as an alternative to Freud's approach. Over the years, Adler's system, with its practical applications to psychotherapy and counseling, has continued to experience steady growth after a period of neglect that followed Adler's death in 1937. Today, Individual Psychology is acknowledged as the precursor of many current systems of thought and approaches to psychotherapy. Its impact can be detected in countless areas—among them, child rearing, marriage and family therapy, and school counseling.

A BRIEF BIOGRAPHY

Alfred Adler was born on February 7, 1870, in Penzing, a suburb of Vienna. He was the second of six children. His father was a middle-class Jewish merchant, and his mother was a housewife. In his early childhood, Adler suffered from poor health and was run over by a vehicle. As he grew older, his health steadily improved. His interest in medicine, which arose when he was very young, led to a medical degree at the prestigious University of Vienna in 1895.

Adler became a practicing physician in Vienna. In the fall of 1902, Freud invited him to join his discussion groups, which later grew into the Vienna Psychoanalytic Society, of which Adler became president in 1910. Adler resigned from the society one year later, in part because of Freud's

1

pressures for uniformity and strict allegiance to his theory. It should be noted that, contrary to popular notion, Adler was not a "disciple" of Freud (he was never psychoanalyzed by him); he was a colleague, and his ideas were often in conflict with Freud's.

After he severed his ties with psychoanalysis, Adler devoted himself to developing his own system of thought. In 1912, the Society for Individual Psychology was born and counted among its members a large number of those who had belonged to Freud's Psychoanalytic Society and who had left when Adler did. After participating in World War I as a medical officer, Adler created numerous child-guidance clinics in the Vienna public schools to serve as training vehicles for teachers, social workers, physicians, and other professionals. Adler demonstrated his techniques in front of groups of professionals—an instructional idea that had never been used before. In spite of their revolutionary nature, the guidance clinics grew rapidly in Vienna and throughout Europe, and, at one point, there were nearly 50 of them. But soon political and other obstacles began interfering with the growth of Adler's psychology in Europe.

In 1926, Adler made his first lecture tour in the United States. After that, his visits became more and more frequent, and eventually, in 1935, he fled Europe and settled in the United States, where he taught and lectured extensively. His death in 1937 in Aberdeen, Scotland, while on a lecture tour, left his disciples, many of whom had fled the political unrest of Europe, to carry on his work.

ADLER'S LEGACY

Adler published more than 300 books and articles.[1] Countless lectures and public demonstrations attest to his commitment to a theory that would be useful not only to professionals but to the public at large. Those who inherited Adler's legacy have continued to honor his commitment by being acutely aware of the needs of the community and by keeping alive Adler's practice of public demonstration, parent- and family-education centers, and the dissemination of useful, practical information.

After Adler's death, there was a decline of interest in his work. The Nazi regime and World War II were partly responsible, causing his disciples to scatter across the European continent and beyond. Many of them came to the United States. Here they found extreme resistance to Adler's work, which was seen as the antithesis of Freudian psychology. This erroneous perception of Adler's ideas here, the destruction of Adler's accomplishments in Europe, and the preeminence of the Freudian approach were the main causes of the

---

[1]Of special interest to counselors and psychotherapists are *The Practice and Theory of Individual Psychology* (Patterson, N.J.: Littlefield, Adams, 1958); *What Life Should Mean to You* (New York: Capricorn, 1958); *Understanding Human Nature* (Greenwich, Conn.: Fawcett, 1969); and *The Neurotic Constitution* (New York: Arno, 1972).

temporary decline in the recognition of Adler's contributions and in the number of his followers.

Rudolf Dreikurs

Rudolf Dreikurs, a prolific writer and the founder of the Alfred Adler Institute in Chicago, nurtured the growth of Adlerian psychology in the United States during the period of heavy psychoanalytic dominance. His dream was the establishment of Adlerian child-guidance centers throughout the world. Among the numerous contributions he made to Individual Psychology until his death in 1972, especially important are his understanding of children and his unique insights into the counseling process.

Inspired by the basic Adlerian principle that all behavior has a purpose, Dreikurs formulated the four goals of misbehavior in children. He saw in attention, power, revenge seeking, and display of inadequacy the explanation for all of a child's disruptive behavior. By categorizing misbehaviors in terms of their goals, Dreikurs offered parents and teachers an invaluable tool for dealing more effectively with children's mistaken efforts.

Dreikurs also made some interesting contributions to the area of counseling. He stressed that the interview with a client is a valuable opportunity for the counselor to show that he or she is not perfect and to offer insights not as indisputable truths but as tentative hypotheses. In Dreikurs' opinion, the counselor should look at each interview as if it might be the last. Anytime the client leaves the interview without having learned something, the counselor has failed. Dreikurs would begin each session by asking the client "What do you remember from last time?" stressing the client's responsibility for his or her own change and the continuity from session to session. It was Dreikurs who first introduced the multiple-therapist procedure to psychotherapy as an excellent teaching method for both therapist and client.

ADLER, A MAN AHEAD OF HIS TIME

Adler left a wealth of ideas and techniques that still serve the counseling profession well. His son, Kurt, a practitioner in New York City, has gathered together what he considers to be the most significant examples of his father's pioneering contributions to psychotherapy and counseling (Adler, n.d.). Here are just a few such contributions.

Alfred Adler was the first to work publicly with clients by practicing group and family therapy in front of large audiences of doctors, teachers, parents, and others. He used these demonstration settings so that other professionals could learn by observing the counseling interaction at work. No other practitioner had ever risked or shared as much as Adler did through these public demonstrations.

Neurotic symptoms were explained by Adler as "safeguards" against threats to one's self-image and against the challenges of the outside world. Freud, instead, saw neurotic symptoms as defense mechanisms against the repression of internal, instinctual drives. Freud's interpretation of neurotic symptoms was later amended by his daughter, Anna, who recognized the existence of defenses against external, and not only internal, demands. The existence of such defenses was first recognized in children and later extended to include the whole gamut of safeguarding devices that are employed by humans of all ages.

Adler suggested that a child's bedwetting problem has a psychological, as well as a physiological, component. Contemporary research suggests that many instances of bedwetting are in fact physiologically based but that the physiological element alone is not sufficient to explain the problem. To thousands of pediatricians who rarely find a physiological cause for bedwetting, Adler's understanding of the interaction between psychic and physiological factors is still valid today, just as it was more than 70 years ago.

In the 1920s, Adler predicted that two more generations would pass before women would achieve true equality. Women's successful struggle for equality in this last decade attests to the accuracy of this prediction. Adler didn't see much difference between domination by males and domination by tyrannical regimes like those that oppressed Europe before and during his lifetime. Instead of indulging in the popular contemporary misconception of women's inferiority, Adler stressed that inequality makes loving relationships and mutual cooperation impossible. His commitment to the equality of all people is reflected in Tyra Boldsen's plans for a monument commemorating the enfranchisement of women. Boldsen, a Danish sculptor and an early "liberationist," planned a sculpture that would have many women but only one man—Adler.

FROM AUTOCRACY TO DEMOCRACY

Adler's model fits a democratic era. The revitalization of counseling through Adler's ideas has paralleled the democratic revolution that has profoundly affected not only our institutions but our strategies for changing behavior, beliefs, and feelings. A therapist-dominated approach, like Freud's, was appropriate in an autocratic era. When powerful leaders dominated the masses, parents and schools controlled children, and minorities were ignored, it was fitting that the therapist would authoritatively prescribe and the client would passively accept the therapist's wisdom. The client's passive position on the therapist's couch alluded to the nature of the relationship and to the power of the helper. In an age of democracy, when people demand to be treated as equals, Adler's basic approach offers a model that is consistent with the times, since it views the client as a full and equal participant in the counseling process.

The shift from autocratic to democratic procedures has brought about a revolution in counseling and psychotherapy. In the past, the training of psychiatrists, psychologists, and social workers was often heavily influenced by the psychoanalytic school of thought. Emphasis was placed on cause and effect, on human drives, and on a mechanistic view and explanation of behavior. While the psychoanalytic theory still has a large following, there is an increasing acceptance of other approaches—for example, rational-emotive therapy, behavior modification, reality therapy, transactional analysis, and client-centered therapy (Corsini, 1973). All these approaches share the belief that people are decision-making beings responsible for their own behavior and capable of changing it.

Walter O'Connell (1976), a past president of the North American Society of Adlerian Psychology, referred to the attitude of many contemporary practitioners and theorists as a "yes, but" acceptance of Adlerian principles. He pointed out that none of them (he specifically mentioned Viktor Frankl, Colin Wilson, Ernest Becker, Ira Progoff, Rollo May, and Werner Erhard) call themselves Adlerians, yet their belief in human development parallels Adler's. All of these "friends" acknowledge many of Adler's ideas in their own contributions to psychology, yet they must add qualifiers to their similarities.

CURRENT STATUS

The North American Society of Adlerian Psychology (NASAP) is Individual Psychology's central organization in the United States and Canada. The society was founded in 1952, largely through Dreikurs' efforts. Dreikurs edited the *Journal of Individual Psychology* after Adler's death and disseminated Adlerian concepts across the North American continent, as well as abroad. Through his efforts and those of his colleagues, numerous local societies and organizations have emerged.

There are Adlerian training institutes in several cities—Chicago, New York City, Minneapolis, and Bowie (Maryland), just to name a few. When NASAP recently celebrated its 25th anniversary, it had passed the 1000-member mark. Although numerically not yet impressive, the Adlerian movement is experiencing a steady growth, and so is the number of practitioners who are operating according to its guidelines.

Each year, thousands of parents are taught parenting techniques through books (Dreikurs, 1948; Dreikurs & Soltz, 1964; Corsini & Painter, 1975; Dinkmeyer & McKay, 1973) and a multimedia nine-session kit (Dinkmeyer & McKay, 1976). Notable innovations in educational practices have been made by Corsini and Madden with their Individual-Education approach, which has been successfully applied by a school system in Hawaii for more than six years. Dinkmeyer's *Developing Understanding of Self and Others* (DUSO) programs have found wide acceptance in numerous elementary schools. The application of Adlerian principles to whole therapeutic communities is successfully exemplified by Walter O'Connell's Glass Ark, a unit in a Veterans Administration hospital in Houston, Texas. Successful practical applications of Adlerian tenets across the North American continent are so numerous that they would exceed the scope of this brief review.

REFERENCES

Adler, K. *Alfred Adler, a man ahead of his time*. Unpublished paper, n. d.

Corsini, R. J. (Ed.). *Current psychotherapies*. Itasca, Ill.: Peacock, 1973.

Corsini, R. J., & Painter, G. *The practical parent: The ABC's of child discipline*. New York: Harper & Row, 1975.

Dinkmeyer, D., & Dreikurs, R. *Encouraging children to learn: The encouragement process*. Englewood Cliffs, N.J.: Prentice-Hall, 1963.

Dinkmeyer, D., & McKay, G. D. *Raising a responsible child*. New York: Simon & Schuster, 1973.

Dinkmeyer, D., & McKay, G. D. *Systematic training for effective parenting*. Circle Pines, Minn.: American Guidance Service, 1976.

Dreikurs, R. *The challenge of parenthood*. New York: Hawthorn, 1948.

Dreikurs, R., & Soltz, V. *Children: The challenge*. New York: Hawthorn, 1964.

O'Connell, W. E. The "friends of Adler" phenomenon. *Journal of Individual Psychology, 1976, 32* (1), 5–17.

CHAPTER 2

THEORETICAL FOUNDATIONS OF ADLERIAN COUNSELING

The Adlerian counseling process applies general theories of behavior to specific individual concerns and challenges. The principles that are set forth in this chapter are drawn from the writings of Alfred Adler and Rudolf Dreikurs, as well as from those of their colleagues and students. Adler's ideas have withstood the test of theoretical challenge and empirical evidence, and his contribution is acknowledged by the proponents of many current theories of human behavior. Adlerian concepts have stimulated a number of practical approaches to counseling with individuals, groups, and families and have seen application in schools, universities, and various agencies, as well as in private practice.

The purpose of a counseling theory is to set the foundations of the relationship between counselor and counselee, thereby helping counselors improve their effectiveness. Theory also provides guidelines for making observations about what occurs in the counseling process. It is the position of the authors that counselors must have an explicit theory of human behavior.

The assumption underlying Adlerian counseling theory is that people are indivisible, social, decision-making beings whose actions and psychological movement have purpose. Each person is seen as an individual, within a social setting, with the capacity to decide and to choose. The following principles expand this overall assumption.

ALL BEHAVIOR HAS SOCIAL MEANING

One of the basic premises of the Adlerian approach is that we are primarily social beings and that our behavior can be understood only in terms of a social context. Interaction with others is a continuous, life-long process

7

that begins in infancy, when we are entirely dependent on others for our very survival. Later, we need to cooperate with others in order to realize our goals and function fully.

Each human being is born with the capacity to develop what Adler called *Gemeinschaftsgefühl*—narrowly translated as "social interest." It is the willingness to cooperate with others for the common good and the awareness of the universal interrelatedness of all human beings. As members of the human community, throughout life all of us must meet three major *life tasks,* which Adler defined as society, work, and sex. Adler believed that the extent to which a person successfully shares with others, contributes through work, and forms a satisfying relationship with a member of the other sex is a revealing indicator of the individual's overall personality and level of maturity.

Awareness of the social significance of all behavior allows counselors to understand their clients more effectively. The school counselor looks at the social microcosms of peer groupings and teacher/student relationships for an understanding of adolescent behavior. Although similar microcosms exist in business and organizational structures, an adult's world is more diverse than that of an adolescent, and the adult's social situation is more the result of personal choice. This makes the task of understanding the social significance of adult behavior more difficult. But, no matter what the age of the counselee, without an understanding of the person's social behavior, the counselor may merely focus on causation (for example, unhappy childhood).

A great deal of importance is placed on making the counseling relationship an immediate and warm interaction between equals. Assuming that the counselor has adequate social skills, the counseling relationship can represent a valuable example of the client's current social-interaction skills. Is the client concerned with power or revenge? Is he/she trying to prove inadequacy?

The Goal of Belonging

Throughout life, the goal of belonging is a fundamental expression of human nature. We decide which groups are important to us and strive to gain their acceptance. The countless formal and informal groupings that exist in any society attest to our goal of belonging and to have a certain place that we value. Many of our problems and anxieties stem from the fear that we will not belong or be accepted by groups we seek to join. When we perceive that we cannot do the job or make the grade, we fear that we will not be accepted by others. Our sense of belonging remains unfulfilled, and we become anxious and unhappy.

In the schools, teachers can use the natural social environment of the classroom to provide situations that utilize the need to belong. Effectively organized group discussions enhance both the development of the individual and that of the group. The adult's world is not as easily structured as that of the child, but the same principles operate there, too. Our goal of belonging creates loyalties to family, individuals, professional and social groups, fraternal orders, and athletic teams—to name just a few.

We relate to one another with varying degrees of success. One measure of a person's psychic health is the extent and effectiveness of that person's current interaction with others. Creative negative interpretation of self can be reversed by encouraging the client to increase and improve interaction with others, so he or she can experience self-worth and, at the same time, be given the opportunity to share his or her abilities with others. Thus, the focus shifts from self to others.

THE HUMAN PERSONALITY HAS UNITY AND DEFINITE PATTERNS

Another basic premise of the Adlerian approach is the irreducible wholeness of the individual. The person is seen as a dynamic, unified organism moving through life in definite patterns toward a goal. Fragmenting the personality by causal or analytical explanations denies this wholeness. Through synthesis, the Adlerian tries to achieve an understanding of the individual that is based in the unity and purpose of the individual's behavior. An example will illustrate this point.

> Linda is a 9-year-old child with a high IQ, as measured by individual psychological tests, and with considerable creativity and spontaneity. Yet, she is failing in all of her school subjects. Many might say that this behavior doesn't make sense. However, if one focuses on Linda's patterns of movement instead of focusing on specific elements (such as high IQ and low grades), one sees the meaning and goal of Linda's behavior. By failing to function, Linda becomes special. Mother and Father now give her a great deal of attention by tutoring her every evening and showing great concern. Linda has become a very special case that must be dealt with in a very special manner both at school and at home. If one is able to conceptualize Linda's behavior at its holistic level, one can clearly see that it does have a goal and also social meaning.

The importance of understanding the patterns of behavior is illustrated in typical case studies. No matter how much information the institution gathers about an individual's intelligence, interests, and achievements, these data cannot speak for themselves. Until one is able to see the relationship between behavior and data and observe the pattern and purpose of the behavior, it is difficult to develop remedial or corrective actions. Counseling techniques that gather much data and concentrate heavily on a counselee's past history often fail to take into account this tremendously important relationship. For the counselor to be effective, the meaning of behavior must be clear with regard to its unity and central function. As Dreikurs (1953) indicated, "The doctrine of the unity of the personality gave Individual Psychology its name. This name, which is so often misunderstood, is derived from the latin word 'individuum,' which literally means 'undivided,' 'indivisible' (in-dividere)'' (p. 56).

This view requires that we take a holistic, rather than reductionistic, approach.[1] It suggests that we look at all actions in the light of the individual's chosen style of life. The way in which people organize themselves as whole persons influences their perception of life and their transactions with others. For example, if Susan is primarily concerned with being noticed, in some instances she will try to be recognized by being the best in anything she can do well—such as tennis, cards, or other activities. In other instances, however, she will not even try, because she will receive equal recognition for her failure to function. Since it is more important for Susan to be noticed than to be successful, she may be a "noticeable" failure in some aspects of her life. Thus, both failure and success can make sense in terms of the person's particular style of life.

BEHAVIOR HAS A PURPOSE

According to Adler, all human behavior has a purpose. Behaviors that may seem inexplicable become understandable once we know their goal, or purpose.

The contrast here is obviously with those who believe that behavior is governed by causality alone and that it can be explained in mechanical terms. From an Adlerian point of view, all our actions are seen in relation to their goal-directed nature, and the goal can have urgent, imperative quality. The goal, then, gives direction to our striving, and it becomes the final cause—the final explanation. Thus, instead of always looking back to a possible cause, we look to the future goal as the "cause."

This is how Adler stated the importance of goals:

> If we know the goal of a person, we can undertake to explain and to understand what the psychological phenomena want to tell us, why they were created, what a person has made of his innate material, why he has made it just so and not differently, how his character traits, his feelings and emotions, his logic, his morals, and his aesthetics must be constituted in order that he may arrive at his goal [Ansbacher & Ansbacher, 1956, p. 196].

Adler's view is echoed by Allport, Rogers, and Faust. In his book *The Nature of Personality* (1950), Allport concludes that goal striving is the essence of

---

[1]Freudian psychology is reductionistic—for example, id-ego-superego. Adlerian psychology is holistic, because it sees the individual as indivisible.

personality and that knowing the goal provides an understanding of the ways in which the person is moving psychologically.

Rogers (1951) observes that "behavior is basically the goal-directed attempt of the organism to satisfy its needs as experienced, in the field as perceived" (p. 491). He also makes a point of noting that from this concept of motivation "all the effective elements [of motivation] exist in the present. Behavior is not 'caused' by something which occurred in the past. Present tensions and present needs are the only ones which the organism endeavors to reduce or satisfy" (p. 492).

Faust (1966) describes essentially the same principle when he states:

> In the modification of behavior it is not so much whether a particular stimulus does, in fact, assure the organism of survival that counts, as it is a matter of how the organism perceives the stimulus or the meaning which the stimulus possesses for the organism's survival. . . . While frequently individuals appear to engage in behavior which according to adults and even peers is destructive, the premise is that from the individual's point of view or interpretation this behavior has certain kinds of meaning to him in terms of his personal significance, self-esteem and method of finding a place and thus he behaves in the way in which he must.

This teleological approach implies that the goals of behavior are always created by the individual and are not the result of preceding events, as the causal approach maintains. Our uniqueness ultimately rests in this "creative power." Behavior is thus understood not only as a response to a stimulus but also in terms of the intervening variable of the person who makes a creative decision about that stimulus.

This emphasis on the purposive nature of behavior is a recognition of humans' freedom of choice; it indicates that people evaluate and interpret life according to the goals they choose for themselves. In pursuing the goal, the individual employs his or her own unique cognitive and emotional abilities. We speak of *private logic* when we refer to the individual's cognitive constructs that serve that person's pursuit of a goal and that represent a set of "personal truths" guiding the individual. It should be noted that the private logic is not necessarily in line with common sense. For example, "I haven't gotten any mail today; therefore, no one cares about me" is a statement that may make sense in terms of a person's private logic but not in terms of what we may call "common logic."

Besides cognitive constructs, the pursuit of a goal involves emotions as well. A common misconception is that human emotions are uncontrollable, passive reactions to environmental input—like the tears produced by the tear ducts in response to an onion. Emotions can be used purposefully to control others and to achieve goals. The cliché "Control your emotions!" may actually mean (often more accurately) "Don't use your emotions to control me!'' The child who screams until he gets his way already understands emotions as a useful goal-achieving tool.

All forms of behavior, including misbehavior, are the results of the creative choices we make in selecting and pursuing our goals. When we are confronted with a bright adolescent who doesn't perform in school and has become a ''juvenile delinquent,'' we may say ''It doesn't make sense,'' simply because we don't recognize his or her purpose. Behavior always makes sense to the person, if not to others. The goal may not always be fully known to the individual; nonetheless, the person operates in the direction of the goal and according to the interpretation he or she has given to the goal.

Awareness of the goal, therefore, provides the counselor with some clues for corrective action. A study of the causes, on the other hand, may provide only a list of factors that are likely to seem beyond the counselor's and counselee's control.

The Goals in Children's Actions

The goal-directed nature of behavior can perhaps be best understood in terms of the goals of child misbehavior. Dreikurs (1957) refers to these goals as: (1) attention getting, (2) struggle for power or superiority, (3) desire to retaliate or get even, and (4) display of inadequacy or assumed disability.

Dreikurs describes in detail all these goals. Children who use attention-getting techniques (for example, annoying behavior) desire attention so much that, rather than being ignored, they will seek attention negatively. Some children receive attention by being successful, some by demonstrating their charm, and others by being a nuisance.

Children whose goal is power are out to show you that they can do as they please and that they will not do what you want them to do. Even when you defeat them, they are all the more convinced of the value of their goal, and the next time they will only employ a more effective method to seek out their goal, to be the boss.

Children whose goal is revenge seek their place by being extremely dislikable. Their feelings have been hurt, and they want to hurt in return. It is their pride to develop a mutual antagonism. These children do not mind being called vicious; after all, their goal is to retaliate. For them to be the most horrible is a form of success.

Children whose goal is to display inadequacy are so discouraged that they cannot believe they can be significant. They use or develop inadequacy as a protection, so that nothing is required or expected. Since they don't partici-pate or contribute, they hope to avoid what they see as an even more devastat-ing experience—to try and to fail.

We counselors can become more aware of these goals by observing the child's behaviors, by checking our own spontaneous reactions to such be-havior, and by noting the child's responses to correction. As we observe our spontaneous reactions, we keep in mind that what we feel most inclined to do often points to the child's intentions. If we feel annoyed and want to admonish and correct, the child is probably just trying to keep us busy with him. When we feel personally challenged and want to show to the child that he can't do that to us, we are engaged in a power contest. Feeling hurt and outraged points to the child's desire to get even with us or society. Most certain of all these clues is the despair we feel with a nonproducing but able child. School and parents don't know what to do, and we are impressed with the child's total inability. By leaving him alone, we do what the deeply discouraged child expects.

Another indicator of the child's goal is his response to correction. If he desires only attention, he will stop when corrected, although not for long. If he wants power, an adult's efforts to stop him will worsen his behavior. The vengeful child will become more violent, while the child who displays inadequacy will continue to endure, possibly without any sincere attempt at action.

Ambivalence or indecisiveness can also be seen as purposive activity, in that it permits the child to gain time and postpone a decision in order to keep things as they are. The fact is that all psychological behaviors and transactions are purposeful, whether active, passive, or supposedly ambivalent. There is no behavior without a goal, and close observation of child, as well as adult, behavior will reveal such goals. In the adult, the goals are more complex, but they still govern the individual's actions.

What we said earlier about counseling in general also applies to child counseling. If satisfactory change is to occur, counselors must understand the significance of the purpose of children's behavior, as well as their feelings. A school counselor, for example, may see Linda's inexplicably poor grades as the "problem," when they are only symptoms that lead to the purpose of her behavior. Instead, viewing the problem as the result of Linda's belief and goal—"I can get more attention by being the worst"—gives the counselor direction for the counseling process. If one remains focused on the grades, one is likely to emulate the blind man who tries to figure out what an elephant is like by feeling its tail and then concludes that elephants are similar to snakes—confused about the "facts"!

THE STRIVING FOR SIGNIFICANCE EXPLAINS OUR MOTIVATION

The striving for significance receives its direction from the individual's subjectively conceived goal of success (self-ideal). In our highly competitive society, we are urged, expected, and even demanded to excel, to be *more than* others. From birth, a person experiences the subjective feeling of being less than others. Adlerian psychology recognizes the family as the first group in which each individual strives to find a significant place. The search for significance occurs when a person experiences the subjective feeling of being less than others (inferiority feelings) and then engages in various attempts to compensate.

Our inferiority feelings are generally the result of faulty self-evaluation. We arrive at faulty self-evaluations by answering "incorrectly" such questions as "Who and what am I?" and "How do I master the environment?" There is abundant proof of our capacity to give the "wrong" answers to these and similar questions and to mistakenly conclude that we are worthless. Even the extreme act of suicide is often the result of subjective inferiority feelings rather than the outcome of an objective assessment of our true worth.

The striving for significance is in essence a movement toward the fulfillment of the goal to achieve unique identity and to belong. This movement toward a unique identity is the motivating force behind all human activity—the master motive. Adlerians see this process, too, from a teleological, rather than causal, perspective—as a pull by the goal rather than a push by the drive. It should be noted that most organismic approaches share the Adlerian recognition of one master motive. The positive attainment of the goal has been variously called self-actualization, self-expansion, or competence.

The power of the striving for significance is most apparent in the adolescent struggle for uniqueness, a struggle that often sets the young in conflict with adults. Defiance of traditional norms, sometimes expressed in unusual style of clothes, unique language, and unconventional behavior, is one way in which adolescents will affirm the difference between themselves and their parents and other adults, thus satisfying in some way their increasing need for personal autonomy. Similar techniques are used by other groups that need to proclaim their uniqueness in order to achieve the goal of being different and yet relate to others in the group through common beliefs and behavior.

Each of us seeks identity in different manners. As we have previously noted, this search often takes the form of "bad" behavior, from children's misbehavior to adult resistance or even illegal actions. Sometimes we observe an individual who is putting all of her energy into her work, essentially giving up in other areas. This behavior, too, is a manifestation of the striving for significance. If we ask "How does this behavior help the person to be significant, as she perceives significance?" we soon discover that the individual perceives that she can be significant only in her area of work. Thus, she gives all of herself to something in which she can succeed and be special and withdraws from other areas in which she cannot do so. In other cases, when an individual recognizes that he cannot succeed at being the best, he will try to succeed at being the worst. Failure to function can at times, as we have seen, bring as much attention and power as brilliant performance.

Because motivation must be seen in the light of a person's striving for significance, as he/she perceives significance, it is imperative that counselors recognize that a person's particular behavior, set of attitudes, and series of relationships reveal how that person believes he/she fits into his/her social context. A question that counselors always ask themselves is "How is the person seeking to be known?'' Most of the ways of behaving that are eventually accepted by the person reflect the person's current concept of self. When individuals see themselves as inadequate in social skills, inept in social relationships with the opposite sex, or unable to cope with other tasks, they tend to behave on the basis of their beliefs, not on the basis of facts (Fullmer & Bernard, 1964). This ''unrealistic'' view of self and environment, however, can also be positively utilized. Many explorers and adventurers throughout history would have never made it if their convictions had not contradicted ''facts.''

BEHAVIOR IS A FUNCTION OF SUBJECTIVE PERCEPTION

We learn to perceive life; that is, early in life, we acquire a perception of our own selves and of the world around us—what is called a subjective point of view. As it was pointed out earlier, in order to understand people's behavior, one must come to recognize the significance of the inner, subjective experience and its influence on all of our decisions.

The discouraged individual actually is in a different internal environment than the individual who feels adequate and has self-esteem. Discouragement anticipates lack of success, and the behavior of the discouraged person actually provokes responses from others that, by validating this anticipation, reinforce the discouraged interpretation of the life situation. Each person plays a dynamic role in the development of his or her subjective view of self and life. People are not reactors; they are actors.

For the Adlerian, it is crucial that the individual be understood in terms of the meaning that a given event possesses for that person. This position is similar to Arthur Combs' view that all behavior is a function of the individual's field of perception at the instant of behaving (Combs, 1954). We tend to behave according to how things appear to us, and, when our perception changes, our behavior changes accordingly. Perception, then, determines behavior perhaps more than ''reality'' does. Combs (1954) also indicates that when perceptions are vague and indistinct, behavior will be similarly ambivalent. Conversely, when perceptions are clear and accurate, behavior will be precise and efficient. In essence, behavior is a function of perception.

Thus, the Adlerian counselor is engaged in a continuous attempt to see with the client's eyes and hear with the client's ears—to get into the client's world for the purpose of making it available to the client and to the significant others in the client's environment. This is how Rogers (1951) cogently states the reason for this constant attempt: ''The best vantage point for understanding behavior is from the internal frame of reference of the individual himself'' (p. 492). It is because of this reason that the Rogerians place great emphasis on the helping relationship and on the need of developing the necessary empathy for the counselor to perceive more accurately the client's point of view. It is apparent that, the more accurately we communicate, the more adequately we will comprehend the client's vantage point.

This position has far-reaching implications for the counselor. For example, it implies that the counselor must avoid as much as possible any personal bias. If a counselor feels that a client's chosen life style needs to be changed, the counselor must ask himself or herself whether this feeling reflects what appears to be a real concern of the client or the counselor's own bias.

In sum, the counselor must have the capacity to comprehend what counselees are really saying and to help them clarify why they feel that way. Once clients examine and become aware of their own points of view, the counselor can assist them to consider alternate views and different behaviors.

Idiographic versus Nomothetic Laws

Adlerians are more concerned with concrete laws that apply characteristically to a specific individual in relation to his/her style of life (idiographic laws) than with abstract laws that apply generally but include many exceptions (nomothetic laws). This point of view is shared by Combs and Snygg (1959), who indicate that the real challenge to psychology is the phenomenological, or subjective, approach. This means that the counselor must seek to understand the behavior of the counselee from the counselee's point of view. As we said earlier, the focus is on understanding people as they are perceived by themselves rather than as they appear to others.

The idiographic approach assumes that psychology will have meaning only insofar as it postulates a theory that helps us to assist a specific human being to live in a manner that is personally satisfying and socially acceptable. It should be clear, therefore, that this approach goes beyond the general normative descriptions that arose in child-development theory and in Freud's psychoanalytic psychiatry regarding certain predetermined characteristics and stages.

The idiographic view implies that the counselor needs to comprehend how the person acquired a particular value system and how that system presently operates in the decisions the client makes with regard to life and the life tasks. The counselor will then be able to understand the basis of the individual's decisions, the goals that the person is trying to achieve, and the things that the person values. Also, the counseling process becomes a channel through which the individual is better able to develop value systems that, by being consistent with his or her particular society and community, permit the person to live more effectively. In some instances, the counselor helps the individual explore a new set of values through a value-conflict situation.

For example, after complaining about four successive unhappy romances, a young woman concludes "They were all so unsatisfactory. Men are such disappointments!" If the counselor is able to see an idiographic rule in this woman's life style—"My man must be perfect, or I must move on"—he or she may also be able to help the client become aware of her self-defeating approach and do something about it.

✍ ADLERIAN PSYCHOLOGY IS A PSYCHOLOGY OF USE, NOT OF POSSESSION

Adlerians believe that, at any given moment, one will do that which is most useful or which best accomplishes one's purpose and striving; that which interferes with one's goal is not done. This principle can be seen at work in the varying ways in which individuals make use of their heredity and environment. If we see someone who appears to have considerable physical or intellectual capacity but chooses not to utilize it, we see someone who has determined that he or she is not adequate and cannot function in terms of those specific capacities. The concern should, therefore, be "What does the person *do* with his or her ability?" rather than "What does the person possess?"

Whether in school, agency, institutional or private setting, the counselor is often given much data concerning a client's intelligence, achievement, and personality. We believe that sometimes this mass of information may be counterproductive, since it may even hide the patterns and meaning of behavior. The Adlerian counselor is more interested in what *use* the person makes of his or her heredity, environment, and experiences. By focusing on the client's motivation, decisions, and conclusions, a more practical and effective counseling relationship is achieved. A simple review of test scores and reports is seldom useful in counseling, unless it points to patterns.

REFERENCES

Allport, G. W. *The nature of personality.* Reading, Mass.: Addison-Wesley, 1950.

Ansbacher, H. L., & Ansbacher, R. R. (Eds.). *The Individual Psychology of Alfred Adler.* New York: Harper & Row, 1956.

Combs, A. W. Counseling as a learning process. *Journal of Counseling Psychology,* 1954, *1*(1), 31–36.

Combs, A. W., & Snygg, D. *Individual behavior: A perceptual approach to behavior* (Rev. ed.). New York: Harper & Row, 1959.

Dreikurs, R. *Fundamentals of Adlerian psychology.* Chicago: Alfred Adler Institute, 1953.

Dreikurs, R. *Psychology in the classroom.* New York: Harper & Row, 1957.

Faust, V. Role of the elementary school counselor: Freeing children to learn. Invited address to U.S. Office of Education, Washington, D.C., July 1966.

Fullmer, D. W., & Bernard, H. W. *Counseling: Content and process.* Chicago: Science Research Associates, 1964.

Rogers, C. R. *Client-centered therapy.* Boston: Houghton-Mifflin, 1951.

White, R. Motivation reconsidered: The concept of competence. *Psychological Review,* 1959, *66*, 297–333.

CHAPTER 3

THE DEVELOPMENT
OF PERSONALITY AND
THE LIFE STYLE

What makes a human being unique? Why do even identical twins display distinctly different personalities? When are personality differences first visible in human development? An infant at birth has already been alive for nine months and has accumulated many experiences and responded to many stimuli. But even a fetus is not only a reactor but an actor, as any woman in late pregnancy can testify. Furthermore, clear-cut evidence of learning in utero has been demonstrated (Hooker, 1954). However, we know very little about parental influences on personality development, and, although many elegant classification schemes have been developed, neonatologists and newborn-nursery nurses are seldom willing to divide infants into more than passive and active categories as far as personality is concerned.

Human infants enter the world with certain genetic endowments and find themselves in particular human environments. But they continue after birth their tendency to not only react to external stimuli but also play an active role that influences their environment. This is particularly true of their social environment—that is, the small group of humans that each child relates to on a fairly constant basis. Through what appears at first to be almost a trial-and-error process, children "learn" what works and what doesn't work. Whatever seems to work, they persist in; whatever fails to influence the significant persons about them (their social field), they discard. Then each new situation is met with an ever-increasing backlog of "experience." But the experience is not reality; it is the infant's subjective interpretation of reality and the conclusions that he or she draws from experience.

Some critics may say that we are imposing our own adult biases on an incomplete human who is only a bundle of disorganized drives and instincts. In our opinion, such a view fails to take into consideration the tremendous creative power of infants and small children. There exists an unrecognized prejudice against children. Actually, even at birth a human being has the capacity to make important contributions to another human being. Through nursing at the mother's breast, the baby facilitates the third stage of labor, reduces maternal hemorrhage, and relieves breast congestion. Yet, this unique ability is often overlooked and denied, and a subtle dehumanization process begins as the infant is whisked off to a sterile nursery.

We can learn a great deal about the infant's ability to perceive and make choices when we see a normal baby with deaf-mute parents. The infant soon "learns" that sound is ineffective, so he screws up his face, gets red, flails his arms and legs, and "cries" without sound. Later he may learn to have a temper tantrum by stamping on the floor so that his parents can feel the vibrations. O. K. Moore demonstrated that ordinary toddlers could be taught to operate electric typewriters, to take dictation, and to read with comprehension.

The above data help us understand how actively children create their personality. But, although children may be good observers, they are often very poor interpreters; that is, they come to conclusions about themselves and life that are based on faulty judgments. As they create their guidelines and establish their blueprints for the future, children tend to operate with an "only if" absurdity. For example, a child may conclude "Only if I am pleasing (or in control, or comfortable, or good, or competent, or right), can I really belong." This kind of thinking is based on the faulty assumption "I don't really belong." Actually a newly born child is already a full-fledged member of the human community and can never become more human—can never belong more than he or she already does (Chess, Thomas, & Birch, 1965). Yet, most of us spend a great deal of time and energy looking for a place that we already have, not realizing that we have our place just by virtue of our existence.

The "only if" absurd premise is based on what we fear the most. If we are bent on pleasing, our most awesome fear is of rejection. If control is our priority, humiliation is what we hope to avoid. If comfort is given precedence, the worst thing is stress. And if moral superiority is what we value most, the feeling of meaninglessness is what we must avoid at all costs. The Adlerian view is that infants establish a number-one priority very early, perhaps within the first few weeks of life, and that it is along this guiding line that they begin to construct their personality, which will include a complex of prejudices, biased apperceptions, conclusions, and convictions.

Since all of this process is going on preverbally, as older children or adults we are only dimly aware of our own style of living—that is, the personality we have constructed for ourselves. Developing a life style is, however, not only economical for the child (he doesn't have to start from scratch with each new experience) but absolutely essential for his survival.

The prototype of the style of living is well developed within the first few months of life, and it appears that the child selects out a few moments of time that he "tape-records" to remind himself of his conclusions. These are the early recollections recalled in adolescence or adulthood, which help the counselor to pinpoint the basic themes of an individual's personality.

INFLUENCES ON THE DEVELOPING
PERSONALITY

Genetic Factors

At the present time, we have no evidence to support genetic effects on the development of the personality. In fact, in identical (one-egg) twins, who have exactly the same genetic makeup, we often see strikingly different personalities. One explanation for the difference may be related to an experience we frequently have when we interview adult identical twins. After relating precisely the same early recollection, the twins usually reach quite opposite conclusions about the incident—which is another way of saying that it doesn't matter so much what we are born with or what we are born into but how we perceive it and what we do about it.

Constitutional Factors

We are unable to measure the effects of the various body systems, such as the endocrine system or the central nervous system, on personality development, except in cases of obvious physical or mental defect. But we know that intelligence, although not static, still is somewhat of a factor in influencing the life style, since intelligence is a necessary tool for coping behavior. A healthy, handsome boy (or girl) will experience certain environmental reactions and find certain opportunities that are different from those that some of his other friends will meet. Similarly, intelligent children see alternatives that duller children miss. But we must emphasize that it is not the constitutional trait itself that is causative; what is important is how the youngster perceives the trait.

> Sally was always a gifted child and grew into a talented art student. As she approached young adulthood, her work drew increasing attention and praise from her teachers. But Sally's number-one priority was pleasing, which is a way of saying that she never really believed that she was gifted, and her talent, which eventually propelled her into a highly successful career in the graphic arts, was always much more appreciated by others than by Sally.

If a child is born with a physical defect, she may be discouraged and operate as if she had a deficiency, or she may overcompensate and, for example, become an outstanding athlete, despite her deficiency. All children make their own decisions concerning how they perceive their genetic endowment and the environmental situation that they find themselves in.

Critical Periods

Montessori and others have quite clearly demonstrated that there are *critical periods* for developing certain traits or abilities. Some human skills require practice from a very early age. If they are learned later, they are acquired only with great difficulty, if at all. According to Montessori, a critical period is a short span of time during which a particular learning—for example, reading—takes place with relative ease. If the child does not develop some reading skills during this critical period, it is often difficult later to teach the child to read. "Children pass through definite periods in which they reveal psychic aptitudes and possibilities which afterwards disappear" (Montessori, in Standing, 1962, pp. 119–120).

Examples of skills that are developed during certain critical periods include the newborn's ability to swim with fishlike movements when immersed in water—an ability that is subsequently lost and never recovered in the same form. For many children and adults, learning to swim the second time may be quite difficult. Newly born infants, if held upright over a flat surface, will also "walk" with well-coordinated alternating steps. This ability, too, is lost, only to be retrieved—often with considerable effort—in the latter part of the first year or in the first part of the second year of life.

Cultural Factors

Culture provides a child with a particular way of looking at the world, thus emphasizing some tendencies in the development of the life style. For example, in Greece and in some of the Latin American countries, the culture is still quite autocratic and male dominated. It is not surprising that, in these countries, both boys and girls tend to grow up with overexaggerated ideas about the importance of males. In North America the culture can be characterized as competitive. Competition seeps into all our relationships, including family relationships, providing a cultural influence that leads most children to be very competitive.

Prenatal and Perinatal Factors

Although the methods of studying the developing fetus are becoming more and more sophisticated, we know very little about the first nine months of life. Nevertheless, it seems logical to assume that the fetus processes stimuli and decides in some primitive sense what to make of the stimuli. Legend has George Gershwin developing his gift for syncopated rhythm as a result of the paroxysmal tachycardia that his mother had during pregnancy; that is, he was subjected for nine months to irregularity of heartbeat, which perhaps predisposed him toward syncopated rhythm.

Perinatal is the term used to describe the critical period just prior to, during, and immediately following birth. Although only very recently have scientists paid much attention to this period, studies are already showing that this is a critical time of life. For example, if a mother holds her unclothed newborn baby immediately after delivery, she is significantly more likely to talk with the child as a 2-year-old than the mother who has been denied that experience.

Family Influences

Each child is born into a certain social milieu, and his interpretation of his role in that cast of characters is crucial, as the following sections will show.

Birth order. Myriads of studies have been published concerning birth order, but most of them are relatively meaningless, since they don't take into consideration the child's attitude and movement, the formation of alliances and opposing groups within the family, and the unique ways in which children approach the social situation in their search for a place for themselves. In other words, these studies don't take into consideration children's perception of their birth order. For example, if a firstborn child is severely retarded, the second child may take over and function as the firstborn. Another child, apparently firstborn but actually preceded by a stillborn sister, can be a much more special "firstborn" than usual.

Birth order, then, needs to be used as a dynamic explanation that takes into consideration how much the child influences the other members of the family, as well as how they influence the child. It is important to remember that all of a child's strivings are directed toward satisfying a feeling of belonging. Pepper (1971) emphasizes that no two children are ever born into the same family situation. With the birth of each child, the situation and, therefore, the environment change because (1) the parents are older and more experienced or more discouraged; (2) the parents may be more prosperous; (3) the parents may have moved to another neighborhood; and (4) because of divorce or death, there may be a stepparent.

The *only child* has a potentially difficult start in life, since he spends his early childhood among adults. But this is not necessarily a disadvantage. It is true that the only child may be pampered and, as a consequence, may expect to be the center of interest. But it is also true that he has the opportunity to be the only beneficiary of the adults' roles as models and educators and, therefore, may become a more competent and cooperative participant in the life of the family.

The *firstborn*'s position often puts the oldest child in a favored spot, but this may be only temporary, since all first children undergo the experience of being dethroned. First children, then, have the choice of trying to maintain the number-one position, or holding their competitor back in the number-two position, or becoming discouraged and letting themselves be overrun by the second child. Naturally, there are innumerable variations in between these alternatives.

The *second child* may feel that he is in a constant race and often develops a personality that is the opposite of the first child's personality, particularly if the two children are close in age and of the same sex. If a third child arrives, the second child also becomes a "squeezed" child. As such, he has one of two general tendencies—to let himself be pushed down by his older and younger siblings or to elevate himself at their expense.

The *youngest child* has the tendency to either try to overtake all the others or to remain a baby, expecting help, service, and consideration. In large families, the children usually divide into subgroups. A family of seven, for example, may be seen by the youngest as made up of three older kids, two middle kids, and two little kids. This means that, when we look for subgrouping in a family, we must do so from the point of view of the person whose life style we are trying to understand and keep in mind that this point of view is not the same for all the children in the family.

Shulman (1973) emphasizes that the ordinal positions are "psychological" more than chronological, citing the instance in which a firstborn may be dethroned and play the role of the middle child and the second born, by virtue of overrunning the first, actually plays the role of the firstborn.

Family constellation. This is a term used to describe the sociopsychological configuration of a family group (Shulman, in Nikelly, 1971). The personality characteristics of each family member, the emotional bonds between family members, the birth order, the dominance or submission of the various members, their age differences, the sex of the siblings, and the size of the family are all factors in the family constellation. A child's position in the family constellation exerts a strong influence on the development of the child's personality. Therefore, as we shall see later, it is essential that the therapist or counselor take such position into consideration in order to understand the dynamics of the client.

The developing child is trying to find his or her place in a particular group's order, and it makes a difference how close or distant the family members are, who was born when, how the siblings perceived their position in the birth order, and who is the boss or, at least, who is seen as boss (if there is one). The family constellation does not describe directly a particular child. Rather, it offers a dynamic way of understanding, for example, the fact that first and second children are often quite different in personality, particularly if they are close in age and of the same sex. An only boy among girls, or an only girl among boys, may experience the family constellation in a very special way, particularly if that family favors either boys or girls. The much larger-sized family presents, of course, many more possibilities. As we said earlier, there may be, for example, subgroupings within the sibling group, so that one child who is the "eldest" of the younger group may share some of the characteristics of the firstborn child. In some larger families, there is a need for more cooperation, and the culturally provided competition may not have as deleterious an effect as in smaller families.

Family atmosphere. Dewey (in Nikelly, 1971) describes a number of typical family atmospheres that the growing child reacts to. These reactions can develop in the direction of accepting the attitudes and values shared by the family, in the direction of rejecting them, or in a direction that is somewhere in between these two.

The attributes that the children in a particular family share—such as love of reading, musical aptitude, or athletic ability—are a reflection of the family atmosphere. They express shared family values. In a family that values athletics, it is quite likely that all children will, to some degree, be athletically inclined. The attributes that, instead, are not shared by the children are, to some extent, a product of the atmosphere of competition within the family, which grows out of the competition between the parents. For example, if one parent is neat and the other is messy, some of the children are likely to be neat and some to be messy. If we have a situation in which the mother is constantly passing judgment on her husband, we can expect that the children, following in their mother's footsteps, will get into trouble in their own marriages by constantly passing judgment on their spouses.

This is another example of how children respond to the family atmosphere. All five children in a family exhibit an unusual interest in music (a shared family value, since both parents are musical). However, each child chooses a different instrument, and one child finds a unique place for herself by being "tone deaf" and making her musical contribution through percussion. The musical talent, then, represents the family atmosphere of shared family values. The difference in the way the talent is manifested is the result of the competition among the siblings. In this family, if one parent had been musical and the other one had not, we might have expected two or three children to be musical and the others to be relatively uninterested in music.

Here are some of the family atmospheres described by Dewey and their characteristics.

The *rejective* atmosphere is exemplified by parents who fail to separate the deed from the doer and who constantly criticize and reject their children.

The *authoritarian* atmosphere is rigid, stresses obedience, and is likely to produce either extremely conforming or extremely rebellious children.

In an atmosphere of *martyrdom*, suffering nobly is greatly valued. The spouse of an alcoholic, who by his or her "heroic" behavior ends up by encouraging the partner's drinking, is a classic example of this situation.

In the *inconsistent* atmosphere, the children don't know what to expect of others or what is expected of them. However, Dreikurs often observed that most of the time in such atmosphere it is the adults, rather than the children, who are confused and that it is usually the parents who need to learn to become a match for their children.

The *suppressive* atmosphere limits the freedom to express thoughts and feelings and sometimes stimulates excessive daydreaming or produces children who are very good at "putting up a front." Examples of this kind of family is a family made up of humorless people or a group of very narrowly religious people, who talk little among themselves and are not demonstrative.

The *hopeless* atmosphere can be described with the term used by Satir—"funereal." She says: "Everyone suffers from severe discouragement, which is highly contagious, and boundless pessimism" (Satir 1972, p. 9). Children who grow up in a funereal family are often like dreary little adults—humorless, friendless, nonspontaneous. It is as if they never learned to play.

The *overprotective* atmosphere denies children the opportunity to learn to be responsible for their own behavior.

The *pitying* atmosphere often stimulates the development of "victims," who become so creative and flexible in their capacity to suffer that they can suffer about anything.

The *high-standards* atmosphere leads the children to feel that they are never good enough.

The *materialistic* atmosphere underplays the significance of human relationships and often produces life failures both among those who want to be "the best" and among those who, despairing at being the best, may work at being "the worst."

The *disparaging* atmosphere in characterized by frequent criticism The parents operate as if anybody who is not a member of the family were an outsider, thus teaching their children the basic skills of prejudice.

In the *inharmonious* atmosphere, the children grow up feeling that they are in an enemy camp.

In deeply troubled families, one of two opposite atmospheres may prevail—a very *disorderly* atmosphere or a very *orderly* atmosphere. An example of a disorderly family is a family in which bickering and fighting go on almost constantly, from the time the first family member gets up in the morning to the time the last one goes to bed at night. An example of an overorderly atmosphere is a family in which the new stepmother—long single and highly efficient as a nurse—tries to operate the family like a hospital ward and fails to establish any kind of rapport with her stepchildren, who refuse to accept her disciplinary attitude and avoid her company as much as they can.

Early Experiences

Early experiences, no matter how dramatic or potentially traumatic, are
✗ not specifically causative of personality traits, because each child will determine for himself or herself the significance of the experience. The power of the
subjective interpretation of reality is apparent, for example, if one interviews
adult identical twins about some incident that occurred quite early in their lives
and that they shared. It is clear from their recollections that the twins do
remember the same incident. But, as we indicated earlier, when they are asked
to pinpoint which was the most vivid moment in the incident and how they felt
at that moment, their answers are likely to indicate that they experienced the
incident in totally different manners.

Impasses

We call *impasse* what the child decides he or she must avoid at all costs.
If we are correct in assuming that the number-one priority is chosen very early,
we can make some speculation that the impasse has something to do with the
family situation and the methods of training. People with a number-one
priority of control probably have perceived themselves in their childhood as
being overpowered and overcontrolled. People with a number-one priority of
superiority have often grown up in a family where good and bad, right and
wrong, success and failure were emphasized and shaming was a common
method of child training. People with a number-one priority of superiority
seem to have felt very doubtful about their belonging as very young children
and have probably come to the conclusion that meaninglessness or nothingness is the most difficult thing to imagine. People with a number-one priority of comfort have probably experienced much stress or pain and decided to
organize their life in such a way as to avoid repetition of that discomfort.
People with a number-one priority of pleasing often have literally been rejected in some way and have experienced one or more kinds of behavior on
the part of their parents that betrayed a significant lack of respect for the
dignity of the child.

THE LIFE STYLE

In Adlerian psychology, the term *life style* refers to a person's basic
orientation toward life. As the Ansbachers (1956) observe, it is a term that
denotes a dynamic state rather than a rigid and static entity. The term also
refers to the overall system of psychological phenomena observed and inferred
by the counselor or therapist in a given individual. From this point of view, it
is more or less equivalent to terms such as *personality, psyche, character,*
and *ego*.

Since a person's life style is based on the person's private logic, develops out of the person's life plan, and is powered by the fictional goal that the

person establishes for himself or herself, we begin our discussion of the life style by analyzing these three basic concepts.

The Private Logic

The general knowledge of what is right and what is wrong, of what one should do and what one should not do, can be looked at as a kind of common sense (Dreikurs, 1969). When people don't do what the situation calls for, they are often operating on the basis of their private logic, which may differ widely from the logic of the human community. Behind every action are plans, goals, expectations, and decisions that cause the behavior but of which we are only vaguely aware. Most of our actions are the consequences of thinking processes that we don't recognize and often prefer not to know but that, nevertheless, have a definite influence on our actions. All of these thinking processes, which never reach the threshold of consciousness, can be considered part of the private logic.

> Whenever we act contrary to our conscience then we are acting with the sense of our "private" logic. This does not occur only when we want to evade the requirements of the situation. In daily life we do not deal with actual realities but operate with a subjective impression of the world, which is not always in accordance with reality. We call this subjective evaluation of events the "phenomenological field" within which each human being is moving, and which is valid only for him alone. We never can conceive of "facts" as such. We only have a more or less accurate impression in our imagination of the facts," but these impressions are used in determining our actions, our attitudes and our goals [Dreikurs, 1969, pp. 70–71; quotation translated by Pew].

The mental precursors—that is, the cognitive processes that take place below the threshold of consciousness and, yet, determine our actions—involve a hierarchy of goals that have one characteristic in common: the fact that we are unaware of them. First, there are the far-reaching basic goals of the life style. These are the fictions according to which we act and of which we are not conscious. Different factors contribute to this remarkable situation. First, these attitudes are formed when we are so young that we are hardly able to understand consciously what is happening within or around us. But, more significantly, the reason why we are unable to know these fictitious goals lies in the very necessity of subjectivity. Each of us has to act "as if" his or her judgment were the only possible and absolutely correct one.

Although the long-term goals provide the substance of the life style, we have the power to take different attitudes toward current events. In other words, our own self-created limitations within the life style still do not limit our individual creative power—that is, the ability to make decisions about immediate situations. Since we are never rigidly forced to assume an attitude, to make a decision, or to establish a goal, we must also recognize the short-range goals that we set for ourselves in the immediate experiences of our lives.

In addition to the long-range and the short-range goals, the private logic also includes a certain form of thinking that Dreikurs called the *hidden reason*. Most of us not only don't recognize the reason why we do something but are also unaware of the process that goes on in our minds and that results in that reason. In order for us to be aware of that process, we would have to imagine that we could examine our own mind whenever we said or did something. Nevertheless, when the counselor (or someone else) guesses accurately the hidden reason, the feeling of being understood is often so overpowering that even a psychotic or a juvenile delinquent is unable to hold himself back from admitting the reason for his behavior.

The Life Plan

Small children are ill prepared to deal with the demands of life. In order to cope, they must learn the rules of the game of the human community—a community experienced almost exclusively through the family, which seems to represent "life" and the "human condition." All difficulties children encounter are experienced personally and interpreted as difficulties that everyone encounters, just as all successes are incorporated and interpreted as examples of successful living.

To escape what appears as destiny and to find clarity and predictability in the disorientation of life, children develop safeguarding mechanisms and fictional solutions to problems, without which it would be impossible for human beings to orient themselves. A fiction creates an illusion of secure values. We operate under the assumption that we can feel safe only under some circumstances and that we can be worthwhile only if we act in certain ways. The child constantly creates and operates in terms of dichotomies—good or bad, on top or at the bottom, masculine or feminine, and so on. All that makes up the character of a human is none other than the manifestation of a certain specific plan that the person has laid down as a child in preparation for living. The life plan grows out of the constant repetition of attempts to cope with real or imagined difficulties. Out of this plan develops the life style, which, like a characteristic musical theme, accompanies the individual throughout life.

The Fictional Goal

Each person develops in early childhood a fictional image of what he or she would have to be like in order to be safe, to be superior, to feel belonging, and so forth. The actualization of this fictional image becomes the central goal of the person's life style and, as a consequence, limits to some extent the range of the individual's actions.

The life plan and its fictional goal are the outcomes of the child's assessment of his or her experiences. This assessment is bound to be often inaccurate because, although children are excellent observers and have extraordinarily sharp perception, they lack the experience and maturity necessary to evaluate their observations adequately. Children's perceptiveness is perhaps due in part to their lacking a set style of life. Without such set style, one is open to all possible perceptions instead of having one's perceptivity selectively biased by a style of life that prevents almost completely the experience of "pure" perception. Guided by the fictional goal, children do the best they can to find for themselves a style of life that gives them an immediate feeling of belonging and promises a greater sense of belonging for the future. The style of life they seek is also one that gives them a sense of superiority as they define it for themselves. Once set, the style of life tends to become self-perpetuating.

Because the life style and the guiding fictional goal are so intimately related, the guiding fiction tends to approximate the life style. One's guiding fiction is a certain image of the world and of oneself; therefore, a person's life style is very likely to be such that the observer can rather accurately infer from it the individual's guiding fiction.

It should be kept in mind, however, that the concept of the life style also—and especially—refers to our manner of handling ourselves with respect to our self-chosen guiding fictional goal. This means that, since our inventiveness is practically limitless (most especially when it comes to the manner of staging our own lives), there is nothing in any given guiding fiction that forcibly entails a set style of life. Thus, even after having formulated our guiding fictional goal and, to that extent, limited the range of our actions, we still have a tremendous amount of freedom in the choices we constantly make with regard to our style of living.

The Development of the Life Style

The style of living is created in the course of an ongoing drama that takes place in the theater of the family, with parents and siblings all playing a part—a drama in which the child functions as his own director and whose last act he has already sketched out in broad outlines. The nuclear family *is* society to the small child, and the child's efforts to find a place in this society influence the way in which he creates his life style. In elucidating an individual's life style, the counselor tries to get some idea of what it was like to be in that childhood drama, of what roles were played by the different actors, and of how the "director" interpreted the drama—that is, what role he played and what conclusions he drew about himself and life.

The drama analogy helps us see the role of another element in the construction of the life style. This element is the order of appearance of each actor on the stage—the birth order. We must keep in mind, however, that the importance assigned to this element is always the doing of the "director"; it is a value judgment on the part of the individual whose personality we are trying to understand. We can make some general guesses about someone's personality if we know that person's ordinal position. These guesses, however, will be based on _nomothetic laws,_ such as "Oldest children are . . . ," "Middle children tend to be . . . ," and so on. But the actual case can be quite different, depending on how the individual sees the situation and what he or she does about it—what we call _idiographic laws_. In sum, nomothetic laws concerning the family constellation help reveal the individual's idiographic laws —that is, the individual's life style.

Understanding the role that the family constellation plays in the creation of a person's life style always involves trying to put ourselves in that person's shoes in order to reconstruct the drama from his or her point of view. Drawing a diagram of the family constellation helps the counselor to quickly perceive patterns. An example of a family-constellation diagram (from Mary's point of view) is given in Figure 3–1.

Helen	George
33	35

Mary	Susan	Bobby
13	−2 years	−5 years

Figure 3–1. Diagram of Mary's family constellation as seen by Mary.

The diagram often reveals the existence of more than two "parents." Aunts, uncles, grandparents, and much older siblings can all be "parents" from the viewpoint of the child if they were an intimate part of the family drama during the years (up to age 6 or 7) in which the child was creating his or her style of living. For the diagram to be complete, it should also include those brothers and sisters who died.

Earlier in the chapter, we discussed the various factors that influence personality development. The style of living of any one individual is the result of that individual's subjective interpretation of these factors. The weight of each of them is creatively determined by the individual. We have mentioned, for example, genetic endowment and environmental influences. Both are very important, but it is the individual who will determine the degree of importance. Children create their life style from raw materials, which also include the method of training by the parents, the cultural influences in the immediate and larger community, as well as illnesses, injuries, and hospitalizations—all grist for the mill. Within those first few years, children will have created their own idiosyncratic answers to: Who am I? What is life? What must I do? What is good? What is bad? Children create their own unique private logic, which, to some extent, will make each of them different from any other human being.

Dreikurs points out that we don't know how many typical life plans exist, but probably no two human beings share the same ideas and goals (Pew, in press). Still, we find considerable similarities in the styles of living of different individuals. Perhaps it is the poverty of our language that forces us to use the same words for different observations and experiences. McLuhan has stated "All reading is guessing." Communication in any form, then, will always be an approximation both as it is sent and as it is received. It is also conceivable that each culture has a dominant perceptual mode and that its members share similar ideals and values.

Some styles of living are relatively broad, providing a basis for the solution of almost all life problems, while others have such a narrow base that they are likely to run the risk of failing. Despite the inherent cognitive defects in the life style, any individual can get along quite reasonably until such time as his or her life style is challenged by the realities of life. Remember: the style of living is self-created and is also self-consistent. After the first years of life, each new experience merely confirms the person's convictions. An individual will report the same early recollections with the same basic themes year after year, little influenced by outside reality. In other words, the individual has created his/her own convictions (or fictions) about what he/she must become and what he/she can expect of life, of the outside, and of other people.

Mosak has divided these convictions into four groups: (1) the self-concept—the convictions I have about who I am; (2) the self-ideal (this is Adler's term)—the convictions concerning what I should be or am obliged to be in order to have a place in the world; (3) the Weltbild (picture of the world)—the convictions about the nonself (world, people, nature, and so on) and what the world demands of me; and (4) the ethical convictions—the personal "right/wrong" code (Mosak & Dreikurs, 1973).

The Life Style and Counseling

The concept of life style is extremely useful in counseling, not just as a tool but also as an attitude. Adlerian counselors believe that the life style is self-created; therefore, they are likely to approach their clients with a positive attitude—the attitude that, as long as there is life, people can grow and change. If, instead, personality is seen as the result of inevitable internal or external forces, one has reason to be less optimistic, for genetic influences are relatively unchanging, and the childhood environment cannot be relived.

It should be remembered that children tend to move in line with the expectations of the adults around them. Even in such dramatic cases as those of children suffering from Down's syndrome (mongolism), the parents' expectations can make a great difference. Actually, some of the intellectual deficit in Down's syndrome may not be related to lack of genetic endowment but, rather, to a defect in the facial musculature that makes it difficult for the child to respond nonverbally to the parents. If parents don't provide the retarded child with the variety of stimulation that they would offer to a more responsive child, the intellectual deficit may, in part, be related to sensory deprivation and to distorted interaction with other people. Even institutionalized "retardates" have been shown to be "rootless and rejected, rather than defective, children" (Braginsky & Braginsky, 1971). These children can be quite skillful in the art of manipulating the staff, can appear "dumber" or "brighter" at will, and demonstrate a wide range of adaptive behaviors.

Even the mere gathering of the data necessary to elucidate a style of living, without any interpretation on the part of the counselor, is useful. Hearing clients describe their childhood family atmosphere and constellation and some of the interpretations they made about their position in the family can often provide the counselor with extremely useful information toward the goal of understanding his or her clients. In fact, in some cases, standard history taking and administration of batteries of tests may add little more.

When clients tell about their childhood family constellation and atmosphere, in a sense they are reliving that situation and the vivid moments and emotional experiences connected with that situation. By sharing the clients' emotional experiences, the counselor achieves a deeper understanding and is in a better position to help clients discover more alternatives in their lives. With the help of the counselor, clients are led to see themselves and all of their biases, guidelines, and convictions more vividly. It is as if a mirror were being held up in front of them, and they can then decide which of their basic convictions they want to keep and which of their basic mistakes they choose to alter.

A change in the life style is not necessarily the goal in counseling, because within a given style of living rest a wide range of behavioral alternatives. For example, one man's life style may include the conviction "I must fight to belong." If this conviction is challenged, the person might react with "What do you expect me to be—a doormat?" There are many other alternatives between being a fighter and being a doormat.

Some warnings are in order. Elucidating the life style is *not* for the purpose of predicting behavior—rather, for the purpose of understanding and helping another human being. Also, people often use their style of living as an excuse: "What can you expect of me? It's my life style." Finally, we need to distinguish between life style, as we use the term here, and an individual's modus operandi, such as a suburban life style versus an inner-city life style. The style of living is what makes an individual unique, what distinguishes him or her from every other human being.

Functions and Mistaken Attitudes of the Life Style

Shulman (1973) describes several functions of the life style. In excellent discussion, he refers to the life style as the cognitive blueprint, the "rule of rules," and the "unique law of movement" for each individual. He sees the life style as the "formal cause" of behavior and as governor as well as feedback. Shulman also believes that we can define quite accurately the functions of the life style as we see them in operation.

Shulman points out that oversimplification, exaggeration, and mistaking the part for the whole are three common mistakes in logic that are also common in the style of living. It is useful to list as part of the formulation of the life style (see Chapter 6) the basic mistakes that are usually beneath the threshold of consciousness. Sometimes these mistakes begin as appropriate attitudes; that is, they were appropriate in the childhood situation but are no longer appropriate for the adult man or woman. Shulman (1973) categorizes these basic mistakes into six groups:

1. Distorted attitudes about self—for example, "I am less capable than the others."
2. Distorted attitudes about the world and people—for example, "Life is unpredictable" or "People are no damn good."
3. Distorted goals—for example, "I must be perfect" or "I must never submit."
4. Distorted methods of operation—for example, excessive competitiveness, excessive pride, or ignoring what one doesn't wish to confront.
5. Distorted ideals—for example, "A real man is always heroic" or "The only thing worth being is a star."
6. Distorted conclusions: (a) pessimism—for example, "I am doomed to failure" or "Life is nothing but a trap"; (b) X (love, reason, money, or whatever) conquers all; (c) cynicism—for example, "Everyone is out only for himself" or "There is always an ulterior motive"; (d) fanaticism—for example, "This is the best of all possible systems" or "I'm the only one who has the 'real' truth."

Types of Life Styles

This brings us to the issue of the advantages and disadvantages of typologies. Labeling the client may be a comfort to the counselor but can be a disservice to the client. For, as soon as we have placed someone in a particular category, our tendency is to overlook the person's complexities and subtleties—those special nuances that make the person unique. It is far too easy to move from the position of seeing people in terms of labels to a position of disrespect, however subtle. And most people are quick to pick up on our failure to treat them with dignity and respect. Also, although personality typing may help us organize our thinking, we should be cautious that our clients don't use typology as an excuse: "Well, that's me. I'm a pleaser, you know!" And we should also be aware that personality typing may reduce our expectations as counselors, thus resulting in lack of respect for our clients.

Keeping these warnings in mind, some generalizations can be drawn about types of life styles (Mosak, 1971).

- "Getters" try to expend as little effort as possible, while hoping for extravagant returns. Only if the world will give them special due are they willing to contribute. Generally, they look for the payoff and tend to renege on their side of the deal.
- "Drivers" want to succeed and achieve, often beyond anyone's wildest dreams. They behave as if total success or "nothingness" were the only alternatives.
- "Controllers" like order, their order. They fear chaos and try to keep the unexpected to a bare minimum. Unfortunately for them, other people keep behaving spontaneously, thus disrupting their system.
- "Victims" and "martyrs" are similar in their "noble" suffering. However, a martyr will suffer for a cause, while a victim will suffer for anything. Victims, then, are more flexible and creative—perhaps.
- "Good ones" satisfy their sense of superiority by being more competent, more useful, more right, or holier than others. They narrow their life styles by obeying the rule that only by excelling in whatever area of moral perfection they have chosen can they truly belong. Needless to say, very few others measure up to these people's high standards.

None of these types is inherently bad. It depends always on what the individual does with his or her convictions (see the discussion of the psychology of use in Chapter 2). Thus, each type may make great contributions, but often for the wrong reasons and at times almost accidentally. Actually, in practice we seldom see pure types. More often we see blends, because the styles of living of individual beings are infinitely varied. The more we learn about a person, the more unique and creative that person becomes in our eyes.

It is essential that the therapist or counselor clearly understand the process through which individuals create their personality, their life style. As we said earlier, the prototype of the life style is already apparent in the first few weeks and months of life, and the broad strokes of a personal life style are well developed by the time the child is 2 or 3. Probably, by the time the child is 4 or 5, the basic structure of the life style is well organized and will remain essentially the same throughout life unless challenged by major experiences or through therapy.

This basic structure is like a foundation that remains relatively unchanged but on which can be developed a broad variety of superstructures. The foundation includes the individual's self-created final fictional goal—that is, his or her idea of how security, belonging, superiority, perfection, or completion can be achieved. All aspects of the personality can be seen as movement in the direction of the final goal. All behavior, then, makes sense if we understand people's private logic, where they think they must go and how they think they must get there. All external influences, important as they may be, have been and will be filtered through the "intermediary psychological metabolism." Each individual will have a different reality, because each individual is totally dependent on his or her subjectivity. All of us will always be functioning "as if"—as if perfection or completion were precisely as we have defined it and as if the only way to move in the direction of such perfection or completion were along the guidelines we have set up for ourselves in early childhood.

These concepts of reality, however, are open to change. If the individual has created them in the first place, he or she can create new ones to take their place—new ones that are more in the direction of courage and social interest. Change comes about as the therapist or counselor consistently challenges each basic mistake, thus helping the person see how counterproductive—at times even ridiculous—these concepts of reality are.

REFERENCES

Ansbacher, H. L., & Ansbacher R. R. (Eds.). *The Individual Psychology of Alfred Adler*. New York: Harper & Row, 1956.

Braginsky, D. D., & Braginsky, B. M. *Hansels and Gretels: Studies of children in institutions for the mentally retarded*. New York: Holt, Rinehart & Winston, 1971.

Chess, S., Thomas, A., & Birch, H. *Your child is a person: A psychological approach to parenthood without guilt*. New York: Viking, 1965.

Dreikurs, R. *Grundbegriffe der Individualpsychologie*. Stuttgart: Ernst Klett Verlag, 1969.

Hooker, D. Early human fetal behavior, with a preliminary note of double simultaneous fetal stimulation. *Proceedings of the Association for Research in Nervous and Mental Disease*. Baltimore: William & Wilkins, 1954.

Moore, O. K. Autotelic responsive environments and exceptional children. In J. Hellmuth (Ed.), *The special child in century 21*. Seattle: Special Child Publications of the Sequin School, 1964.

Mosak, H. H. Lifestyle. In A. G. Nikelly (Ed.), *Techniques for behavior change*. Springfield, Ill.: Charles C Thomas, 1971.

Mosak, H. H., & Dreikurs, R. Adlerian psychotherapy. In R. J. Corsini (Ed.), *Current psychotherapies*. Itasca, Ill.: Peacock, 1973.

Nikelly, A. G. (Ed.). *Techniques for behavior change*. Springfield, Ill.: Charles C Thomas, 1971.

Pepper, F. C. Birth order. In A. G. Nikelly (Ed.), *Techniques for behavior change*. Springfield, Ill.: Charles C Thomas, 1971.

Satir, V. *Peoplemaking*. Palo Alto, Calif.: Science and Behavior Books, 1972.

Shulman, B. H. *Contributions to Individual Psychology*. Chicago: Alfred Adler Institute, 1973.

Standing, E. M. *Maria Montessori: Her life and work*. New York: New American Library, 1962.

CHAPTER 4

PSYCHOPATHOLOGY

The term *psychopathology* presents problems. No one has ever seen a psyche or demonstrated its existence. The psyche is a heuristic invention, which may be useful as long as we keep a holistic view. Pathology implies sickness. Most schools of psychology have been constructed on the sickness (or pathology) model, just as medicine built its foundations on pathology. But the advantages of basing human understanding on a pathology model may be outweighed by the disadvantages.

When we are disturbed by behavior and wish to bring about change, we (society) tend to deal with the problem by putting people in special classrooms, by incarcerating them in institutions, by sending them to confession, or by putting them in bed in a hospital. In other words, labeling them stupid, bad, sinful, or sick. The latter may be the least punitive but still carries with it a lack of respect for the individual, an emphasis on his or her weaknesses, and an overlooking of his or her strengths. When we put someone in bed because of troublesome behavior, we may unwittingly reinforce the negative behavior and reduce the possibility of recovery.

NEUROTIC SYMPTOMS

In *The Myth of Mental Illness,* Szasz (1974) has taken what many critics would call an extreme position. What is often referred to as mental illness, Szasz says, may be a variety of human failure based on discouragement and a set of mistaken ideas about how to find belonging in the human community.

This condition of failure and discouragement is often identified as *neurosis*. What is neurosis? Essentially, neurotics are aware and accepting of the common sense, and they know what they should do. But they arrange, through various creative symptom complexes, to avoid certain tasks of life. They have an exaggerated and mistaken idea of what they must do to belong, yet, in one way or another, they are "on strike." (*Psychotics,* instead, tend to function much more on the basis of private logic, ignoring the common sense and making bizarre pretenses at responding to the various challenges of life.) To put it simply: neurotics add two and two and do get four, but they don't like it.

Neurotics are characterized by lofty overambition, lack of courage, and a pessimistic attitude. They lack the courage to be imperfect and suspect the worst. They engage in artistic "smoke screens" that convince them (and some of their associates) that they are really trying—all the time deftly avoiding the basic responsibilities of life. They are not consciously aware of their psychological mechanisms, else they would have a hard time maintaining them.

Usually a neurosis begins when a person's style of living slams up against the reality of life and, in discouragement, the person retreats to a sideshow rather than face the main test. Neurotics are always reassuring themselves about their lofty ideals and grand intentions. The symptoms they create always have social significance; they are meant to avoid some responsibility of the human community or to attempt to control in some way the behavior of those around. Every symptom has meaning. No behavior is irrational if we understand the point of view of the person and his or her peculiar situation as he or she sees it.

Choosing Symptoms

Why is one symptom chosen? Usually, a person stumbles by chance onto the fact that a certain symptom can relieve responsibility or has unusual power in the control of others. Sometimes the symptom is revived from early childhood, and sometimes it is the result of modeling (Uncle John always got out of helping with the dishes by complaining of indigestion after overeating).

Small children often choose symptoms related to what their parents want to avoid most. Anything we want for our children more than they want it for themselves we will not get. In a family in which high premium is placed on the value of proper eating, a child may choose over- or undereating as a symptom. Another family may place great emphasis on bladder function—a marvelous setting for enuresis. If mother controls the family with her headaches, it is not unlikely that one or more of her children may become just as creative. Certain organ inferiorities[1] run in families. Certain illnesses, too—for ex-

---

[1] *Organ inferiority* refers to the fact that, for reasons that are not at all clear, in certain individuals (and even in some families) a particular organ or organ system functions as the point of least resistance. Consequently, that organ or system is likely to be the first to fail to function when the body is subjected to unusual stress.

ample, allergy—may be heavily endowed with psychological overlay. Here are some examples.

David, a junior-high student, has a definite family history of moderate eczema and has been suffering from hay fever and asthma since he was 7 or 8 years old. A complete medical workup reveals that he is sensitive to many inhalants. However, he usually wheezes with asthma only during the week, seldom on weekends, and infrequently during vacations. David's parents desperately want a good education for him; in fact, they are more concerned with his education than he is. David, on the other hand, feels put down and hurt because his parents don't accept him as he is; and he deeply resents their demands on him. His way of "getting even" with them is by doing poorly in school. His tendency toward asthma, particularly during the night preceding a school day, seems to absolve him of all responsibility for his behavior. Of course, David is not consciously aware of these psychological mechanisms. A combination of individual counseling, family therapy, and good medical treatment result in a marked lessening of the frequency and severity of David's asthmatic attacks.

Five members of a large, strict Catholic family have ulcers. They seem to be saying through organ language that they can't "stomach" the atmosphere. Because of the oppressive atmosphere of this family, perhaps that's the only language they dare to use to express their feelings.

A woman has been happily married for many years. Suddenly, because of business frustrations and an overall "middle-age crisis," her husband, once attentive and responsible, starts drinking heavily. The situation "breaks her heart," and she ends up in the intensive coronary-care unit. After extensive examinations, she is dismissed from the hospital because all the tests show that there is nothing wrong with her heart.

A young man loses his job in a plant that emphasizes perfect control of temperature, humidity, and dust. In his new job, which he bitterly dislikes, the conditions are quite different. Among other things, there is a lot of dust. The young man develops nasal allergy, which baffles the physicians particularly because he has no previous history of allergy. Counseling reveals that this young man has always been "nose oriented." As a teenager, he felt that the shape and size of his nose were responsible for his lack of social contacts, especially with girls.

The building blocks of neurosis may include genetic tendencies, family values, past life experiences, and often mere chance alone, which suddenly gives the individual an unexpected excuse. The purposiveness of neurosis is clearly seen in so-called "compensation neurosis," in which it literally pays the individual who is suing for damages to maintain the symptoms until after the court settlement, as the following case illustrates.

A young man suffered a fairly severe back injury at work. He and his family had long been struggling to make ends meet. Suddenly, he found himself in the hospital, relieved of all responsibilities. His problems and what he saw as his own failure were forgotten. After a prolonged hospitalization, his doctors pronounced him able to return to work. His symptoms, however, persisted for two and a half years. But, as soon as his case was settled in his favor in court, the symptoms disappeared. Even in such a clear-cut situation, outside observers, including experts in human behavior, are hard put to tell for sure whether or not a person is malingering. And even if the experts were absolutely certain that the person was malingering, the very fact that he or she found malingering necessary would still be indicative of problems that warrant counseling.

Childhood Symptoms

One of the most common neuroses in childhood is the so-called "school phobia." In dealing with this problem, child psychiatrists tend to make a distinction between the younger children and the older, more experienced students. In general, the symptoms of school avoidance in younger children can be best understood in terms of the goals of their behavior. They avoid school in one way or another to gain attention, to show their power, to get even, or to demonstrate their "disability." Counseling can be quick and effective if it focuses on identifying the goal and teaching the parents and/or teachers and administrators to extricate themselves from the unreasonable demands of the child. With adolescents, significant school avoidance may be a much more complex problem. The youth is likely to come from a family in which fairly severe conflict is present and to lean in the direction of psychotic behavior.

School avoidance, by both younger and older students, is often accompanied by physical symptoms. Dreikurs (1962) has provided us with help in discerning whether the disease is functional—that is, not of organic nature. The youngster is asked how his life would be different if he suddenly had no more abdominal pain or whatever he is complaining of. If the complaint is functional, the youth will answer that he would have more friends, or study better, or get along better at home, or find his relationship with girls improved. In other words, he will point to the life task he is avoiding with his symptom. If the pain is organic, he will answer, instead, that he would feel better, without any reference to avoided life tasks.

Adlerians view all human failures as mistaken efforts to find belonging. Thus, the basic psychodynamics of the neurotic, the psychotic, the person with character disorder, the delinquent, the dropout, and the nonlearner all have many more similarities than differences. Occasionally, children and, somewhat more often, adolescents exhibit schizophrenic or psychotic behavior. In such cases, diagnosis must include careful case history, physical examination, neurological evaluation, and family description. The possibility of organic psychosis, although rare, must be investigated, since certain endocrinological and central-nervous system disorders respond well to medical treatment. On the other hand, we must not be quick to attribute to brain dysfunction what is, instead, the result of parental or teacher failure. Diagnoses are not immune from fads. Minimal brain damage and dyslexia are two examples of current fads. Even if clear-cut organic disorder is found and medical therapy prescribed, the counselor is not absolved of responsibility. The youngster and his/her family have usually experienced many discouragements. A holistic approach to counseling takes into consideration the whole child in his/her family and in his/her community. Adlerians deplore, for example, the tendency to rely on a prescribed medication as the only form of therapy.

In our own clinical experience, we have been aware of an occasional child whose hyperactivity appeared to be part of a cluster of "soft" neurological findings. Such a child can be helped immensely through appropriate use of stimulants. But such therapy should be taken as seriously as starting a young diabetic on insulin, with a comprehensive treatment program involving the ongoing cooperation of the child, his or her family, and *all* of the professionals involved.

Dennis, at 8 years of age, had thoroughly exhausted his kindergarten, first-grade, and second-grade teachers. He was in constant motion —from the time that preceded his birth (his mother described him as very active in utero) throughout his preschool years. Although he had no significant insult to his central nervous system, the electroencephalogram showed some very mild abnormalities. Neurological examination revealed nothing that would point to any specific lesion, but there were a number of tasks that Dennis couldn't do with the dexterity that one would expect of someone his age. His teacher reported that he had a "short attention span" and that he didn't attend to the learning process. Dennis was given a small dose of dextroamphetamine in a time-release capsule each morning. The teacher was not informed that the child was receiving medication. After the dose had been increased three times, the teacher called Dennis' parents and told them that a remarkable change had taken place in the child. Dennis was calm and functioning much more smoothly, his attention span had increased, and he was able to sit still in the classroom. Most remarkable of all, he had actually begun to show some enthusiasm about learning.

During the next several years, Dennis was kept on medication. His pediatrician, however, kept contact with the school, with the home, with Dennis' special-education teacher, and with the elementary-school counselor. From time to time, individual-counseling sessions and family-therapy sessions were held. The dosage of medication had to be changed to take into consideration the boy's spurts of growth. By the time he reached junior high, Dennis had almost caught up with his classmates academically. Attempts were made to withdraw the medication during vacations, but, after a week or so, Dennis usually asked to be put back on the medication. By the time Dennis reached tenth grade, he was able to function very well without medication, was a responsible young businessman with two part-time jobs, and enjoyed school. Contrary to many expressed concerns, Dennis did not become "addicted" to amphetamines. Quite the contrary: he was so tired of taking pills that he was very hesitant about taking any kind of pill whatsoever.

Adolescence Symptoms

In adolescence, a complex value-orienting process takes place, and the task of value formation may outshadow all other aspects of the adolescent's life. Thus, a common syndrome of this age is a vaguely defined existential neurosis, with adolescents appropriately questioning almost everything and, in the process, neglecting the more mundane tasks and producing confusion not only in their own minds but in the minds of their close associates, their parents, and their teachers. If parents, teachers, counselors, and friends are to be helpful at this time, channels of communication must be kept open as adolescents try to use those around them as sounding boards for their newly developing ideas and values.

Although rarely identified as troubled or troublesome, adolescents in crisis sometimes take drastic measures to signal their need for help. Passive withdrawal may approach schizophrenic proportions. Suicidal threats and attempts are common. Bizarre and irresponsible behavior, often related to experimentation with drugs or alcohol, may result in a psychiatric picture that is indistinguishable from serious psychosis. But the adolescent also exhibits remarkable recuperative powers and ability to change. As counselors, we need to walk the narrow line between overreacting and seeing the fluid adolescent in adult mental-illness terms—terms that may keep us from showing sufficient concern to a youngster who is hurting desperately and doesn't know how to ask for help.

The active troublemakers are much more obvious. Much delinquency is related to the pressure of peers and to the striving for excitement, as well as to the fact that we have raised a generation of tyrants who say, in one form or another, "If you don't do what I want, you don't love me!" Because of this attitude and because of the hypocrisy they observe in adult society, adolescents often feel justified to seek out whatever gratification meets their fancy, with little regard for the rights of others. This attitude, however, is usually directed toward the "establishment," and the youth retains a certain degree of social interest with regard to the immediate peer group.

In the area of sexuality, all evidence points to much earlier and more frequent experimentation than was true in the past. Yet, most of today's adolescent sexual behavior still occurs within the context of meaningful, however brief, relationships. In many adolescent cultures, the norm is monogamy.

Betty lives in a small town. In her high school, couples who "go steady'' take their relationship—even if it is short lived—quite seriously. Betty has two boyfriends, and she also keeps an open, friendly relationship with a number of other boys. Because of this situation, she is considered by many of her peers, as well as by some of the parents and teachers, a "loose woman."

The kinds of problems adolescents present to counselors relate to one or more areas of the life tasks. Occupation—current, as a student, as well as future—is a frequent source of concern. Many of our schools are doing little to stimulate the keen intellectual curiosity so common in adolescence. This is why school is often seen as a grim sentence to be served. Although dropouts, throwouts, and throwbacks are common, any youth can be reached if he or she can be enlisted as a true partner in the educational process. The work ethic in our society is being seriously challenged. Many youth look at their parents' crowded schedules, fatigue, psychosomatic disorders, pill popping, and alcoholism—and wonder.

Taking a "sabbatical" in late adolescence is becoming more and more common. In the past, most young people went directly from high school to college, even if they didn't have a clear goal in mind or a particular reason for continuing their studies. But today increasing numbers of students, recognizing and accepting their lack of clear-cut goals, choose not to go to college merely for the sake of being in college and decide, instead, to take off a year to work, to travel, to experience another culture, or to otherwise broaden their experience before moving into a specific program.

Another task that confronts adolescents is the social challenge. In a democratic society, this boils down to the challenge of social equality —learning to live together as social equals. As counselors, we could learn a great deal from students, some of whom are literally working full time in this area.

We touched briefly on the task of love. Counselors are likely to hear more and more about feelings of inadequacy in the area of sexuality. In the college population, male impotence is today a more common complaint than female frigidity—quite a switch from a decade ago and a reflection of the increasing equality between the sexes. Retreat from the love task is seen in ever-increasing homosexuality, experimentation with alternatives to sexual dyads, and a wide range of bizarre sexual fantasies and actions. Counselors can start from the assumption that many of their students will have questions and problems related to sexuality. To be effective, counselors need to be knowledgeable in this area and to have thought through their own values, while avoiding imposing those values on their student—a difficult task indeed.

Another life task that is particularly problematical in adolescence is that of getting along with oneself. The young are subjected to many put-downs, subtle and not so subtle. Watch a long-haired 14-year-old try to get waited on by a clerk, for example. In many instances, the only source of encouragement will be the adolescent's peers, but relationships among the young are often fluid. Like all of us, adolescents need to learn to accept themselves as they are at the moment, to develop the courage to be imperfect, and to be willing to do the best they can and let the chips fall where they may.

Spiritual issues, although paramount for many adolescents, are frequently overlooked by counselors. All of us have the task of figuring out who we are, why we are here, and what our relationship is to the universe, to creation, and to God (if we are religious). The search for meaning cannot be underestimated in the counseling process.

Leisure and recreation, an expected part of adolescence, present their own set of problems. Love of excitement, adventure, and fun is normal in adolescence and all too often blunted in "maturity." Yet, the adolescent is faced with the need to put fun into perspective, with the question of participation versus passive spectatorship, and with the whole issue of responsible use of leisure time—an issue that promises to be of ever-increasing proportions in our fairly immediate future.

Parenting is another crucial issue in adolescence. Some adolescents are parents themselves or are contemplating parenthood fairly soon, and others are parenting younger siblings. Many young people witness, and often see so clearly, the errors that their own parents make. In our opinion, specific training for parenthood should begin at least by seventh grade. Counselors will need to play an important role in planning and leading such training.

We have mentioned earlier the results of faulty parenting. One of the most distinctive child-rearing mistakes is pampering. The pampered life style becomes especially clear in the school setting. Pampered youngsters have failed to learn the art of giving and taking. Their social interest is deficient; that is, the willingness to cooperate, to be part of the whole, and to contribute is severely challenged outside the home situation. The school is not set up to give these adolescents the special consideration they demand. Their retaliation is school avoidance, physical symptoms, failure to learn, defective interpersonal relationships, and, occasionally, adultlike neuroses—hysteria, obsessive compulsiveness, anxiety, and depression, to name a few. Personal protest may take the form of joining with other malcontents and disrupting the efforts of the school. If these youngsters can be recognized in their discouragement, their deficient social interest, and their high-flown ambitions, counselors are in a position to lead them toward greater social interest by capitalizing on their ambition and leadership abilities.

Psychopathology is often explained by defeated and pessimistic observers as the result of various relatively unchangeable socioeconomic factors. As members of the human community, we must, of course, do all we can to make sure that the basic survival needs of others are met. However, we must also be careful not to use sociological studies and pseudoscientific classifications as a means of alleviating our personal responsibility as counselors. We must, therefore, be aware of the special areas of concern that beset youth, keeping in mind that we live in a society that provides little opportunity for young people to be contributing partners in their own education or in the community at large. We must be sensitive to the needs of those adolescents who feel locked in by economic deprivation and by racial or religious discrimination. Our task is to meet students where they are, so to speak, building on strengths and overlooking weaknesses. As long as a student is alive and breathing, no matter what kind of psychopathology he or she is burdened with, he or she can *grow* and change. One counselor with faith in the powerful creativity of humans can literally mean the difference between life and death.

> It was about this time that I discovered Papanek's secret. It was really very simple. He had the ability to see everybody as they really are—just people, no more and no less. Also, he saw children as people, little young people with individuality, not as some separate group of beings called children, dominated by the so-called adult world. Having this ability alone made him a giant at understanding people; being Papanek . . . made him irresistibly likable.
>
> Papanek had a way of making the whole world seem beautiful and making everybody in life seem to be important. And he made life important from the standpoint of the individual. He made life big, not only in relation to people. He made it go over a whole lot of nonsensical things like color, like handicaps, like looks [Brown, 1965, p. 125].

CLASSIFICATION OF MENTAL DISORDERS

Any theory of psychopathology is based on the assumption that there are certain specific psychopathological entities that can be named, described, and explained in some manner. Or there may be entities that, because of the current state of scientific development, are recognizable but are beyond explanation. The *Diagnostic and Statistical Manual of Mental Disorders* (DSM-II), published by the American Psychiatric Association (1968), provides a nomenclature that is commonly used in mental hospitals, psychiatric clinics, and office practice. It is also used in general hospitals—both in psychiatric wards and in consultation services to patients in other hospital departments—in community mental-health centers, as well as in consultations to courts and in industrial health services.

The manual uses suitable diagnostic terms that are meant to facilitate communication in the mental-health field, keeping confusion and ambiguity to a minimum. In their foreword to the manual, the authors point out that different names for the same manifestation imply different attitudes and concepts—that is, different theories of psychopathology. The manual, however, tries to avoid terms that carry with them "implications" regarding either the nature of a disorder or its causes and is explicit about causal assumptions when they are integral to a diagnostic concept (American Psychiatric Association, 1968).

In the DSM-II, the authors vigorously attempt to avoid any general view of the nature of mental disorders. Individuals may have more than one mental disorder. For example, a patient with anxiety neurosis may also develop h␣ addiction. Many mental disorders, particularly mental retardation and t␣ various organic brain syndromes, are reflections of underlying physical conditions. If those conditions are known, they need to be taken into consideration not only in the diagnosis but in the theory of psychopathology.

The diagnostic nomenclature in general use in the United States includes ten categories of mental disorders.

1. Mental retardation
2. Organic brain syndromes
   a. Psychoses associated with organic brain syndromes
   b. Nonpsychotic organic brain syndromes
3. Psychoses not attributed to physical conditions
4. Neuroses
5. Personality disorders and certain other nonpsychotic mental disorders
6. Psychophysiologic disorders
7. Special symptoms
8. Transient situational disturbances
9. Behavior disorders of childhood and adolescence
10. Conditions without manifest psychiatric disorder and nonspecific conditions.

In an attempt to elucidate a teleoanalytical holistic theory of psychopathology,[2] we will discuss each of these categories, considering how childhood experiences, inferiority feelings, compensation, approach to the life tasks, and specific symptom formation can offer some understanding of why a particular person behaves the way he or she does. We will also discuss how a psychotherapeutic or counseling approach can contribute to the client's holistic rehabilitation—that is, the achievement of maximum function and self-actualization physically, spiritually, and mentally. Such achievement is seen within the context of the person's genetic endowment, environmental situation, personal life style, and the realities of the specific medical problems that are contributing to the mental disorder.

MENTAL RETARDATION

Mental retardation is subnormal general intellectual functioning. It usually originates during the developmental period and is associated with impaired learning, defective social adjustment, or delayed maturation. Although many Adlerians decry the overuse and abuse of intelligence testing, the

[2]A teleoanalytical holistic theory of psychopathology regards any troubled or troublesome behavior as a reflection of one indivisible, unified, whole organism moving toward self-created goals.

various degrees of mental retardation can be specified by referring to the IQ range.

Borderline mental retardation: IQ 68–85
Mild mental retardation: IQ 52–67
Moderate mental retardation: IQ 36–51
Severe mental retardation: IQ 20–35
Profound mental retardation: IQ under 20

All available intelligence tests measure only a limited number of attributes. More specifically, no reliable tests are available to measure that nebulous capability that we refer to as *adaptation*. Adlerians believe that even significantly handicapped individuals still influence their social milieu and are influenced by it and that many of them can make significant contributions to society. Many children who have been diagnosed as mentally subnormal have no demonstrable defects whatsoever; rather, they have become highly skilled at training adults to treat them as if they were defective.

We believe that at least half of the so-called borderline mentally retarded children in the public-school system are actually pseudoretarded. These are desperately discouraged children, who operate in most situations with one goal in mind: to be left alone and to be treated as if they were disabled, thus avoiding challenges or the possibility that their true limitations may be revealed.

Mental retardation includes many clinical subcategories. A significant number of cases can be classified according to known causes. Among these causal factors are infection or intoxication; psychological or physical trauma; disorders in metabolism, growth, or nutrition; gross brain disease (postnatal); diseases and other conditions due to unknown prenatal influences; chromosomal abnormality; prematurity; psychosis and other major psychiatric disorders in early childhood; and psychosocial (environmental) deprivation. In the cases associated with this last condition, the degree of retardation is usually mild.

ORGANIC BRAIN SYNDROMES

These disorders are associated with pathological disturbances in the brain—that is, with impairment of brain-tissue function. They may be acute or chronic and may be the result of vascular disease, disturbances of circulation of the cerebral spinal fluid, intracranial masses, various toxins, certain genetic conditions, postinfectious conditions—for example, Parkinson's disease, which develops many, many years after a bout of influenza—metabolic disorders, convulsive disorders, and a number of poorly understood conditions, such as multiple sclerosis. Whenever possible, it is important to move from the general diagnostic category of organic brain syndrome to a diagnosis that clearly indicates etiology. Even mild cases of organic brain syndrome show self-centeredness, difficulty in assimilating new experiences, and childish emotionality. Deterioration may be minimal or progress to vegetative existence.

As we said earlier, Individual Psychology is a psychology of use rather than a psychology of possession. Best estimates indicate that most of us use no more than 10% of our total brain capacity. As Adlerians, we are less interested in what a person "possesses" in terms of pathology than in what he or she does with it. The senile and presenile dementias, for example, would seem to have tremendous significance with regard not only to the individual's expectations but also to the expectations of those in the person's milieu. In other words, whatever causes senile or presenile dementia and whatever amount of actual brain damage has occurred will not alone be sufficient to account for the way the person behaves.

Two people with identical amounts of measurable brain damage may still have strikingly different degrees of troublesome behavior. The more a person expects to be dysfunctional, the more dysfunctional he or she is likely to be. Also, clients tend to move in line with the expectations of their caretakers. We have seen many cases of so-called backward patients in mental hospitals who, with the help of medication, are mobilized and reintroduced into the community, functioning at a much better level than anybody would have previously imagined. Resocialization has also made it possible for seriously handicapped inmates of mental-retardation units to function at a higher level and sometimes even become self-sufficient.

Psychoses Associated with Organic Brain Syndromes

The *alcoholic psychoses* are said to be caused by alcohol poisoning. Psychosis, psychoneurosis, and other disorders may also be aggravated by alcohol intake. *Delirium tremens* is an acute brain syndrome characterized by delirium, coarse tremors, and frightening visual hallucination. Clinically, this condition is related not only to the ingestion of alcohol but to nutritional deficiency and to the physical and social surroundings of a person with whom the use of alcohol has become a severe problem. The fact that delirium tremens can be greatly alleviated by the attitude of the helper and by the physical surroundings gives credence to the view that chemically stimulated psychopathologies have tremendous social implications.

Because alcohol is such a frequently misused chemical, a number of other syndromes have been associated with it, including *Korsakoff's psychosis,* which is a variety of a chronic brain syndrome characterized by memory impairment, disorientation, peripheral neuropathy, and, most of all, confabulation. Other terms, such as alcoholic hallucinoses, alcohol paranoias, acute alcohol intoxication, alcoholic deterioration, and pathological intoxication, merely describe the wide range of psychopathology connected with the misuse of alcohol in our society. Alcoholism is being seen more and more as a family problem, with the "enabler" (most frequently, a spouse) being as much of a problem as the individual who is misusing alcohol.

There are a number of psychoses associated with intracranial infection, either bacterial or viral. Here, too, the degree of disability is strongly related to the preinfection life style as well as to the attitude of the helpers and the attitude of the significant others.

Another large number of psychoses are associated with insult to the central nervous system. Among them are psychosis with cerebral arteriosclerosis, psychosis with other cerebral vascular disturbance, psychosis with epilepsy, psychosis with intracranial neoplasm, psychosis with degenerative disease of the central nervous system, and psychosis with brain trauma. Of course, not everyone with cerebral vascular problems, epilepsy, neoplasm, degenerative disease of the central nervous system, or brain trauma develops psychosis. Whether or not psychosis becomes a problem depends in part on the personal life style of the patient, on the expectations of the therapist, and on the expectations of the intimate others.

There are a number of psychoses associated with other physical conditions, such as endocrine disorders, metabolic or nutritional disorders, systemic infections, drug or poison intoxication, and childbirth. Many people who belong in this category appear to use, involuntarily and unconsciously, the physical condition to say no to life, in the broadest possible sense, by developing some form of psychosis. That is, each of the above physical disorders may provide the stimulus and the excuse for the patient to reject life in whatever creative form he or she may produce the psychotic symptoms. A holistic treatment must include not only treatment of the psychosis but also, depending on the causative factor, correction of endocrine disorders, specific treatment of metabolic or nutritional problems, treatment of infection, identification of poisons, or a complete evaluation of the psychological significance of childbirth, not only for the individual but for the spouse and other members of the family.

Nonpsychotic Organic Brain Syndromes

All of the conditions that we have discussed can also be found in nonpsychotic organic brain syndromes. A common syndrome is found in children with mild brain damage and is often manifested by hyperactivity, short attention span, easy distractibility, and impulsiveness. At other times, the child is withdrawn, listless, perseverative, and unresponsive. These symptoms are deeply affected by the interaction between the child and his or her parents and teachers.

PSYCHOSES NOT ATTRIBUTED TO PHYSICAL CONDITIONS

Schizophrenia

The two groups of mental disturbances that belong in this category are schizophrenia and affective disorders. Both are called *functional distur-*

bances, since both prevent the patient from functioning properly, although there is no definite evidence of brain injury or disease.

Schizophrenia includes a group of disorders with characteristic disturbances of thinking, mood, and behavior. The thinking disturbances may lead to misinterpretation of reality and sometimes to delusions and hallucinations. Mood changes may include ambivalent, constrictive, and inappropriate emotional responses and loss of empathy with other people. The behavior may be withdrawn, regressive, and bizarre.

Simple schizophrenia is characterized chiefly by slow and insidious reduction of external attachments and interests and by apathy and indifference. These manifestations lead to impoverishment of interpersonal relationships, mental deterioration, and adjustment to a lower level of functioning. *Hebephrenic schizophrenia* reveals disorganized thinking, shallow or inappropriate affect, unpredictable giggling, "silly" and regressive behavior and mannerisms, frequent hypochondriacal complaints, as well as transient and poorly organized delusions and hallucinations. *Catatonic schizophrenia* includes two types; one is expressed in excessive and sometimes violent motor activity and excitement, and the other in generalized inhibition accompanied by stupor, mutism, negativism, or lack of flexibility. *Paranoid schizophrenia* is characterized by persecutory or grandiose delusions, frequent hallucinations, sometimes religiosity, and a hostile and aggressive attitude, with behavior consistent with the delusions.

During acute schizophrenic episodes, the patient often manifests confusion, perplexity, ideas of reference, emotional turmoil, dreamlike dissociation, excitement, and repression or fear. Schizophrenia is accompanied by a variety of often antithetical symptoms, such as pronounced elation or acute depression. Occasionally a form of schizophrenia is manifested before puberty. Besides those that we enumerated, there are also chronic undifferentiated varieties (Shulman, 1968).

Major Affective Disorders

The other group of nonorganic psychoses includes the major *affective disorders,* which are characterized by extreme depression or elation that dominates the mental life of the patient. Such disorders of mood also have an all-pervasive effect on the people closest to the patient. Acute depression is a dysjunctive emotion and, as such, has the effect of creating distance between the patient and important others. Elation, on the other hand, is per se a conjunctive emotion—that is, an emotion that brings people together. But, as a major affective disorder, elation is such an extreme mood that it usually drives people away.

Although the affective disorders are generally considered functional rather than organic, there is considerable controversy with regard to the origin of these disorders. Particularly those cases that are cyclic in nature and whose shifts do not relate directly to precipitating life experiences are the most likely to be considered by many as organically based. Naturally, people with major affective disorders also have psychological and social problems. Even when the extreme mood swings can be controlled with medication, the patients often reveal quite limiting neuroses or personality disorders. To put it another way, their style of living is narrow and limiting, and they often fail to fulfill the responsibilities of one or more of the life tasks.

The *paranoid states* are psychotic disorders in which a delusion, whether persecutory or grandiose, is the basic problem. Whatever disturbances in mood, behavior, and thinking are noted seem to derive from a specific delusion. Most authorities believe that the paranoid states are variants of schizophrenia or of a paranoid personality.

If a person develops a reactive depression—that is, in response to some stimulus—accompanied by impaired reality, a diagnosis of psychotic-depressive reaction may be made.

NEUROSES

We said earlier that, from the Adlerian point of view, a neurotic is a person who generally accepts the common sense but doesn't like it. Fear or anxiety characterizes the neuroses. Neurotics, with their high-flown ambitions, fear losing their place, however they may define it. Adler (1972) once said that all neurosis is vanity. The neurotic is a person who approaches life with a "yes, but" attitude. And, of course, if a person always goes through life "but" first, he or she will surely "save face"; thus, his or her vanity will be satisfied.

Neurosis may be manifested in a variety of different patterns. *Anxiety neurosis* is characterized by apprehension or fear so acute that it may reach the point of panic and is often accompanied by somatic symptoms. *Hysterical neurosis* generally involves an involuntary psychogenic loss or disorder of function. The symptoms appear suddenly in very frightening or highly emotional situations. Here is an illustration.

> Charlene, a 19-year-old woman, got into a major conflict with her father one Sunday afternoon. Later, she recalled being afraid that she would hurt him with her cutting remarks or even physically. By the time she was admitted to the hospital, she had lost her voice and the function of both arms.

In the *conversion* type of hysterical neurosis, the person attempts to deal with anxiety through blindness, deafness, anesthesia, paralysis, or ataxia. Although these symptoms may be quite severe, the person exhibits an inappropriate lack of concern about them. In the *dissociative* type of hysterical neurosis, a portion of experience is cut off from conscious awareness through various mechanisms, such as amnesia, multiple personality, or somnambulism.

The *phobic neuroses* relate to an intense fear of an object or situation that the person recognizes as presenting no actual danger. The condition is accompanied by palpitation, perspiration, fatigue, nausea, tremor, and even panic.

> Charles was a very successful executive but also a "workaholic." Whenever he got out of his work situation, he developed physical withdrawal symptoms. Having been permanently disabled since childhood, he had unconsciously reached the conclusion that, when he was not working, he was "only a disabled person." When he stopped working, the nausea, flushing, perspiration, and panic would appear.

Different neuroses have become more popular at different times in history. For example, the hysterical neuroses were much more popular at the turn of the century, while today probably the most popular kind is some variation of *obsessive-compulsive neurosis*. People who suffer from it are plagued by thoughts, urges, or behaviors that seem to be beyond their control. While striving for godlike superiority and perfection, these people escape all kinds of responsibilities in interpersonal relationships, at work, or at play. They are aware of the nonsensical nature of their thoughts and urges and, yet, cannot do anything about them, since their patterns of responses seem to be beyond their control.

The *depressive neurosis* is usually related to some kind of loss. A depression is a silent temper tantrum, a sit-down strike for higher wages. Depressed persons feel that life has deprived them in some way, and all they want to do is pick up their marbles and go home. The purpose of depression, like that of any other temper tantrum, is to influence or control other people. Depressed people seldom realize the tremendous power that they exert.

People who complain of chronic weakness, fatigability, and exhaustion may be suffering from *neurasthenic neurosis*. Although it is important that such people undergo a thorough medical examination, the psychological basis for their symptoms can often be discovered by asking the question "If you suddenly were no longer weak and exhausted, how would life be different for you?" If the condition is organic, the person will say "I would have no more symptoms." But if the condition is psychogenic, the person will usually reveal which of the life-task areas he or she is avoiding with the symptoms. For example, the person may say "My marriage would be better," or "I would be more successful at work," or "I would make friends more easily."

Hypochondriacal neuroses are characterized by preoccupation with the body and fear of disease. Although the fears don't have a delusional quality, these neuroses have profound social significance.

PERSONALITY DISORDERS AND CERTAIN OTHER NONPSYCHOTIC MENTAL DISORDERS

The term *personality disorders* refers to life-long patterns of maladaptive behavior. This category includes a large number of disorders, which we shall discuss in brief.

The *paranoid personality* is characterized by hypersensitivity, rigidity, jealousy, excessive self-importance, and tendency to blame others. The *cyclothymic personality* is a behavior pattern with recurring and alternating periods of depression and elation. It is the extremeness of the mood swings that differentiates this pattern from the normal degree of mood variation found in most people. The *schizoid personality* is a disorder distinguished by shyness, oversensitivity, seclusiveness, and often eccentricity. The *explosive personality* is expressed in gross outbursts of rage or of verbal or physical aggressiveness. The *obsessive-compulsive personality* reveals excessive concern with conformity and adherence to standards of conscience. People with this personality disorder may be rigid, overinhibited, overconscientious, overdutiful, and unable to relax easily. Those with a *hysterical personality* are often excitable, emotional, overreactive, and dramatic. The *asthenic personality* shows easy fatigability, low energy level, lack of enthusiasm, marked incapacity for enjoyment, and oversensitivity to stress. It should be noted that all these personality disorders must be distinguished from the psychotic or neurotic patterns of which they are milder variances.

Antisocial personality is a term used to refer to people with sociopathic or psychopathic life styles. These persons say no to life in a qualitatively different way than both neurotics and psychotics. Individuals with an antisocial personality make their own laws, denying and flaunting the common sense. This means that they have serious problems adjusting to society's rules. Therefore, they are often found in the delinquent and criminal groups.

If we study the childhood family constellation and atmosphere of people with an antisocial personality, we frequently find a history of pampering, often for a relatively short period of time, followed by neglect. Such individuals go through life as if it were an enemy camp, feeling perfectly justified to take whatever they want and whenever they want it. They are often overambitious and may display real or apparent courage to a considerable degree; their social interest, however, is very low. Although they are often described as incapable of loyalty, they do show loyalty to their own subgroup. Easily frustrated, they seem not to learn from their mistakes. They tend to blame others and often present complex rationalizations to excuse their antisocial behavior.

The term *passive-aggressive personality* represents an excellent example of labeling something without understanding its meaning. The apparent stubbornness and procrastination that characterize this disorder and that are said to reflect hostility and resentment are best understood in light of their purpose.

For example, retiring in the face of danger or exempting oneself from the demands of reality serves as a safeguard for self-esteem.[3]

Inadequate personality refers to the personality of individuals who, although not defective in any way, seem inept, socially unstable, and lacking in stamina. The specific prescription for this disorder is a large dose of encouragement and sustained recognition of the person's strengths.

Sexual deviation is defined by the American Psychiatric Association as "sexual behavior at variance with more or less culturally accepted sexual activities." Here George Bernard Shaw's advice "Do not do unto others as you would have others do unto you; their tastes may be different" is appropriate. Living in a time of sexual revolution, we must take into consideration the fact that many people sincerely believe that any sexual behavior between consenting adults cannot be called in any way pathologic. Also, when our goal is zero population growth, our view of sexual behavior must in some way be consonant with that goal.

Any particular sexual behavior other than autoeroticism conducted in private has social significance, but most of our sexual mores are open for reconsideration at this time. If a person displays marked deviations, we need to understand this behavior in light of the personal life style. For example, in our experience, a significant number of so-called transsexuals—that is, individuals who wish to be surgically changed from one sex to the other—are adults operating within a very pampered life style. They want everything their own way; this includes even determining their own sex.

By *chemical dependency* we mean dependency on drugs, alcohol, nicotine, and caffeine. Alcohol and nicotine are the two most dangerously misused chemicals in our society today. But caffeine, too, can stimulate significant symptomatology. The vast amount of exploration that has been done in the last decade has revealed that the variety of drug dependence is almost unlimited. The chemicals most frequently misused fall into four categories: "uppers," or central nervous-system stimulants; "downers," or central nervous-system depressants; intoxicants; and chemicals that produce significant altered states of consciousness, including psychotic-like behavior. A variety of combinations of these drugs are used as well.

Some drug users may be seeking merely excitement, peer approval, and the thrill of exploration; some may be seeking a new personality; and some may be seeking oblivion. The widespread availability of "legitimate" drugs and street chemicals makes it difficult to comment on what is still an unstable picture. We feel, however, that it is a mistake to categorize or diagnose a person according to his or her particular choice of chemicals. What is important is to understand the significance of the chemical abuse and then treat the

[3]For a detailed discussion of the various purposes of symptoms, see Shulman and Mosak (1967), pp. 79–87.

whole person, keeping in mind that family members and society at large are profoundly affected by a person's chemical abuse.

PSYCHOPHYSIOLOGIC DISORDERS

Psychophysiologic disorders are physiological changes in the function or structure of an organ that are brought about by psychological disturbances. These changes are more acute and last longer than those that normally accompany certain emotional states. Here, too, it is important to understand for what purpose a person "creates" a particular symptom or group of symptoms.

> A 37-year-old father of three children has left his family to live with another woman. Unwilling to make a final decision about divorce, each time the issue of divorce is raised, he has an attack of asthma, often severe enough to require hospitalization.

The choice of particular symptoms may be related to organ inferiority, to a particular body function that has been overemphasized by parents, to mere chance discovery, or to imitation.

SPECIAL SYMPTOMS

Occasionally, we encounter individuals who seem perfectly normal except for a single symptom, such as speech disturbance, specific learning problems, sleep or feeding problems, or tics. Here, too, the purpose of the symptom is usually easily determined by asking the question "How would your life be different if you suddenly didn't have this problem anymore?" Assuming that the symptom is not organically based, the person's answer is likely to reveal in which of the life-task areas he or she is escaping responsibility through the creation of the particular symptom.

TRANSIENT SITUATIONAL DISTURBANCES

This category includes disorders that are transient, even though they may be very severe. People who manifest such disturbances often have no apparent underlying physiological problem and seem to be responding to overwhelming environmental stress, such as death of a parent or divorce, either of which can be felt as a major stress. The diagnosis is based on the patient's developmental stage—for example, adjustment reaction of adolescence. It should be noted, however, that each individual will assign his or her own unique meaning and respond in his or her own creative way to stress situations. Therefore, there is no predictable cause-and-effect (one-to-one) relationship between the stress and the symptom.

BEHAVIOR DISORDERS OF CHILDHOOD AND ADOLESCENCE

The disturbances that are included in this category are more stable than those we just discussed but less stable than psychoses, neuroses, and personality disorders. The diagnoses for these disorders are primarily mere descriptions of what kind of behavior is observed in the child or adolescent. Such diagnoses generally make use of the term *reaction*—for example, hyperkinetic reaction, withdrawing reaction, overanxious reaction, runaway reaction, unsocialized aggressive reaction, or group-delinquent reaction. The problem with this term is that it fails to take into consideration the fact that children and adolescents are not merely "reactors"; they are active participants, even though they may not be aware of the purpose of their disturbed and disturbing behavior.

CONDITIONS WITHOUT MANIFEST PSYCHIATRIC DISORDER

Some patients who are considered psychiatrically normal nevertheless have problems severe enough to warrant psychiatric evaluation and treatment. The categories of marital maladjustment, social maladjustment, and occupational maladjustment can be related to Adler's original three life tasks. The category of dyssocial behavior, instead, can be used to classify predatory and more or less criminal people, such as dope pushers, prostitutes, gamblers, and racketeers.

Although the various diagnostic categories described in DSM-II are helpful as a form of shorthand in communication and are apparently needed for administrative purposes, it is essential that the therapist or counselor constantly keep in mind the uniqueness of the individual. Therefore, an Adlerian diagnosis would always be at least a paragraph, if not a page, long, and it would probably take into account the items that Adler listed under "general diagnosis." They include (1) what produces the feeling of deficiency (the critical problem), (2) the direction in which the person strives to overcome the perceived deficiency, (3) the relationship between such direction and the "right degree of cooperation," (4) the life-task area or areas in which the person is failing to function with courage and responsibility, (5) the way in which the person shows a hesitating attitude and evades the problem, (6) the way in which the person arranges to feel superior, even though he or she is avoiding the problem, and (7) what in the person's past history explains why the person is improperly prepared for life.

If one takes this approach, many "diagnoses" become mere descriptions of behavior. Adlerians believe that much more information is necessary for an adequate understanding of the particular patient and his or her particular social milieu.

REFERENCES

Adler, A. *The case of Mrs. A.: The diagnosis of a life-style.* Chicago: Alfred Adler Institute, 1969.

Adler, A. *The neurotic constitution.* New York: Arno, 1972.

American Psychiatric Association. *Diagnostic and statistical manual of mental disorders* (2nd ed.). Washington, D.C.: Author, 1968.

Brown, C. *Manchild in the promised land.* New York: New American Library, 1965.

Dreikurs, R. Can you be sure the disease is functional? *Consultant,* 1962, *2,* 34–36.

Shulman, B. H. *Essays in schizophrenia.* Baltimore: Williams & Wilkins, 1968.

Shulman, B. H., & Mosak, H. H. The various purposes of symptoms. *Journal of Individual Psychology,* 1967, *23,* 79–87.

Szasz, T. S. *The myth of mental illness.* New York: Harper & Row, 1974.

CHAPTER 5

COUNSELING THEORY

PRINCIPLES OF ADLERIAN COUNSELING

The theory of Individual Psychology is socioteleological and understands people as social, creative, active, decison-making beings moving toward unique goals and influenced by unique beliefs and perceptions.

This statement gives considerable direction to the counseling process, as we hope to make clear in the following discussion. Before we begin, however, a clarification seems in order. Our discussion focuses on counseling rather than on therapy. There are differences between the two situations, as well as similarities. Counseling is concerned chiefly with enabling the person to modify self-defeating behaviors, make effective decisions, and solve problems efficiently. Psychotherapy is more concerned with influencing the life style; changing faulty, mistaken, and self-defeating perceptions; and actually influencing the beliefs and goals of the individual. But the same "model of man" and techniques apply to both counseling and therapy.

Socioteleological Orientation

Seeing the purposive nature of all behavior. Adlerian psychology is unique in its focus on purpose. This teleological orientation, in contrast to a historical-causal approach, has real significance for the transactions between counselor and counselee. The emphasis is not only on the removal of symptoms and the changing of behavioral patterns but on the understanding on the

57

part of counselees that they are not the powerless victims of circumstances and that they act of their own accord.

All of the counselee's discouragements are understood in terms of their purpose. Lack of success on the job or at school and failure to get along with people are seen not as static problems but as valuable indicators of the pattern of the person's psychological movement. What happens as a result of this ineptness? By displaying ineptness, children may get their parents to do their homework or house chores for them. By revealing that they cannot handle certain situations themselves, adults may get someone else to handle the situations on their behalf. In the same manner, the inability to face any other challenges of living may enable a person to be treated as special, may afford him or her control over a relationship, or may make it possible for the person to exert power in some other area. The counselor's goal is to help clients see these motives and, consequently, accept the notion that all of their behavior makes sense in terms of their premises about life and that they act in a certain way because it serves some purpose for them.

For example, if a counselee complains that he is unable to find satisfaction in his relationships with women, the counselor will try to understand the purpose of this behavior—that is, how ineffectiveness with women pays off. Perhaps, because of such ineffectiveness, the person feels excused from functioning in that arena and puts all his efforts into his work—an area of life in which he feels secure. Or, maybe, the man's ineptness worries his friends, and they double their efforts to "find him the right girl." Actually, he may have a large number of people concerned and involved in establishing contacts for him. Once the counselor sees the payoff of the client's behavior—in other words, the motives, often unconscious, of the behavior—he or she can help the client become aware of these motives himself and see how they affect his life style.

Stimulating social interest. As you may recall from our earlier discussion, Adlerian psychology sees people as social beings who cooperate with others in order to realize their goals and function fully. Thus, Adlerians believe that a person's mental health can be measured in terms of his or her social interest—that is, the person's willingness to participate in the give and take of life and to cooperate with others and be concerned about their welfare. A typical Adlerian suggestion for people who are discouraged is to become involved in helping others and to look outward instead of inward. Social interest and concern for others are contrasted with self-interest and concern for what is good for oneself only.

People Are Creative, Decision-Making Beings

The view that people don't merely react to the stimuli about them implies that people have an active influence on the course of their lives. A simple counseling lead that helps counselees see this and assume responsibility for the events in their lives is the question "How do *you* keep *yourself* from _____ or from being involved with _____?" If a client says "I can't cooperate more with my (husband, teacher, boss)," the counselor asks her to rephrase the statement as "I will not cooperate . . . ," thereby taking on full responsibility for the relationship. The counselor makes it clear that the counselee can always decide to change but that, for some reason, it apparently suits her purpose not to change. The counselee then examines her payoff, which, as we said earlier, may involve being treated as special, getting service, being in control of a relationship, getting even, or whatever else is rewarding to the person.

THE GOALS OF ADLERIAN COUNSELING

Adlerian counseling has four main objectives, which correspond to four stages in the counseling process:

1. Establishing an empathic relationship between counselor and counselee, in which the counselee feels understood and accepted by the counselor.

2. Helping the counselee understand the beliefs and feelings, as well as the motives and goals, that determine his or her life style.

3. Helping the counselee develop insight into his or her mistaken goals and self-defeating behaviors.

4. Helping the counselee consider available alternatives to the problem behavior or situation and make a commitment to change.

Establishing an Empathic Relationship

The relationship that Adlerian counselors seek to establish is a relationship between equals, a collaborative effort in which counselor and counselee are active partners working toward mutually agreed-upon goals.

The counselor is responsible for providing the necessary conditions for an effective helping relationship and for utilizing skills that enable the counselee to initiate and sustain action related to his or her concerns. The counselee is not a passive recipient "being counseled" but an active party in a relationship between equals. This relationship is sometimes spelled out in a contract. The contract indicates the goals of the counseling process and specifies the responsibilities that each equal partner in the process undertakes. This emphasis on equality and responsibility is counter to the popular notion that one goes to counseling to be "cured." In Adlerian counseling, clients recognize that they are responsible for their behavior.

The goals of the relationship are made explicit so both counselor and counselee are able to evaluate progress. Mutual goal alignment expresses respect for the person's capacity to direct his or her life and move in directions that are personally satisfying. It also ensures the counselor's willingness and commitment to help the counselee move in those directions.

Throughout the counseling process, the counselor helps the counselee become aware of, accept, and utilize his or her assets. Instead of engaging in a continual analysis of deficits and liabilities, the counselor, recognizing the power of encouragement, offers sustained support. Only if counselees are aware of their strengths and personal power to change, can they begin to change their beliefs, feelings, goals, and behavior.

This positive approach that stresses assets rather than liabilities permits counselees to perceive in less threatening terms the barriers and obstacles they must face and overcome. A poor relationship at work or in the home, a mistake, or a failure is understood as an opportunity to learn and grow—not as a frightening display of inadequacy.

Confidentiality and privacy are essential elements for the establishing and maintaining of an effective counseling relationship. Such a relationship is more effective when the counselee is voluntarily engaged in the process. Individuals assigned to counselor custody or probation may agree to cooperate only to avoid more onerous consequences. Until the client chooses to cooperate, "counseling" will not progress.

Understanding Beliefs and Feelings, Motives and Goals

Adlerians see the life style as a personal construct—a structure built on one's beliefs, perceptions, and feelings about oneself and others. Therefore, in order to gain true understanding of the client's life style and communicate such understanding to the client, the counselor listens closely, trying to identify the person's beliefs, perceptions, and feelings. It is a special way of listening—an active attempt to understand all the verbal and nonverbal components of the person's communication. A holistic synthesis takes place in Adlerian counseling: all material is understood in terms of how it fits with the person's life style and how it can be used to increase the person's understanding of his own dynamics, so he can become more effective in life.

The counselor is not interested in fragmentary analysis of elements. IQ, interest scores, and past history are only elements, and they must be understood in relation to the pattern. Instead, the counselor looks at the meaning of the total psychological movement. The focus is on the counselee's purpose as revealed through the counseling communication. This is particularly significant, since it affects the whole counseling process.

Each statement is understood in relation to the preceding and ensuing statements—that is, in terms of its relationship to the counselee's pattern. When a client says "I do my best, but others are often not satisfied; yet, I keep trying to make them happy," the counselor deals not only with the feeling of discouragement and despair but with the belief about the importance of pleasing and the purpose of pleasing. Is the client attempting to be a victim, even a martyr, through pleasing? By "doing it only for you," perhaps the goal is to make others feel indebted. Again, it is appropriate to ask "Is it that you can't or that you won't please?"

Once the counselor, by actively listening and applying the principles of holistic synthesis, has reached a thorough understanding of the client's life style, he or she is in a position to help the client reach the same understanding and see how his own basic beliefs and perceptions influence his life style. The very act of communicating to the counselee that his life style makes sense and showing him explicitly how this is so has a therapeutic effect and a profound influence on the counseling relationship. Instead of a rapport of simple empathy, the relationship becomes a rapport of understanding and acceptance. True understanding of someone's life style is the highest form of empathy. Once clients feel understood and accepted, they can confront their problematic behaviors and faulty premises and attempt to change them.

What are the beliefs that are revealed in the counseling process? Here are a few: "Life is unfair," "People are no good," "I must be right," "I must please," "I'm something only if I'm first," and "Winning is everything." Even such a short list of beliefs clearly reveals people's different approaches to the challenges of living.

> *Michele*: I do everything I can to please the boss, but he's never satisfied. I can't figure him out.
> *Counselor*: Perhaps what you're feeling is that, if you can't please, there's no sense in trying.

Beliefs result in feelings. By empathizing with the counselee—listening closely and reflecting back feelings of anger, compassion, joy, discouragement, and excitement—the counselor helps the counselee identify her feelings, the beliefs behind them, and the purpose that the feelings are supposed to achieve.

> *Michele*: I do everything I can to please the boss, but he's never satisfied. I can't figure him out.
> *Counselor*: You're confused.

This response on the part of the counselor leads the conversation into a discussion of feelings and enables counselor and counselee to explore more intensively such feelings. However, until Michele becomes aware that her basic belief is "I must please or I won't be successful," just exploring the feelings will not enable her to become aware that her belief is influencing her feelings. Remember: it is the Adlerian position that beliefs influence feelings, that your belief about being shy creates your panicky feelings and not the other way around.

Hence, while the Adlerian counselor explores feelings to understand motives, develop empathy, and improve the relationship, he or she always goes beyond the feelings to discuss the beliefs behind them. It is through confronting the faulty belief and seeing it as faulty that the counselee becomes aware that she is not at the mercy of her feelings but in control of them and able to change them.

> *Michele*: I do everything I can to please the boss, but he's never satisfied. I can't figure him out.
>
> *Counselor*: Is it possible that you believe that, if you can't please, there is no point in trying? Your boss' failure to recognize your efforts justifies your becoming less cooperative or even quitting.

The counselor would make this type of response only after having clearly heard the client's feelings and getting in touch with her beliefs. It is a response designed to go beyond empathy and understanding and to stimulate action. Note that the communication is tentative—"Is it possible . . . ?"—so Michele can decide for herself. At the same time, the counselor's response moves the transaction toward a consideration of purpose. It is our position that, until the counselee is in touch with her goals and intentions, she is not going to be motivated to make significant moves toward change. Awareness of purpose is accompanied by the awareness that one has chosen his or her purpose and has the power to change it.

The following example illustrates the need for the counselor to go beyond empathy and deal with the purpose of the client's feelings, instead of merely reflecting them.

> Jim, a first-year teacher, is explaining how things go for him with his students. He says "I spend hours preparing for class. I attend special workshops and even use my personal funds to purchase materials. Despite my best efforts, the students don't appreciate my concern. They are disorderly in class, don't get involved with the material of the class, and seldom do the assignments. I give up. Why try? It's useless!"
>
> It is apparent that Jim is deeply discouraged about his progress as a teacher. The purpose of his complaints is to give himself the justification to stop working so hard. He believes that, if he shares his despair, the counselor will be sympathetic and excuse him from the responsibility of constructively facing the challenge of his students.

If the counselor focuses *only* on understanding and empathizing with feelings, without trying to get at the purpose of these feelings, the dialogue between Jim and the counselor may proceed like this:

> *Jim*: Wow! I've tried everything with these students, but nothing works.
> *Counselor*: It seems pretty hopeless.
> *Jim*: Nobody could do anything with students like these.
> *Counselor*: Sounds like there's no way you can be successful. You're feeling discouraged.
> *Jim*: That's not all. At home . . . .

The example clearly illustrates that mere empathy tends to stimulate more feelings of inadequacy in the counselee. A more appropriate approach is that of hearing and sharing the feelings first and then moving beyond the feelings into cognition, beliefs, attitudes, and purposes, so that Jim can become more aware and motivated to change:

> *Jim*: Wow! I've tried everything with these students, but nothing works.
> *Counselor*: I get the idea that you have the belief "I can't be successful."
> *Jim*: I sure don't feel successful.
> *Counselor*: I have a hunch that the students sense that and deal with you on the basis of your belief.
> *Jim*: Well, I'm discouraged; nothing works!
> *Counselor:* Could it be that your belief that the students are impossible justifies your lack of success? By openly declaring your inadequacy, you become the victim.
> *Jim*: Perhaps. But what can I do?

By acquainting Jim with his beliefs and the purpose of his feelings, the counselor makes it possible for Jim to consider other alternatives.

Developing Insight into Mistaken Goals and Self-Defeating Behaviors

Most persons coming to counseling are aware that they are doing something wrong, that they are not effective in their approach to the tasks of life. The primary function of the counselor is to help individuals recognize their mistaken ideas and understand why they act the way they do. In other words, the goal is to have clients understand the purpose of their behavior and how that behavior helps them achieve their goals, which are often unconscious.

While the counselor is empathic and accepting, he or she is also confronting. Insight about hidden purposes and goals occurs through confrontation and encouragement, as well as through interpretation and other techniques designed to facilitate self-awareness and awareness of how we interact with others (these techniques will be discussed in detail in the chapters to come). This insight into what keeps one from functioning more effectively helps clients resolve apparent contradictions and makes it possible for them to see that their mistaken goals must be given up if functional behavior is to be achieved.

Seeing Alternatives and Making New Choices

In the final stage of the counseling process, we move toward reorientation. This is the action-oriented phase of counseling—putting insight into action—in which a variety of active techniques are used to promote movement. The beliefs are understood, the goals and purposes perceived, and the feelings accepted, clarified, and explained in the light of the accompanying beliefs and goals. Now attention is directed toward seeing alternatives and making new choices.

> *Michele:* I do everything I can to please the boss, but he's never satisfied. I can't figure him out.
>
> *Counselor:* You're discouraged and believe that, unless you please, you're a failure. This is an idea *you* have decided to accept for yourself. You could believe, instead, "I will do my best, and, if he's not pleased, that's his problem." What do you think about that?

The counselor hears the feelings, clarifies the belief and purpose, but does not reinforce it. This is often the point at which the neophyte counselor gets bogged down—for example, by echoing the counselee's ideas. The experienced counselor, instead, offers alternative ideas or beliefs for consideration.

There are certain elements that can contribute to the success of the reorientation phase. Encouragement is the prime factor in stimulating change in the counselee. Encouragement generates the self-confidence and self-esteem that enable a person to act upon his or her concerns. As we have indicated, discouragement is one of the basic factors in failure to function. Encouragement increases confidence and courage and thus promotes change. When courage is stimulated, there is a tendency to move in more positive directions and be open to encouragement and support from others. In turn, when counselees learn to encourage others, they experience encouragement themselves. This becomes a reinforcing cycle in which behaving courageously stimulates greater self-confidence.

Another element that promotes consideration of viable alternatives and commitment to change is the explicitness of the purposes of the counseling process. Clearly stating specific goals and purposes fosters the counselee's involvement and commitment to change.

A study of what produces change in the client, conducted by Edmund Kal (1972), revealed that insight is the factor most frequently mentioned as instrumental to therapeutic change and that change occurs through interpretation of the person's goals and purposes. However, the clinicians surveyed in the study also stressed the importance of action outside of therapy—that is, putting insights into practice by experimenting with alternative ways of behaving. Thus, insight should be considered as a powerful adjunct to behavioral change but not as a prerequisite, since people can make abrupt and profound behavioral changes without developing much insight.

GETTING STARTED

It is important that the counselee understand the nature of the counseling relationship from the very beginning. Most individuals coming to the counselor have had no previous exposure to this type of relationship. Because of lack of experience and inaccurate impressions derived from popular magazines, movies, and television, the counselee is likely to have a number of faulty expectations about what will happen in the setting. There may be an anticipation that the counselor will simply listen or perhaps serve as an advisor supplying answers to questions. There may even be the hope that the counselor has the magical power to solve problems quickly and single-handedly.

It is, therefore, essential that, on the very first session, the counselor spell out clearly his or her role—a helper who works with the person to gain greater insight into the person's behavior in order to help him move toward the change he desires. The counselor must also clarify that he or she can help the person consider alternatives but that the decisions are up to the individual.

From the start, the relationship is collaborative—two people working together in an equalitarian manner and in a relationship that has no superiors and inferiors. No movement can occur until the goals for counseling are spelled out and mutually agreed upon. It is our belief that from the first session clients should begin to formulate a plan or contract concerning what they want, how they plan to get there, what is keeping them from being successful in their pursuit of their goals, how they can modify their nonproductive behavior, and how they can use their assets and strengths to achieve their purposes.

> *Beth:* I understand that you can help people like me.
> *Counselor:* Tell me something about yourself and why you are here.
> *Beth:* I've been told I have good ability, but I get poor grades in school. I can't seem to get interested. My reading is weak. Do you tutor in reading?
> *Counselor:* I'm not a reading tutor, but I can help you find one. You seem to feel you're not living up to your expectations.
> *Beth:* It's not just *my* expectations. My parents are very disappointed. I'm afraid I may be flunking.
> *Counselor:* There is pressure from home also.
> *Beth:* Yeah. Dad is really mad. He says I'll never grow up and be responsible. I'm so confused I don't know what to do.
> *Counselor:* There's a lot of pressure from home, and you also sound discouraged about yourself. What would you like to get from our counseling sessions?
> *Beth:* I'd like to understand why I'm not motivated, and I'd like to learn how to get my parents off my back.
> *Counselor:* What should we talk about first?
> *Beth:* Why I'm not motivated.
> *Counselor:* Our purpose, then, will be to understand your motives as they relate to school and to determine what keeps you from succeeding.

During the initial stage, the counselor listens very closely and moves consistently toward helping the counselee establish why she is there and what she hopes to accomplish. The interview is not open ended but focuses on clarifying what is being sought. Beth may later change her goals, but focus and purpose for the original contract have been established.

It is essential that counselees understand what the counselor offers and how they are expected to participate in the relationship. This necessitates that the counselor have a clear conceptualization of the process and be able to articulate it to the person seeking help.

It may also be helpful to invite a new counselee to ask questions about the counselor, such as who he or she is, what he or she is about, and how counseling is conducted.

THE EFFECTIVE HELPING RELATIONSHIP

Motives and Expectations

As we said earlier, people often have faulty expectations about counseling. Since some of the counselor's expertise is in the area of motivation, he or she is well equipped to discern from the start the individual's motives for seeking help.

In an insightful article, Mosak and Gushurst (1971) have clarified some ways in which the purpose and real meaning of the person's statements concerning his motives can be determined.

For example, a person may say "I'm confused and immobilized. I feel as if I'm pulled in two directions, and I can't decide." As soon as the counselor attempts to help the person attack the dilemma, the counselee will respond with a "Yes, but . . . ," indicating that the counselor has a good point but must certainly weigh the considerations on the other side of the issue. If a person goes through life with a "yes, but" approach, although he will surely save face, he will not go far. Neurosis is face saving, and the stance of the neurotic is a "yes, but" stance. As Mosak and Gushurst (1971) observe,

> His statement, in other words, contains the hidden intention "I'm not going to go anywhere" and the "conflict" is his method of immobilizing himself. The reasons for such immobilization vary from patient to patient, but they tend to fall into one or the other of two major categories: protection from a loss or retention of a gain [p. 428].

By not taking a stand or choosing a direction, the person doesn't run the risk of losing something and can reap the subtle benefits while protecting his good intentions. In other words, by being undecided, a person can maintain more than one position. For example, a student complains "If I quit my job and put full effort into my studies, I can't afford school; but if I keep my job, I don't have the time to do well in my studies." As a result, this student can continue to put less than full effort into academic work. The counselor helps the counselee see that he is describing only two extremes and that there are many other alternatives in between.

Another statement heard frequently is "I guess you'd say I'm a dependent person." As Mosak and Gushurst (1971) indicate,

> From an Adlerian perspective, however, dependency is a life movement in which the individual places others in his service. Convinced of his own inadequacy and consequent exemption from responsibility, the dependent person concentrates on evoking and maintaining the assistance of others whom he sees as stronger and therefore obligated to help him. Another way of declaring impotence is contained in the statement "I can't seem to let go of myself"—and here the patient is generally referring to his feelings and his inability to live spontaneously. In reality, the manner of stating the problem conceals the patient's investment in keeping himself "held in"—keeping himself safe, in control, free of blunders and exposure. This kind of statement is frequent among controllers[1] and perfectionists, people who want to keep their best profile forward [p. 429].

It is important that counselees be aware from the start that the counselor understands their motives, even those that may be hidden from their consciousness. When the counselor responds not only to the feeling or belief but also to the purpose, the counselee's awareness is expanded and the possibilities for change are increased. Furthermore, the recognition by the counselor that the person's statement makes sense—that is, the counselor's acceptance of the person's private logic—is a way to establish instant rapport. The ensuing task for the counselor is to move the person from his or her faulty private logic to acceptance of the common logic.

Real and hidden meanings. As the counselee speaks, it is important that the counselor catch the meaning of his or her words and their purpose. Let's consider two ways of leading.

> *Christopher:* I can't seem to let go of myself.
> *Counselor:* It's very discouraging, and you feel defeated.
> *Christopher:* Yes. I'd like to relax like other people, but it doesn't seem right.
> *Counselor:* You're really tied up.

In the above dialogue, the counselor focuses on feelings and alludes to beliefs. The following dialogue, instead, moves on to possible purpose.

> *Christopher:* I can't seem to let go of myself.
> *Counselor:* You're afraid to relax.
> *Christopher:* Yes. If I relaxed, I could make a mistake and look like a fool.

[1]For a discussion of the life style of the "controller," see Mosak (1973).

> *Counselor:* It is dangerous to make mistakes. Is it possible that you feel comfortable only if you are in control and can predict what will happen?

In this dialogue, the counselor is empathic but quickly moves to talking about beliefs and the purpose of Christopher's movement. This more active role on the part of the counselor has the effect of influencing the client to become more actively involved in looking at his life and the choices he is making.

Often the stated problem is not the real problem. The concerns the client expresses in the first sessions may be a way of testing whether the counselor is really listening and how perceptive he or she is. If it appears that the counselor is naive or overly accepting, the counselee may not have the necessary confidence to share his or her true concerns. Involvement with the real and hidden meanings at an early stage increases the counselee's faith in the counselor's ability and enhances the possibility of early entry into the change process.

In some instances, particularly with children and spouses, there may be indications on the counselees' part that they are there because someone referred them or "made me come here." In these instances, it is important to openly discuss how the counselee feels about being sent by someone else. There may be anger and feelings of inadequacy or unfairness, and these should be discussed. It is also important to clarify the counseling relationship and to build a bridge toward goal alignment by helping the person choose what he or she would like to work on. For example, a parent may send a child to the counselor, so she may become more motivated about school. The child's major problem is with a sibling or a peer. It is more productive to begin with the child's goals than to attempt to force her to discuss what she was sent to discuss. As the relationship unfolds and as the counselor proves an effective resource in dealing with the concern expressed by the child, she will be more willing to become involved in working at the problem for which she was referred.

If a person is sent to counseling in order to appease a spouse, the counselor helps the individual determine his or her concerns, which may be different from those of the spouse. The client is encouraged to discuss the feelings he or she has about being sent to be counseled, and it is made clear that the counselor will work with the client's perceptions of the marital relationship and will make no attempts to make the person over to the spouse's specifications.

Negative and unrealistic expectations. People come to counseling for a variety of reasons and with different expectations. Some who are pessimistic may believe "I can't change," "Nobody can help me," "Life is unfair," or "People are no good." They expect little to happen, and their negative expectations often become self-fulfilling prophecies, since their discouraged outlook and faulty self-defeating beliefs about life actually interfere with their involvement in counseling. It is important to get a clear contract with those who have negative expectations, otherwise they may even decide to stay in counseling in order to prove that nothing can be accomplished. The purpose of negative expectations—to keep from moving—or the purpose of resisting counseling—to prove that nothing can happen—should be confronted. Only when counselees see how their mistaken perceptions influence their experiences can they possibly be helped to change.

Other persons may have ridiculously high expectations with regard to the counseling process. They may also be very dependent and attempt to transfer the responsibility for their progress to the counselor. They may believe "Life owes me everything," "Others must protect me," "I can do no wrong," "Others are at fault," or "My problems are simple. If you are competent, you should be able to help me in a short time." This last type of person, if he or she doesn't see rapid changes and many encouraging signs of progress, is quick to put the blame for the lack of progress on the counselor or the situation.

In the very first session, the counselor should clarify what he or she can offer—careful listening, empathy, understanding, clarification of counselee beliefs, and insight into counselee purposes and behavior in order to stimulate action and change. Counselees are expected to be honest, open, congruent, involved, and committed to considering alternatives and making choices. The counselor can help, but, for movement to occur, counselees must put their understanding to work and be committed to specific change.

As counselees recognize that counseling is work and that the counselor anticipates their full involvement and cooperation, they understand the process as a collaborative one, in which the counselee must not only talk but decide and act.

Ingredients

Education and training of counselors and psychotherapists were originally accomplished in a less systematic manner than they are today. It was believed that counseling skills could be developed just by reading the theories of established leaders in the field, almost as if by osmosis. Professionals had some supervision during their training, but such training was not carried out systematically. Specific programs focusing on skill development were not available.

The research of Rogers, Gendlin, Kiesler, and Truax (1967) and that of Truax and Carkhuff (1967) presented the first evidence that professional counseling and psychotherapy may be "for better or for worse." Such evidence was based on research showing that the results of professional counseling are difficult to predict and that all counselors are not equally effective and therapeutic, even if they have had the same training.

These findings led to studies of the ingredients of effective helping. It became apparent that the counselor's ability to function in specific emotional and interpersonal dimensions has a significant influence on the counselor's "for better or worse" effectiveness.

The interpersonal dimensions determined to be essential ingredients of the helping relationship were identified by Rogers and his colleagues (1967) as empathy, unconditional regard, and congruence and by Truax and Carkhuff (1967) as accurate empathy, nonpossessive warmth, and genuineness.

Carkhuff (1972) reported:

> Perhaps the most important extension within helping has been to expand the helper dimensions from responsive to initiative dimensions. Thus, the original formulations emphasizing helper empathy, unconditional regard and congruence were complemented by the more action-oriented dimensions of helper concreteness (Truax & Carkhuff, 1967), confrontation and interpretations of immediacy (Carkhuff, 1969) [p. 7].

The Helper's Perceptual Organization

It has become increasingly apparent that counselors need more than theory. They need a clear understanding of the dynamics of behavior change and the specific skills necessary to implement this change. But, in order to be effective, counselors also need a perceptual organization (that is, a system of beliefs and perceptions) that is conducive to a helping relationship with their clients.

Combs and his colleagues at the University of Florida (Combs, Soper, Gooding, Benton, Dickman, & Usher, 1969) researched the perceptual organization of workers in the helping professions—for example, counselors and parole officers—and found a high degree of similarity of perceptual organization among effective workers in the numerous helping professions. More specifically, these researchers identified the beliefs that effective helpers share. Here are some of them.

Beliefs about what people are like. Effective helpers perceive others as having the capacity to deal with and find solutions to their own problems. They don't doubt people's capacity to handle themselves and their lives. They see others as friendly and essentially well intentioned. They recognize and respect the worth and dignity of others.

Effective helpers see others as essentially developing and unfolding *from within,* not as the products of external events, easily molded and directed. They regard people's behavior as dependable, because they believe that behavior is predictable and understandable. They see others as being potentially fulfilling and enhancing, rather than impeding or threatening, to the self.

Beliefs about what they themselves are like. Effective helpers feel fundamentally adequate. Thus, they can attend to the needs of others and identify with them. Effective helpers see themselves as essentially dependable and as having what it takes to cope with events. They see themselves as wanted and basically likable.

Beliefs about what their purpose is. Effective helpers perceive their purpose as one of freeing, rather than controlling, people—assisting, releasing, and facilitating rather than controlling, manipulating, and coercing.

Effective helpers tend to be more concerned with large than with small issues. They are more likely to be self-revealing than self-concealing. They are more concerned with furthering processes than with achieving goals. Their purposes are altruistic rather than narcissistic.

Beliefs about the approach to the counseling task. The basic approach of the effective helper is a concern with people rather than with things—be they objects, events, rules, or regulations. Effective helpers are likely to approach others subjectively, or phenomenologically, since they are more concerned with people's perceptual experience than with objective facts.

Combs and his colleagues' contribution to the understanding of the counseling process cannot be stressed enough. Not only have they directed attention to the importance of the helper's perceptual organization; they have also provided the counseling field with valuable guidelines concerning the beliefs that make a helper effective. If a counselor's beliefs are not congruent with those described by Combs, it is likely that the client's chances of benefiting from the counseling relationship are reduced.

It should be clear from an examination of the list of beliefs held by effective counselors that the opposing beliefs can truly interfere with a successful counseling process. It is, therefore, important that all counselors in training be exposed to intensive experiences in interpersonal communication, which will help them get in touch with their own beliefs and with the ways in which these beliefs may help or hinder the counseling process. It is also important that experienced counselors continue to participate in group experiences in order to keep receiving feedback about their beliefs and the effect of such beliefs on their practice.

THE ADLERIAN COUNSELOR

Characteristics

The counselor's portrait that emerges from the studies we have discussed is remarkably similar to the portrait of the good Adlerian counselor. Throughout this chapter, we have stressed the elements that constitute the essence of the Adlerian counselor's role. In light of the preceding discussion, some of these elements are worth mentioning again here, however briefly.

It has been observed that counselors frequently choose a theory of counseling that fits with their personality as well as their values. We Adlerians are no exception; we, too, have models that influence the way in which we approach the counseling process. First of all, we are active participants; we collaborate with the counselee, and, at the same time, we recognize and accept responsibility for the process. We bring this active dimension to the counseling process by being concerned with the purpose of behavior and the unique laws of psychological movement of each individual. As we listen to the counselee, we are more than merely empathic and reflective; we also attend to how the client's message reveals beliefs and goals and how we might intervene most productively to help the person see how his or her beliefs and goals influence his or her feelings and approach to the life tasks.

Through chosen responses, we direct the discussion toward a considera-tion of all these elements, since we are constantly aware that moving from empathic reflection to tentative confrontation accelerates the process. We do not wait for some magic moment in which the person, having processed all of this information, develops a sudden awareness of why he or she is functioning in a certain manner and how he or she might change. Our commitment is to active procedures, such as confrontation, interpretation, and disclosure. These procedures not only challenge the person's beliefs and goals but influence the individual to translate insight into specific actions and behaviors that reflect the change that has occurred in the person's beliefs, self-concept, and goals.

It is increasingly apparent that our personalities are principal tools in the helping process (Combs et al., 1969). While it is important to have a theory of personality and be acquainted with a variety of counseling techniques, this knowledge must be integrated into the personality of the helper. The counsel-ing process necessitates acting creatively and spontaneously in response to the changing interpersonal demands of the helping relationship. Regardless of our theoretical orientation, we are behavior models for our counselees. They are influenced by our views, values, goals, and feelings, and this is a fact we must keep in mind all the time.

Here are some of the most important characteristics of the good Adlerian counselor.

Awareness of one's beliefs. The counselor must be able to answer clearly the questions "Who am I?" "What do I believe?" and, most important, "How do my beliefs affect my counseling?" Good counselors are aware that they too (not just the counselees) can have mistaken beliefs about counseling and the counselor's role. Thus, they explore their reasons for being in a helping profession and know well the motives, goals, attitudes, and feelings that can create "blind spots."

Awareness of one's feelings. Counselors are trained to listen to the feelings of others and to pick up nonverbal indicators of feelings. But they must also be aware of their own feelings, particularly insofar as these feelings affect the counseling process. Involvement with their counselees may cause counselors to become enthusiastic about progress and discouraged about setbacks or lack of movement. When this occurs, counselors need to ask themselves why they are so personally tied to the fluctuations in the lives of their counselees.

If the counselee grows, such growth is a result not only of the counselor's good work but also of the counselee's understanding and initiative. In the same fashion, failure to make progress is often a result of the person's unwillingness to apply what he or she has learned. Although failure to progress may be due to faulty diagnosis or to the counselor's inability to help the individual move from insight to outsight, counselors should not assume that there is an automatic relationship between their behavior and progress. A skilled consultant can be most helpful to a counselor who is experiencing difficulties in a counseling relationship. The consultant can help clarify if the lack of progress is due to faulty diagnosis, ineffective communication by the counselor, or lack of motivation on the part of the counselee. But the essential point that the counselor must keep in mind is that no progress can occur without the counselee's cooperation.

Awareness of the counselor's modeling role. Counselors serve as models to their counselees, whether they intend to or not. The counselee is sensitive to the counseling relationship and expects the counselor to be able to handle his or her own personal relationships effectively, so they don't interfere with the counselor's professional life. A counselor with a confused and stormy personal life is less believable as a professional resource. If a counselor's own children, marriage, or friendships are not satisfying, that counselor's ability to help others may be questioned. This does not suggest that counselors must be free of problems but that counselors must be aware of the powerful impact that their own life styles have on their counselees.

In order to effectively influence the counseling process, counselors must understand how they are perceived by their clients and be in touch with the type of model they communicate. Our counselees often learn more from what we do and how we approach our own challenges in living than from what we say.

Schmidt and Strong (1970) studied the factors that distinguish "experts" from "inexperts" from the standpoint of those being helped—factors that are especially relevant in the Adlerian counseling relationship. Helpers perceived as expert treated counselees with friendly, attentive behavior. They spoke courageously and with confidence and were able to move quickly to the heart of the problem. Those perceived as "inexpert" were tense, fearful, rambling, and uncertain, and they communicate their disinterest.

High ethical standards. Counselors must be trustworthy and concerned about their counselees' welfare. Personal information confided to them must not be revealed. Although ultimate allegiance is to society, the counselor's primary responsibility is to the counselee. Whatever is discussed in the private session can be shared with others only with the counselee's consent and only when there is clear danger to the counselee or others. Counselors must be dependable and responsible; that is, they must have a strong commitment to a set of ethical behaviors. Counselors who work in school districts will need to clarify their ethics to students, teachers, and administrators.

Awareness of the conditions that are essential to the development of the counselee. If counselors are to help counselees to lead a more satisfying life and achieve the purpose for which they come to counseling, certain conditions are essential. Good Adlerian counselors are aware of the following conditions and willing to meet them.

1. *Empathy*—seeing the world the way the counselee perceives it. It comes by accurately perceiving the individual's feelings and by being able to communicate this perception to the counselee. It involves understanding of the individual's private logic and beliefs as well as emotions.

2. *Caring and concern.* It is demonstrated by verbal and nonverbal attending and by showing deep and genuine concern about the welfare of the counselee.

3. *Genuineness and openness.* Both are greatly facilitated by the counselor's self-disclosure. Self-revelation can become the basis of a constructive relationship, since the counselor's words are congruent with his or her actions.

4. *Positive regard and respect* for the counselee's individuality and worth as a person.

5. *Understanding and clarification of the meaning and purpose of the individual's behavior.* Through the counselor's tentative hypotheses and disclosure, counselees develop insight into the motivational factors that direct their lives.

6. *Action-oriented techniques.* The use of these techniques, such as confrontation and encouragement, enables the counselee to change.

REFERENCES

Carkhuff, R. R. *Helping and human relations: A primer for lay and professional helpers* (2 vols.). New York: Holt, Rinehart & Winston, 1969.

Carkhuff, R. R. New directions in training for the helping professions. Part 1: The development of systematic human resource development models. *The Counseling Psychologist,* 1972, *3*(3), 4–11. Part 2: Toward a technology for human and community resource development. *The Counseling Psychologist,* 1972, *3*(3), 12–30.

Combs, A. W., Soper, D. W., Gooding, C. T., Benton, J. A., Jr., Dickman, J. F., & Usher, R. H. *Florida studies in the helping professions* (University of Florida Monographs, Social Sciences No. 37). Gainesville: University of Florida Press, 1969.

Dreikurs, R. *Fundamentals of Adlerian psychology.* Chicago: Alfred Adler Institute, 1953.

Dreikurs, R. *Psychodynamics, psychotherapy, and counseling.* Chicago: Alfred Adler Institute, 1967.

Kal, E. Survey of contemporary Adlerian clinical practice. *Journal of Individual Psychology,* 1972, *28*(2), 261–266.

Mosak, H. H. The controller: A social interpretation of the anal character. In H. Mosak (Ed.), *Alfred Adler: His influence on psychology today.* Park Ridge, N.J.: Noyes Press, 1973.

Mosak, H. H., & Gushurst, R. S. What patients say and what they mean. *American Journal of Psychotherapy,* 1971, *25*(3), 428–436.

Rogers, C., Gendlin, E. T., Kiesler, D. J., & Truax, C. B. *The therapeutic relationship and its impact.* Madison: University of Wisconsin Press, 1967.

Schmidt, L. D., & Strong, S. R. "Expert" and "inexpert" counselors. *Journal of Counseling Psychology,* 1970, *17*, 115–118.

Truax, C. B., & Carkhuff, R. R. *Toward effective counseling and psychotherapy: Training and practice.* Chicago: Aldine, 1967.

CHAPTER 6

THE PHASES OF THE COUNSELING PROCESS

THE RELATIONSHIP

As we indicated in Chapter 5, the Adlerian counseling process consists of four phases: establishment of the relationship, analysis and assessment, insight, and reorientation. All leading theorists, from Freud through Rogers and Carkhuff, have stressed the importance of the counseling relationship, and its necessary conditions have been set forth in a variety of ways. This section is devoted to amplifying the points we covered in the preceding chapter about the Adlerian view of the relationship between counselor and counselee.

Dreikurs (1967) states the nature of the relationship lucidly:

> The proper therapeutic relationship, as we understand it, does not require transference but a relationship of mutual trust and respect. This is more than mere establishment of contact and rapport. Therapeutic cooperation requires an alignment of goals. When the goals and interests of the patient and therapist clash, no satisfactory relationship can be established. Winning the patient's cooperation for the common task is a prerequisite for any therapy; maintaining it requires constant vigilance. What appears as "resistance" constitutes a discrepancy between the goals of the therapist and those of the patient [p. 65].

Mutual Trust and Respect

Mutual trust and respect are essential elements of the Adlerian helping relationship—an equalitarian relationship in which there are no superiors and inferiors. By working in the context of a collaborative effort directed at creating psychological movement, counselees feel responsible for their own lives. They are made aware of the counselor's belief that they have the power to change. This belief is demonstrated by helping the individual to see how "can't" often really means "won't." When a client says "I can't stop from supervising my son's homework," he may be asked to reword his statement so it is more accurate and say, instead, "I *won't* stop supervising my son's homework."

This simple technique often leads clients to recognize that they are choosing to behave in a way that keeps them in trouble. At some point, they may feel uncomfortable even when they say "I won't," because these words clearly imply that they are acting by choice. Thus, full responsibility is placed on counselees for their behavior. The counselor conveys this sense of responsibility in a respectful manner that indicates the belief that, once the person is aware of the decisions he is making, he will decide for his own good.

Goal Alignment

As Dreikurs' statement above clearly indicates, Adlerians place much emphasis on the alignment of the counselee's and the counselor's goals. The session does not consist merely of friendly conversation, acceptance, and support. It is a working session in which the conversation has the purpose of developing awareness, generating insight, and stimulating movement. Cooperation and focus on a common therapeutic task are essential if change is to occur. Thus, small talk is kept at a minimum, and attention is devoted to the beliefs and mistaken perceptions that interfere with the person's progress in meeting the challenges of life.

An important aspect of the helping relationship is the establishment of a contract that clearly states why the counselee is seeking help and what he or she expects from counseling. Dreikurs' statement provides some clear guidelines for recognizing when lack of movement or resistance are due to a discrepancy between the goals of the counselor and those of the counselee. For example, the counselor may have decided that it is important for Tony to recognize that her poor schoolwork is due to a power struggle with her parents. The counselor sees Tony's behavior as an attempt to prove that no one can make her study and as an indication that she enjoys the power of defeating her parents' efforts. Tony, on the other hand, seems to be more concerned with getting her parents off her back and with developing her own social skills. The counseling process can be effective only if it deals with things that the counselee recognizes as important and wants to discuss and change. Eventually, by working with her concerns as she perceives them, Tony may also become motivated to develop a new approach to schoolwork.

Tentative Hypotheses and Encouragement

In Adlerian counseling, a great deal of effort is put into providing tentative hypotheses about the purpose of the counselee's behavior—

hypotheses that are offered and discussed even in the early stages of counseling. It is important that the counselor help the person understand the purpose of his behavior. The counselor's recognition that the person's behavior makes sense from the person's own point of view demonstrates that the counselor's empathy goes beyond simple understanding of the feelings expressed and extends to a recognition of the meaning behind the behavior. For example:

> *Tina*: I've been trying to listen to my husband's opinions; but I find they don't make sense, so I follow my own ideas.
> *Counselor*: You're disappointed you can't count on him.

Here the counselor only empathizes with the counselee, and this could lead to a lengthy exploration of feelings. An alternative course would be to formulate a tentative hypothesis about the relationship between husband and wife.

> *Tina*: I've been trying to listen to my husband's opinions; but I find they don't make sense, so I follow my own ideas.
> *Counselor*: Is it possible that you have to be in control? You seem to believe that you must be right, and this justifies negating your husband's views.

Here the counselor focuses on beliefs and meanings and conveys the message that the behavior makes sense from Tina's point of view. At the same time, by dealing with the movement instead of simply identifying the feelings, the counselor makes it more likely that the goals and beliefs influencing the feelings and the behavior will be modified.

The counseling relationship is actually enhanced by the discussion of tentative hypotheses. By sharing a view about the hidden motives and goals of behavior and by dealing with them through interpretation, the Adlerian counselor conveys a form of empathy that makes the relationship more effective.

Encouragement is also part of the relationship from the very beginning. The whole process of attending closely to verbal and nonverbal messages, focusing on the counselee's concerns, and being sensitive to both verbalized and implied feelings is encouraging because the person feels valued. For some people, it may be the first caring and close human relationship they have ever experienced.

Disturbances That May Interfere with the Relationship

Certain psychological disturbances may interfere with the counselee's cooperation. For some, the counseling relationship is an implicit threat— a threat to self-esteem and to the habitual mode of dealing with people and meeting the challenges of living (Shulman, 1973). In his article, Shulman identifies some of the disturbances that interfere with the counseling relationship.

The fear of being defective. Coming for counseling is an admission of weakness, since one should be able to handle one's problems alone.

> Abe, a self-made man who has fought his way to the top in his profession, has nothing against his wife's and adolescent daughter's going for counseling. However, he feels very strongly that, if he should have some problems of his own, he should be able to work them out by himself.

The fear of being exposed. Sharing one's thoughts and feelings will destroy the image one wants to project.

> Betty, a 38-year-old single woman, is very interested in sex and greatly enjoys it. A successful teacher, she has learned to project the image of a well-organized, self-controlled person who is not flustered by anything. She fears that even talking of her true feelings about sex will make her attitude apparent to perceptive people around her and that it will make it even more difficult for her to control her sexual impulses.

The fear of being disapproved of. Revealing oneself will produce disapproval even on the part of the counselor.

> Carla, like so many women, has been trained to believe that she can belong only when she is pleasing, particularly to men. Therefore, she finds it very dangerous to reveal the anger, even rage, that underlines her incapacitating depression.

Counselees may also use certain defenses to save their self-esteem or to defeat the counselor. Shulman (1964) has categorized such defenses as follows:

1. *Externalization* ("The fault lies outside of me"). It is employed to preserve self-esteem and shun the responsibility for one's own behavior. By externalizing, the person puts the blame on others and considers himself or herself the victim of circumstances. The varieties of externalization include:

A. *Cynicism* ("Life is at fault"). These individuals escape responsibility for their own behavior by blaming those in charge, the "system," and so forth. They see people as getters, concerned only with meeting their own needs.

> Dean, 30, has won and lost a fortune. He is understandably distressed but puts the blame for what happened on others. He concentrates on their behavior rather than on his own and overlooks his own greed and poor judgment, which led him to financial disaster.

B. *Inadequacy* ("I'm just an innocent victim"). The person demonstrates incapacity and an inability to function.

At age 32, Lynn has a long history of running away from responsibility. She never completes a program or task she sets for herself and spends months at a time incapacitated. A victim of incest as a child, she still detects injustice everywhere she turns, and, whenever demands become too pressing, she "takes a vacation."

C. *Rebellion* ("I can't afford to submit to life"). These individuals challenge all the ordinary rules of life. They battle with life not just to win but to defeat the commonly accepted rules of society.

Hugh, a 25-year-old man, has pushed his crusade against the current "rules of life" and his attempt to create his own rules so far that he is hardly able to eat a meal for fear that the food has some noxious additive or lacks the appropriate nutrients. He is a very sad Don Quixote who sees windmills wherever he turns.

D. *Projection* ("It's all their fault"). The person suspiciously blames others and shuns all responsibility for what has happened.

In a large business corporation, several of the department managers are doing poorly. The president blames them for the company's slow progress, instead of recognizing his share of responsibility for not supplying them with the information and resources they need in order to do a good job.

2. *Blind spots* ("If I don't look at it, it will go away"). By refusing to face a problem, the person pretends that the problem is not there.

Despite the fact that three of her five children have had serious psychiatric disturbance, Mary consistently avoids counseling for herself, vigorously insisting that hers is a completely normal, healthy family.

3. *Excessive self-control* ("I won't let anything upset me"). Self-control is so powerful that all emotions, pleasant or unpleasant, are strongly suppressed and the person is protected from both joy and sorrow.

Although John's 16-year-old daughter is failing in school, has no friends, and is very obese, John is always smiling when he tells others that everything he tries as a father fails.

4. *Arbitrary rightness* ("My mind is made up; don't confuse me with the facts"). The person makes arbitrary decisions and allows no doubts.

Claire is a highly successful attorney. Her steel-trap mind is an advantage in her profession, but her arbitrary rightness is intolerable to her husband and children.

5. *Elusiveness and confusion* ("Don't pin me down"). These individuals attempt to conceal themselves from others by lying, pretending ignorance, or changing the subject.

> Kay is a scatterbrain. She is always confused, and this gives her a convenient excuse to avoid responsibility or decision making.

6. *Contrition and self-disparagement* ("I'm always wrong"). These individuals express feelings of guilt that permit them to continue the behavior while affirming good purposes that they have no intention of carrying out.

> Fred is an intelligent, verbal adolescent who tyrannizes the household with temper tantrums and then wallows in guilt feelings. When the counselor suggested that, although no living person had ever been made a saint, Fred—with his contrition and noble suffering—might be a candidate, he almost took it seriously.

7. *Suffering as manipulation* ("I suffer to control others"). These persons get what they want by protesting how much they will suffer if they don't get it. They may even put on the martyr act to glorify themselves in the eyes of others.

> Things are always going wrong for Jill, and she is very willing to let her family know how much she suffers. Through family counseling, the members of Jill's family are finally beginning to understand why she is always so successful at getting things her own way.

ANALYSIS AND ASSESSMENT

The phase of analysis and assessment has two purposes: understanding the life style and seeing how the life style affects the individual's current functioning in the life tasks (Mosak & Dreikurs, 1973). The counselor begins by exploring the current situation and the ways in which the person approaches social relationships, work responsibilities, and the sexual role, as well as his or her feelings about himself or herself. Although this investigation may be carried out in an open-ended manner in which data are permitted to surface, information regarding the life style is generally gathered systematically by inquiring how the person copes with the life tasks. Here are some of the questions the counselor is likely to ask.

Social relationships: How are things going in your social life? Do you have a few close friends, do you have many acquaintances, or do you feel isolated? Are you satisfied with the number of friends you have? Do you find satisfaction in your relationships with other people? Do you feel belonging and acceptance?

Work: How do things go for you in your work? Do you enjoy what you are doing? Are you successful? Are you a workaholic—overinvolved with and overcommitted to your work? What do your fellow workers (or students) think of you? How do you respond to authority? Is work a rewarding and fulfilling task, a chore, or an all-encompassing part of your life?

Sexuality: Are you glad you are a man (or a woman)? Do you wish you were of the opposite sex? Are you very masculine (or feminine)? How do things go for you in your relationships with women (or men)? Do you feel any special concerns in relating to women (or men)?

Feelings about self: How self-satisfied and self-accepting are you? What do you do for fun? How do you enjoy yourself? Do you pressure yourself? Do you feel good about yourself? Do you like yourself?

Sometimes the interviewer may also ask: What are your goals? What are the meaning and purpose of your life as you understand them?

The investigation may also involve asking counselees to rate their current feelings about success in the areas of social relationships, work, sexuality, self, spiritual life, leisure, and parenting (1 is excellent, and 5 is very unsuccessful and discouraging).

Priorities

The counselee's priorities in making decisions are also investigated. Adlerians believe that determining a person's number-one priority is a useful clinical method for quickly ascertaining one facet of the life style. For teaching purposes, Adler presented four types of number-one priorities: ruling, getting, avoiding, and socially useful. Adler indicated that each type of priority, unless challenged, continues to characterize the individual, thereby determining the unity of the person, or life style.

One point should be made clear. The concept of priorities is not used to categorize people, since the individual is too complex a being to be classified on the basis of type. Priorities are used to understand short- and long-range goals and to get at core convictions.

The number-one priority is determined on the basis of the person's answers to the self-questions "What is most important in my quest for belonging?" and "What must I avoid at all costs?" Kefir (1972) originally defined four number-one priorities: comfort, pleasing, control, and superiority.

Important to my belonging	To be avoided at all costs
Comfort	Stress
Pleasing	Rejection
Control	Humiliation
Superiority	Meaninglessness

Thus, if Sally's number-one priority is comfort, she will give precedence to comfort over pleasing, control, or superiority. Her priority is based on the mistaken conviction "Only when I'm comfortable do I truly belong." The avoidance stance would, instead, be "The worst thing for me is to be under stress. I must avoid it at all costs." These priorities have a crippling effect on our lives, since they severely limit our courage and social interest.

In pinpointing a counselee's number-one priority, the counselor might ask the person to describe in minute details his typical day—what he does, how he feels, and why he does it. Usually these descriptions will reveal a consistent pattern. The person's number-one priority may also be determined by finding out what it is that the person avoids at all costs and what feelings he consistently evokes in others.

Superiority. Possibly the most common number-one priority is superiority in its various forms, such as being competent, being right, being useful, being a victim, and being a martyr. People whose number-one priority is superiority will always move toward it regardless of circumstances or the behavior of others. They will also consistently evoke certain feelings in those who encounter them—usually various degrees of inferiority or guilt feelings.

The price for superiority is overinvolvement, overresponsibility, fatigue, stress, and uncertainty about one's relationship with others. Each number-one priority has a price, which is often quite steep. People coming for therapy are seldom interested in changing their number-one priorities, but their discomfort leads them to seek ways of avoiding paying the price. However, this is impossible; so one goal of therapy (or counseling) may be to help the person see his or her number-one priority, accept it, and learn to cheerfully pay the price from time to time.

Control. Another common number-one priority is control, which usually comes in two varieties: in one type, the emphasis is on control of others; in the other type, the emphasis is on control of self. People whose number-one priority is control of others consistently achieve, or at least move toward, their goal, but they also evoke feelings of challenge and resistance in those around them. The method of control may vary widely, but the number-one priority is the same. The price for this priority is distance from others.

People whose number-one priority is self-control are well known to all of us. We call them "uptight." All of their orifices are tight, their skin is tight, their guts are tight, and their smile is tight. The feeling these people evoke in others is frustration, often leading to disinterest. Our self-controller pays a price, too: diminished spontaneity and creativity.

Comfort. Those whose number-one priority is comfort or self-indulgence won't wait for gratification; they want their pleasure their way and right now. They get what they are after, but they annoy others in the process. The price they pay is diminished productivity, since they won't risk frustration and don't want responsibility.

Pleasing. Pleasers neither respect themselves nor expect respect from others. An immediate reaction to the pleaser is "Here's a nice guy," but further acquaintanceship often evokes very negative responses—rejection, disgust, intense frustration, despair, and exasperation. The price the pleaser pays is stunted growth, alienation, often institutionalization, and retribution.

These are just a few of people's number-one priorities, and each one contains many varieties. One way to look at priorities is on an active-to-passive spectrum. An active person with a number-one priority of superiority may lean toward martyrdom or righteousness, while a passive person may lean toward saintliness and victimization. Other-controllers may accomplish their priority actively, and be tyrants, or passively, and be artful dodgers. Self-controllers are likely to be more passive. Comfort seekers may pursue their goal actively by behaving like spoiled brats or passively by sitting around, expecting to be served by others.

Pleasers may be very passive, always subordinating their desires to those of others, or they may be exceedingly active, continuously looking for someone to please. Passive pleasers evoke pity and, at first, elicit in others the desire to help them. These feelings, however, are soon replaced by frustration and despair. Active pleasers infuriate us, and we often openly, or not so openly, heap abuse on them to express our disgust.

Dealing effectively with priorities. Once a person's number-one priority has been pinpointed and understood by counselor and counselee, alternatives can be considered. The counselor doesn't usually work toward changing the priority. It is likely that, if a number-one priority is discarded, a number-two priority will replace it and be just as troublesome. The counseling goal is to help clients understand the feelings they evoke in others and the price they pay. Then they can decide how much distance they want from others and how much they are willing to pay. The goal is to lead the person away from the absurd position of "only if" ("Only if I please, can I belong" or "Only if I'm in power, can I find my place") into recognizing that he or she can belong and find his or her place without going to such extremes.

As we have stressed many times before, a cooperative working relationship is necessary for all counseling. Such a relationship can be quickly established if the counselor can make the counselee feel understood. Pinpointing the number-one priority is one of the best and most efficient methods for doing so. A connection is established, and, as soon as a discouraged, mistaken human being has made a real connection with one other human being, he or she is well on the way toward change.

FORMULATION OF THE LIFE STYLE

As you know, the life style denotes the basic premises and assumptions on which the person's psychological movement through life is based. The life style can be expressed in terms of the syllogism "I am . . . ; the world is . . . ;

therefore, ..." (Allen, 1971b). We believe, feel, intend, and act upon these premises, and we move psychologically to justify our point of view. Our life style is formulated from our pattern of beliefs, convictions, and attitudes.

The investigation of the life style begins with the first psychological transaction between counselor and client. Body language, tone of voice, and expressed attitudes reveal a person's style of life. Therefore, one needs to learn to understand the scripts and what the scripts really mean (Mosak & Gushurst, 1977). It is essential that, when the self-defeating or maladaptive patterns are discussed, the counselee not be made to feel accused. As Mosak and Dreikurs (1973) indicate, "the therapist will have to assist him in distinguishing between being assessed, i.e., understood, and being blamed, a distinction not easy to make or accept" (p. 55).

Analysis of the Family Constellation

The life style is formulated by assessing the individual's family atmosphere, as it emerges from the person's answers to a family-constellation questionnaire, and the individual's early recollections. The family atmosphere is understood by asking questions that seek to determine the relationship between the counselee and his or her parents, as well as the family's values, attitudes, and disciplinary procedures. In asking these questions, the counselor is guided by a life-style form. Some examples of this form are included in Appendix A.

Adlerians believe that siblings often influence one another as much as the parents influence the siblings and that, in many families, the children influence the parents as much as the parents influence the children. The parents, however, do set the tone for the family atmosphere, particularly in the early years.

The family-constellation questionnaire. The questionnaire provides insight into the individual's perception of self, the relationships between the siblings, the influential forces to which the person reacted, and the experiences that affect the decisions the person makes about life.

The questionnaire investigates factors that Adlerians believe to be influential, such as birth order, sibling characteristics and ratings, and transactions and interactions between siblings and between children and parents. Great emphasis is placed not on birth order per se but, rather, on the child's psychological position in the family—that is, how the child perceived his or her position and what he or she did with it. Since the topic of birth order (ordinal position) was covered at length in Chapter 3, we refer the reader to our discussion there.

Guided by the questionnaire, the counselor begins by asking the client why he or she is seeking counseling and how satisfied he or she is with the way things are going in the basic life tasks. Next, the counselor asks for a description of the counselee's parents, their names and ages, occupations, and a brief list of their outstanding personality traits. After this initial information, the counselor asks "Who was your father's favorite? And your mother's? Did your parents have ambitions for their children? What was your father's relationship with the children? And your mother's? Who was the sibling most like your father? In what ways? Most like your mother? In what ways?" Then the counselor inquires about the relationship of the client with his or her parents and finally, about other parental figures in the family and the effect they may have had on the client's outlook on life (Eckstein, Baruth, & Mahrer, 1975).

After posing questions about the parents and their relationship with their children, the questionnaire asks for a description of the client's siblings. The client lists each sibling, beginning with the oldest and including himself/herself, giving his/her name, age, and a description of his/her character and personality traits. If some of the siblings are deceased, they are noted in their respective positions and identified in some way—for example, with a broken circle around the name (Eckstein et al., 1975). The family-constellation questionnaire then asks "Who among your siblings was most different from you? In what respect?" If the client is an only child, he/she is asked "Who in your peer group was the most different from you? In what ways?" The next question is "Who was most like you? In what respect?" This gives the counselor an understanding of how the client views himself/herself, the traits with which he/she identifies most, as well as those with which he/she identifies least.

Other questions that can be asked with regard to the client's siblings are "Which siblings fought and argued? Which played together? Who took care of whom?"

Now the focus shifts to the client himself/herself. The counselor asks "What kind of child were you? Did you have any unusual talents, achievements, or ambitions? What was your physical development like? Were there any physical or psychological handicaps?" The client then is asked to describe his/her sexual development in terms of his/her first relationships with the opposite sex, including the first sexual experiences. If the client is a woman, she may be asked to state how she experienced her first menstrual period.

The next item in investigating the family constellation is the rating of the client in relation to the siblings in terms of a list of attributes. To do this, the counselor takes one of the 24 attributes listed in the questionnaire—for example, intelligence—and lists, on one side, the sibling who was most intelligent and, at the opposite side, the sibling who was least intelligent. If the client is at neither extreme, the counselor indicates the client's position in relation to the siblings.

Attribute	Most	Least
Intelligence	Mary (Sam)	George

Hence, Sam, the client, is closer to Mary in his intelligence rating.

Family dynamics. There is an infinite number of personalities that can result from the family atmosphere, ordinal position, psychological position (the way in which the individual perceives and interprets his or her position in the family), and methods of training employed. The oldest child may adopt the patterns of the parent believed to have more power. For example, if father is gruff and demanding and gets his way, the child tends to copy these traits. On the other hand, if mother controls by passive-destructive methods, such as withdrawing and using silence, the child may adopt these tactics. The first child may attempt to emulate the parent's traits he or she considers most important or may give up because he or she cannot live up to those standards.

The second child is usually very perceptive of what is expected and what is needed to become important in the family. By noting the behavior of the first child and the behaviors valued by the parents, the second child may choose to adopt parental traits that the older child has overlooked. The second child also closely identifies areas in which the first child has not succeeded and, if this provides acceptance and belonging inside the family unit, quickly moves into those territories. As Shulman (1973) states, "divergence in behavior between siblings is partly due to competition between them for a place in the sun; the second avoids the territory of the first and goes elsewhere to seek his fortune" (p. 49).

> According to Dreikurs, personality traits are the children's responses to the power politics within the family group. "Similarities and differences . . . indicate alliance and competition" (Dreikurs, 1957). The siblings who are most alike are the allies (Dreikurs, 1952–53). Conversely, the siblings most different from each other are the main competitors, even though there may have been no open rivalry. Dreikurs distinguishes between rivalry and competition, describing the first as an open contest, the second as having "a much deeper impact on each child, leading to the development of opposite character traits . . . as each child seeks success where the other one fails" (Dreikurs, 1957). Competition develops mainly with the proximal sibling, the one who always had to be taken into account during the formative years [Shulman, 1973, p. 49].

It is clear that siblings have a very significant influence on the emergence of one another's personality traits. The psychological position in the family may be as important as the method of training used by the parents.

> Thus, in summary, the analysis of a family constellation requires four things: first, a solid and comprehensive familiarity with the factors that Adlerian theory considers most influential in personality development, the implications that Adlerians find in certain types of phenomena, and the common life styles identified by Adlerians; second, the ability to

recognize, discover and characterize patterns; third, the ability to compare patterns for the presence of similarities and differences; and, fourth, the ability to make accurate inferences, either by extrapolation within an already identified coherence, or through an intuitive, empathic grasp of a particular phenomenal world [Gushurst, 1971b, p. 32].

Interpretation of Early Recollections

Early recollections are another crucial type of information collected by the Adlerian counselor in the course of the formulation of the life style. Early recollections are specific incidents recalled from early childhood—incidents that the person can remember in clear detail, almost as if he or she could see them, and including the person's feelings and thoughts at the time of their occurrence. They are not merely reports that tell about a person's early life; they reveal beliefs, basic mistaken attitudes, self-defeating perceptions, and unique laws of psychological movement. Early recollections are valuable because, according to the Adlerian theory of personality, they are indices of present attitudes, beliefs, and motives (Mosak, 1958; Gushurst, 1971a) and because Adlerians believe that *people remember only those events from early childhood that are consistent with their present views of themselves and the world* (Adler, 1958). As Gushurst (1971b) indicates, early recollections "provide a brief picture of how an individual views himself, other people, and life in general, what he strives for in life, and what he anticipates as likely to occur in life" (p. 33).

Gushurst (1970, 1971a) has attempted to describe in an objective format what the diagnostician does when interpreting an early recollection. Gushurst has also moved toward a strategy for objectifying in a reliable and replicable manner the interpretation of early recollections. Here are other writers' comments about the interpretation of early recollections.

[Early recollections] are first interpreted thematically and second with respect to specific details. . . . The characters incorporated in the recollection are not treated in interpretation as specific individuals but as prototypes. They represent people or women in general or authority figures rather than the specific individuals mentioned. While the content of the recollection is given primary consideration, a sequential analysis provides a more rounded picture of the individual. The characteristic outlook rather than the characteristic behavior is portrayed [Mosak, 1958, pp. 107–108].

The main theme or pattern is to be interpreted in a manner similar with the TAT theme or the figure drawings, and are not to be broken into separate fragments. Starting with hunches, individual themes are brought together and their unity and pattern spell out a message—the client's feelings and emotions provide the main interpretative clue [Nikelly & Verger, 1971, pp. 57–58].

The individual selects only certain events from the vast number of experiences that occurred earlier in life; he or she emphasizes certain aspects of each memory, while downplaying or completely omitting others. Memory is a product of selective and evaluative processes; hence, it can be used to provide projective data from which we infer the basic elements of the current life style (beliefs and goals). These elements influence and shape the recollection as it is articulated to the counselor.

Kopp and Dinkmeyer (1975) present a standardized procedure that can be used in the interview.

> Think back as far as you can to the first thing you can remember . . . something that happened when you were very young (it should be before you were seven or eight years old). It can be anything at all—good or bad, important or unimportant—but it should be something you can describe as a one-time incident (something that happened only once), and it should be something you can remember very clearly or picture in your mind, like a scene.
>
> Now tell me about an incident or something that happened to you. Make sure it is something you can picture, something specific, and something where you can remember a single time it happened.
>
> As the student begins to tell the memory, listen for the visual and specific part of the memory. Some background details may be appropriate. Do not, however, spend too much time setting the stage with facts leading up to or surrounding the incident itself. Instead, concentrate on what actually happened.
>
> Phrases such as "we were always . . . ," "would always . . . ," "used to . . . ," or "would happen" suggest incidents that occurred repeatedly. Ask the student to choose one specific time which stands out more clearly than the others and tell what happened that one time. If one particular incident does not stand out over others, eliminate this event and choose a different early memory which can be described as a single incident.
>
> Before moving on to the next memory, ask the following questions and write down the student's response:
>
> Do you remember how you felt at the time or what reaction you had to what was going on? (If so), please describe it. Why did you feel that way (or have that reaction)?
>
> Which part of the memory stands out most clearly from the rest—like if you had a snapshot of the memory, it would be the very instant that is most vivid and clear in your mind? How did you feel (what was your reaction) at that instant?
>
> Our experience indicates that, although we can begin to see a student's basic beliefs and motivations in the first memory, the accuracy of these interpretations increases when they are based on additional memories. The counselor's assessment thus should be based on at least three memories. Typically, from three to six memories are collected [p. 24].

The counselor can make the directions less specific by stating "I want to record a particular incident that you recall in the first seven or eight years of your life. Tell me what happened, what moment is most vivid, and how you felt at that moment." If the counselee follows the directions, the counselor then proceeds to take down verbatim what the counselee says. If the counselee doesn't follow the directions, the counselor may have to resort to a whole variety of other tactics. If the counselee is resistant or says "I can't remember any specific incident," the counselor might ask the person to make one up—to invent one. Most people at that point will suddenly remember an incident that actually occurred. When that happens, the counselor is likely to suspect that the person is someone who tends to do the opposite of what is expected of him or her. Some people, on the other hand, are much more creative. They may intermittently invent and recall incidents; they may embellish a partially recalled incident; and, at times, they may claim that they are unable to invent an incident. Of course, an invented incident is just as useful diagnostically as something that actually happened. Other creative variations are the attempt to offer recollections from a later age period and the attempt to give reports.

When people are very unwilling to cooperate with the early-recollections process, the counselor should discuss with them the fact that probably they are unconsciously unwilling to reveal much about themselves —which is, of course, their prerogative. This insight often prompts the person to bring in some early recollections at an ensuing session.

Sweeney (1975) provides some additional guidelines about how to utilize the early recollections.

- Is the individual active or passive?
- Is he/she an observer or participant?
- Is he/she giving or taking?
- Does he/she go forth or withdraw?
- What is his/her physical posture or position in relation to what is around him?
- Is he/she alone or with others?
- Is his/her concern with people, things, or ideas?
- What relationship does he/she place him/herself into with others? Inferior? Superior?
- What emotion does he/she use?
- What feeling tone is attached to the event or outcome?
- Is detail and color mentioned?
- Do stereotypes of authorities, subordinates, men, women, old, young, etc. reveal themselves?
- Prepare a "headline" which captures the essence of the event; for example, in relation to the woman's recollection of the ice cream: Girl Gets Job Done!
- Look for themes and an overall pattern.
- Look for corroboration in the family constellation information [p. 49].

Identification of the Basic Mistakes

The summary of the family constellation and the interpretation of early recollections enable the counselor to specify the person's mistaken and self-defeating perceptions. These perceptions are often very different from the guidelines of Adlerian "social interest," which emphasize the give-and-take, cooperative, equalitarian, and responsible nature of human relationships. Early recollections and the investigation of the family constellation frequently indicate self-interest, concern with power, avoidance, and withdrawal—all of which are identified as mistaken perceptions.

Mosak and Dreikurs (1973) offer the following classification of the basic mistaken and self-defeating perceptions.

1. Overgeneralizations. "People are hostile." The "all" is often implicit. "Life is dangerous," with the "always" implicit.
2. False or impossible goals of "security." "One false step and you're dead," "I have to please everybody."
3. Misperceptions of life and life's demands. In the extreme, one can observe these in the delusions and hallucinations. Typical convictions might be "Life never gives me any breaks" and "Life is so hard."
4. Minimization or denial of one's worth (Adlerians accept the worthwhileness of every individual). "I'm stupid" and "I'm undeserving" or "I'm *just* a housewife."
5. Faulty values. "Be first even if you have to climb over others" [p. 57].

Integration and Summary

One of the counselor's major tasks is integrating and summarizing the information gathered from the investigation of the client's family constellation, from the interpretation of early recollections, and from the identification of the basic mistakes. The goal of this diagnostic task is to extract from the information

a brief description of the individual's role within his family (either alone or in comparison with the roles played by the other members of the family), his major areas of success and failure, the major influences which seem to have affected his decision to adopt the role that he did, and perhaps also an inferential statement about his apparent major goals and/or conceptions of himself, others, life in general, or of some particular aspect of life, such as sexuality, physical handicaps, religion, and so forth [Gushurst, 1971b, p. 31].

This process of integration should result in a clear, concise summary that reveals the client's mistaken and self-defeating perceptions, as well as his or her assets, in such a manner that the individual can easily recognize his or her own dynamics. The summary is presented to the counselee for his or her consideration and can be refined by discussing specific points.

> In summary, the Adlerian diagnostician proceeds by extracting the major features that appear in an individual's answers to the family constellation questionnaire, thereby obtaining a brief picture of his nascent personality; the individual's current outlook on life is then obtained by interpreting his early recollections; and the mistaken elements in his approach to life are then specified by comparing his contemporary convictions with those which seem to be required by the "logic of social living." Most importantly, when these diagnostic procedures have been completed, the individual has before him some very specific problem areas on which to focus, should he decide to change his life [Gushurst, 1971b, p. 34].

Sometimes it is useful to dictate the summary of the life style in the presence of the counselee. Then the counselee, at the next session, reads it aloud. This procedure offers the opportunity to stop and discuss areas that raise questions. The counselor can learn a lot from hearing the counselee read and by being alert to slips and to the kinds of emphasis the counselee places in the reading.

Although this procedure may appear deceptively simple, it requires a good grasp of Adlerian theory if it is to be clinically useful. One can synthesize and integrate the life-style material only by understanding the basic concepts of Adlerian psychology. The diagnostician must be able to recognize and articulate patterns.

> That is, he must learn to note that certain traits, because of an inner logic or necessity, tend to cohere; that if two or more traits of a certain kind are present in a given personality, certain other traits are likely to appear; and if these other traits do not appear, some explanation must be found for their absence [Gushurst, 1971b, p. 31].

For example, if a person is passive and requires service from others, one can anticipate that she may feel helpless and tend to give up or that she will get her way by displaying ineptness and by withdrawing. If she cooperates, one can expect that she will do it by proving her "stupidity." Thus, the counselor must not only discern discrete patterns in the life style but understand how certain behaviors reinforce certain beliefs.

Because of the basic unity and pattern of the personality, one can identify a number of common life styles. Mosak (1971) provides a set of guidelines that can facilitate the analysis of common syndromes. As he states, "The life style forms a unifying principle, a gestalt to which behavior is bound in accordance with the individual 'law of movement' " (p. 77). Mosak illustrates some commonly observed life styles, such as:

- The "getters," who exploit and manipulate life and others.
- The "drivers," overtly overambitious, overconscientious, and dedicated.
- The "controllers," who keep spontaneity and feelings in check in order to control life and ensure that life will not control them.
- The persons who need to be right and hence feel superior to those whom they perceive as being wrong.
- The persons who need to feel superior. These individuals, when they cannot be the best, settle for being the worst.
- The persons who want to please everyone and who are always dependent on the approval and evaluation of others for their own self-esteem and worth.
- The persons who feel morally superior because of high standards that elevate them over others.
- The "aginners," who oppose all expectations and demands of life and who rarely know what they are for but who always seem to know what they are against.
- The "victims," who pursue disaster and elicit the sympathy and pity of others. Victims are very creative. They are willing to suffer for anything—not just for a cause, as martyrs do—and they reveal a great deal of flexibility and imagination.
- The "martyrs," who suffer like the victims but die for a cause. Often referred to as the "injustice collectors," they either silently endure or make their suffering very visible.
- The "babies," who find their place by exploiting others through their charm and cuteness.
- The "inadequate" individuals, who behave as if they couldn't do anything correctly and, therefore, constantly needed the help of others.
- The "rationalizers" and the "intellectualizers," who avoid feelings and spontaneity and who are comfortable only in situations in which intellectual talents are valued.
- The "excitement seekers," who despise routine and repetitive activity and who create and stimulate excitement.

This and similar typologies merely represent examples of various kinds of psychological movement. They are useful in that they give a concise word picture of behaviors and beliefs. But, remember, each life style is unique and must be understood in terms of its unique pattern.

The aforementioned patterns are, of course, not the only life styles we observe. The counselor, therefore, must develop the capacity to see relationships among the various data and formulate new patterns. Once certain patterns are identified, they are compared for similarities and differences. The areas of difference between the client and the rest of the family may be areas of competition, while the areas of similarity may reflect alliances between the siblings, role modeling, or the acceptance of family values. It should be noted that a highly competitive atmosphere set by the parents will stimulate differences in the attributes of the siblings.

The information obtained in the life-style analysis is valuable not only because it helps the counselor understand the perceptions of the counselee but, more importantly, because it helps the individual feel understood. As we discussed in detail in Chapter 5, this type of understanding transcends the establishment of rapport and of a good working relationship; it creates faith in the counselor and stimulates hope that things can change. The counselor's reflection of feelings and empathy are important, but the kind of understanding we are describing has the power to stimulate movement. There is a great difference between dealing with someone who simply recognizes that you are angry and receiving from someone the insight that your anger is dictated by the belief "I know what is best." This kind of understanding goes beyond empathy and confronts you with the fact that you yourself are deciding to display a particular emotion (for example, anger) and, therefore, you can also choose to respond differently.

The analysis of the life style helps counselor and client develop a plan for the counseling relationship and for the nature and direction of the counseling process. The life style and the mistaken or self-defeating perceptions, which are presented to the counselee, point to a number of beliefs and mistaken ideas that will reoccur in the course of counseling. The life style, then, is not a static, one-time diagnostic formulation but a consistent theme that is continuously discussed in relation to the person's approach to the various challenges of living.

INSIGHT

As you know, Adlerians believe that behavior develops not from what we are but from what we believe we are; that is, behavior is not the result of our experiences but of how we interpret them. Our behavior is based on our expectations and on the resultant self-fulfilling prophecies. We approach people in a friendly or hostile manner, and they respond in kind.

The insight phase of counseling is concerned with helping clients become aware of why they choose to function as they do. Although the counselor does not lecture or give advice, counseling is an educational process in which counselees learn about themselves. Through constant emphasis on beliefs, goals, and intentions, the individual's private logic is explained and discussed.

All of us operate with varying degrees of common sense and private logic. People who exhibit dysfunctional behavior, however, don't see life in terms of common sense but in terms of their private logic only. They solve their problems in a self-centered manner that shows a lack of normal social interest and willingness to cooperate with others.

As we pointed out in Chapter 5, Adlerians interpret the pattern of behavior holistically—that is, in terms of its unity. Therefore, they don't accept a dualism of intellectual and emotional insight and don't believe that the counselee should defer dealing with a problem while seeking to develop insight. Besides, intellectual insight may be only a ploy designed to keep the person involved in counseling instead of becoming involved in problem resolution.

Those people who clearly indicate that they understand and, yet, make no attempt to change their beliefs or try on new behaviors must be confronted with the purpose of such behaviors. By staying in counseling, clients publicly declare their good intentions to the counselor and to those close to them. However, by refusing to become involved or to make a commitment to change, these people defeat others' attempts to help them, while protesting their good intentions and well-meaning efforts. This is the situation that Adler called the "yes, but" game—"I know I should stop, but . . . "—with all its concomitant excuses, which reveal the person's psychological movement.

Interpretation is concerned with creating awareness of (1) the life style, (2) the current psychological movement and its direction, (3) goals, purposes, and intentions, and (4) the private logic and how it works. Insight is created through constant reference to the basic premises of the person's life style and to the ways in which these mistaken, self-defeating premises keep the individual from leading a successful and satisfying life.

The information that represents the basis for interpretation is derived from the person's here-and-now behavior and position in the family constellation. It also comes from hunches about the client's ordinal position and from an understanding of the individual's psychological position in the family constellation. As we said earlier, early recollections are used to clarify and sharpen the interpretation. Finally, the inquiry about the various challenges of living—work, social contacts, sexual relationships, self-image, and spiritual concerns—provide insight into the motives and purposes of behavior.

Adlerian interpretation can be clearly differentiated from classical psychoanalytic interpretation. Adlerian interpretation is done in relation to the life style, which is the central theme. The interpretation is not done statically—in terms of a person's present position—but is, instead, continuously related to one's movement. It refers to the direction and course of the person's transactions with others. It also alludes to where the person is going and to what the person expects to get by his or her behavior—to be special, to be in control, or to obtain special service. Thus, the interpretation enables the person to see the pattern of movement and its meaning.

Characteristically, the interpretation deals with the purpose of the behavior and its consequences. No time is spent with the investigation of causes, which Adlerians see as unproductive. The focus is on the here-and-now behavior and on the expectations and anticipations that arise from the person's intentions. The interpretation is always done holistically—in terms of the meaning and scope of the pattern of movement. No attempt is made to analyze elements as discrete from the pattern.

Method of Presentation

The method of presentation of an interpretation is very important. Interpretation is generally made in a tentative fashion: "Could it be . . . ?" "Is it possible . . . ?" "I have an idea about you I'd like to share." The open-ended sharing of hunches and guesses is powerful, because it relieves the counselor of the burden of being always right; one doesn't have to be perfect in order to offer a hunch or guess. It also provides a mirror through which the counselor can look at the client's behavior. Because the interpretation is offered in a tentative manner, the client is not forced to defend himself or herself and is truly free to agree or disagree. And when the counselor is wrong, this method of presentation enables both parties to consider other alternatives. The guessing method is a perfectly acceptable scientific process and is very functional within the counseling relationship. If the counselor guesses correctly, the counselee feels understood. If the counselor guesses incorrectly, he or she has an opportunity to demonstrate the courage to be imperfect and to contribute another valuable element to the relationship.

There are times, however, when the interpretation is presented in a confronting manner. This happens when there is a discrepancy between what the person says he or she intends and what he or she actually believes. The discussion of the purpose of this behavior can help the individual get in touch with the basic beliefs and goals that motivate his or her transactions in life.

At times, counselees are encouraged to interpret for themselves. Some believe that, if clients are able to interpret for themselves, the interpretation will be retained better. As counselees become familiar with their own life styles, they can start to contemplate their alternatives. In order to elicit the counselee's own interpretation, the counselor may ask "From what you understand about your life style, how would you explain the current experience that you have just been describing to me?"

Goals

The counselor may at times offer an interpretation that is deliberately exaggerated. This is done so that the person can see the ridiculous elements in his or her behavior. This type of interpretation has the same purpose as the paradoxical intention (see Chapter 7); both can, by their very extremity, influence or even create movement.

Generally, interpretation should not take place before trust and rapport have been established. However, it is important to note that a meaningful interpretation may actually build and solidify the relationship.

Since the interpretation is directed at the movement and purpose of the behavior, it is also designed to help counselees begin to "catch themselves." An example of what we mean by that is found in people who muddy up conversation by introducing the phrase "you know." Each person has his or her own idiographic meaning for that phrase. For some, it means "You know, don't you?'' For others, it means ''You don't know'' or ''Could you possibly know?'' or ''No one has ever known.'' And for still others, it means ''You ought to know.'' Most people are unaware of how frequently they interject the phrase ''you know.'' If they are interested in making their communication clear, they will learn to catch themselves in the act of mudding up what they are saying. Often we maintain a symptom by being constantly on guard against it. Instead of fighting the habit of using the phrase ''you know,'' the counselee is advised to catch himself or herself saying ''you know'' and laughingly say ''There I am, up to my old mischief again.''

This ability to intervene in one's own self-defeating perceptions as they are about to occur or to become aware of the purpose of one's own behavior as it is happening epitomizes the goal of insight. By catching oneself and interfering with the undesirable behavior, one is learning to stop self-defeating patterns. This opens up the opportunity for the person to practice active-constructive behavior and to replace faulty goals with positive goals. Examples of new beliefs and new positive goals that may result from such opportunity are ''I belong by contributing'' (goal: involvement), ''I can decide and be responsible for my behavior'' (goals: autonomy and responsibility for one's own behavior), ''I am interested in cooperating'' (goals: justice and fairness), and ''I can withdraw from conflict'' (goal: acting maturely by avoiding power contests and by accepting and understanding others' openness).

The manner in which the individual reacts to the counselor's interpretation provides guidelines for the next steps in the counseling process. Remember that interpretations are always made tentatively (''Could it be . . . ?'' ''Is it possible . . . ?''), so there is no need for the counselor to be always right. Also, this tentative approach ensures that, if the counselor is wrong, the counselee will not be harmed. The counselee will simply indicate that that's not how he or she perceives things. If the client's response indicates that the counselor is wrong and the counselor is not upset by his or her failure to guess correctly, the counselee may benefit from learning that counselors too can make mistakes and survive them unharmed. The courage to be imperfect is being modeled, and it often teaches as much as an insightful interpretation. The counselee begins to see that the world does not come apart just because a person makes a mistake.

Results

If the interpretation is accurate and helpful, several things may occur. At the time of the interpretation, the individual may give a recognition reflex—a grin or smile indicating that what the counselor just said makes sense to him or her. In other words, the interpretation ''rings a bell'' and is personally applicable. The counselee may, instead, have a contemplative look, which generally indicates that the person is seeing some of his or her behaviors and attitudes in a new light for the first time.

Interpretation from the Adlerian frame of reference is never nomo-thetic—that is, dealing with generalities—but idiographic—designed to fit the unique life style of each individual. Interpretation involves communica-tion about all kinds of interpersonal transactions, with emphasis on purpose rather than on cause and on movement rather than on description. In other words, Adlerian interpretation is dynamic rather than static.

By exposing the counselee's hidden intentions responsible for the self-defeating behavior and by clearly illustrating them, the counselor helps the counselee see these intentions as very unpalatable. This is what Adler was talking about when he used the expression "spitting in the patient's soup," which means that the person may still eat the soup, but it will never taste quite the same. The person may still engage in a self-defeating behavior, but he or she will not like it.

REORIENTATION

In the reorientation phase, counselor and counselee work together to consider alternative attitudes, beliefs, and actions. The approach is to reedu-cate and remotivate the counselee to become a more effective person in his or her approach to the challenges of living.

However, the counselor must go beyond developing mere awareness of alternatives. The courage to risk and make changes must also be developed. This is often accomplished by focusing on the immediate interpersonal situa-tion rather than on past experiences. By seeing how he or she can change within the counseling relationship, the client develops the motivation to experiment in other relationships.

Establishing Realistic Goals

A beginning step in reorientation is to clarify with the counselee what he or she wants. The relationship phase focused on mutual goal alignment, but now, in reorientation, there must be a clear establishing of the counselee's goals. The counselor attempts to determine whether the client's complaints are about the environment or himself/herself. It is important to make it clear that, as people change themselves, they also change their environments. Changing a belief such as "I must win every conflict" to "I am willing to cooperate, listen to others, and give in when appropriate" can have a major effect on a person's relationships. The change will stimulate totally different responses in others, and, as a consequence, the person's feelings, goals, and actions will also change.

It is important to determine whether the counselee's goals for change are realistic. Unrealistic goals may serve only to discourage. For example, some-one who has not been able to relate to women may decide to become involved with a very popular and attractive woman. If this relationship doesn't work, the person can justify his lack of success by taking the self-defeating approach of ''See? I tried, but I can't make any progress.'' Instead of letting this person ''prove'' his faulty assumption that he is not acceptable to women, the counselor encourages him to establish the intermediate goal of becoming better acquainted with women.

> To initiate behavior change after the client has recognized his basic life pattern, the therapist may suggest, ''Is this the kind of person you want to be? Could you think of another better way to act? What do you suspect will eventually happen if you continue this pattern for a long time?'' [Nikelly & Bostrom, 1971, p. 104].

A new orientation toward people and the life tasks, which is the goal of the reorientation phase, comes about as the client's beliefs, perceptions, feelings, and goals become more appropriate and more in line with the common sense. This phase actually involves showing how a person's behavior and relationships are related to the person's intentions and beliefs. The counselor mirrors to the counselee how his goals and intentions are chosen by him and by him alone and how they influence all of his actions, feelings, and approaches to the tasks of living.

> The therapist must understand that the client behaves according to his interpretation of what is meaningful and significant to him. The client learns or forgets whatever serves his purposes; however, such selectiveness may hamper his sense of social relatedness and inhibit self-realization [Nikelly & Bostrom, 1971, p. 105].

It is at this point in the process that the counselee is made aware that insight has little value by and of itself. It is only a prelude to action. Outsight—the moving of ideas into action—is the real aim of the process.

Seeing New and More Functional Alternatives

The goal of Adlerian counseling is active-constructive behavior that enables the individual to become a more effective and happier person. Any failure to take steps forward should be interpreted in terms of its purpose. Counselees are helped to see such purpose and the payoff of persisting in the self-defeating behavior. To that effect, it may be useful to get the counselee to ask himself or herself ''What is the worst thing that could happen if I changed?'' The person is then likely to recognize that the ''worst thing'' is not so bad after all and that, as a matter of fact, changing the behavior will probably result in positive situations—for example, relating better with others. Through this process, clients learn once again the effects of the choices they continually make about life. Even more importantly, they get in touch with the power they have to change their beliefs, perceptions, and goals—hence, their feelings and actions as well.

The Adlerian orientation is primarily a motivation-modification system, not a behavior-modification system; that is, the focus is on changing attitudes, beliefs, perceptions, and goals, so that behavior will also change. This does not prevent the Adlerian counselor from suggesting from time to time "Act as if . . ."—encouraging the counselee to assume a certain behavior in order to start experiencing the world differently.

It is important to show clients how they create and maintain their own ineffectual approaches to the challenges of life. By creating a goal that is unobtainable or by adopting a belief that is dysfunctional, people set themselves up for failure.

> Jack believes "I can do as I please; I make my own rules" and also "I'm not as much as others." His goal is to find excitement. When things don't go well for him in school, he drops out. Not having salable skills, he gets a menial job that is everything but exciting or rewarding. To find excitement, he becomes involved with hard drugs. His belief that "I can make my own rules and do as I please" leads him to believe that he will not be caught.
>
> The counselor's task is to help Jack see how these self-defeating beliefs get him in deep trouble and that they provide a false base of security. Jack needs to be helped to see that there are active, constructive ways of finding excitement, which will be rewarding instead of destructive. By changing his beliefs about himself and life in general, Jack will be able to consider a new and more challenging type of work and to develop confidence in his capacity to relate successfully to people.

> Maria believes "It is dangerous to express feelings," "People are no good and treat me unfairly," "I must please others no matter what," and "If I'm not on top, I'm nothing." Her goal is to stay ahead of others by being right and in control. Since she is very unwilling to express her feelings, she has difficulty in her social and family relationships. Her hiding behind a facade of inconsequential talk creates and maintains a wall between her and others. Her children don't respect her and keep alluding to how inadequately she provides for the family. Maria uses the children's attitude to fortify her belief that people treat her unfairly. Instead of expressing anger at her family's lack of appreciation, she dejectedly accepts their criticism.
>
> If Maria is to lead a more functional and satisfying life, she must start to express her real feelings and stop pleasing others at her own expense. The counselor helps to point out ways in which she does this and encourages her to find specific new ways to express her feelings and to feel OK about herself even if she is not on top.

Dreikurs (1967) states:

> To motivate reorientation, I employ a mirror technique confronting the patient with his goals and intentions. Moreno also employs a "mirror

technique'' for similar purposes in psychodrama. Interpretation of goals is singularly effective in stimulating change. When the patient begins to recognize his goals, his own conscience becomes a motivating factor. Adler called this process ''spitting in the patient's soup.'' However, insight into goals and intentions is not merely restrictive; it makes the patient aware also of his ability to make decisions, of his freedom to choose his own direction [p. 70].

The focus on change involves helping counselees clearly see their own self-defeating mistaken beliefs, mistaken ideas about human relationships, mistaken ideas about life's demands, and mistaken purposes and goals. When the interrelationships between these factors are comprehended, counselees are in a position to change and move in a positive direction.

Specific Strategies

Adlerians use a variety of interview strategies to reorient the counselee. Here we briefly review some of these strategies, which will be discussed in detail in Chapter 7.

Encouraging the counselee to act. When a counselee complains ''If only I were (or could) . . . ,'' the counselor may suggest that for the following week the counselee act as if she possessed the characteristics or traits she believes she doesn't have and wishes she had. By changing her behavior, the person begins to evoke different responses from her environment and learns that changing is not only safe but often rewarding.

Spitting in the counselee's soup, or besmirching a clean conscience. The emphasis here is on changing the meaning of the behavior to the person who emits it. The focus is on defeating the counselee's purpose—that is, depriving him, in his own eyes, of the gain he obtains from playing his game.

Antisuggestion, or paradoxical intention. This is a strategy that encourages counselees to practice their symptoms, to consciously intend to do that which they appear to be fighting against or resisting. Counselees are asked to exaggerate a symptom or do it on schedule. For example, a child with a tic is asked to practice it in front of a mirror for five minutes a day, perfecting it. The chronic worrier is asked to sit down each day at the ''worry hour'' and list all of his worries. A couple who have a ritualistic fight every evening—she screaming and he hiding behind the newspaper—are encouraged to do the same thing on schedule. The child who won't go to school is encouraged to resist going to school even more strongly. The child who behaves temperamentally is encouraged to put on a bigger performance.

Sweetening the pot. This is how Allen (1971a) describes this technique: ''In employing this maneuver the counselor sets out to imbue the behavior in question with a meaning which makes it extremely difficult for the client to eschew it without experiencing considerable discomfort'' (p. 42). When the behavior is given a new meaning and the counselee becomes conscious of his purpose, the behavior is more difficult to maintain.

Drawing an image or picture. This strategy offers counselees a clear picture of how they face life and portray themselves—for example, as victims or controllers. These mistaken, self-defeating perceptions create images that they live up to. As counselees become aware of their goals, they are able to see the absurd, even ridiculous, side of their behavior.

Avoiding the client's Tar Baby. Adlerians recognize that, no matter how dysfunctional a behavior may be, the person perceives it as the most reasonable for him and defends it even to the extent of fitting the counselor, as well as everybody else, into his plan. The counselor must avoid these traps in order not to confirm the counselee's faulty assumptions; that is, the counselor must avoid the client's Tar Baby (Allen, 1971a). For example, a client who believes that people don't like her will look for evidence to fit the counselor into her belief structure. She may also set the counselor up to make decisions for her, and, when she fails to carry them through, she places the blame on the counselor. Thus, she confirms her private logic by entrapping the counselor. It is crucial that this counselee be shown how she provokes the behavior she anticipates. It is equally important that the counselor break the counselee's cycle of self-defeating expectations by responding in a manner that is contrary to the script programmed by the person's life style.

Confrontation. This method is designed to bring counselees face to face with their perceptions, feelings, or behaviors and provoke an immediate response. Confrontation ''asks in a manner which necessitates an immediate response and thus is more intensive than an interpretation, although interpretation may be done in a confrontive manner. The purpose of confrontation is to provoke therapeutic change'' (Shulman, 1973, p. 197).

The counselor may confront counselees with their perceptions, with their feelings, or with their behavior. In the case of perceptions, the counselor deals with what Dreikurs called the ''hidden reason.'' These are some of the questions the counselor asks to explore the client's hidden reasons: ''What were you thinking of at the moment you took the action?'' ''What reason did you give yourself for doing it?'' ''What did you tell yourself?'' If the counselee says ''I don't know,'' the counselor guesses a number of possible hidden reasons in line with the counselee's psychological movement. Hidden reasons describe the private logic and rationalizations people use in order to make their behavior acceptable to themselves. This technique is very similar to the procedure Albert Ellis uses in Rational-Emotive Therapy (Ellis, 1962).

Confronting clients with their behavior may occur in connection with the here-and-now behavior, with resistances, and with repeated patterns of self-defeating behavior.

Catching oneself. The goal of this technique is to have counselees catch themselves in the midst of self-defeating, counterproductive behaviors, so they can learn to anticipate the situation and avert its occurring again.

Push-button technique. As described by Mosak and Dreikurs (1973), this strategy is used with persons who believe that they are victims of their emotions. Counselees are asked to close their eyes, re-create a pleasant incident from their past, and note the feeling that accompanies the memory. Then, they are asked to re-create an unpleasant incident and to note the accompanying feeling. This technique allows counselees to realize that, through imagination and beliefs, they can create whatever feeling they wish. By showing people that they have the power to decide, this method offers them convincing evidence that they are the creators and not the victims of their emotions.

Encouragement. This is the most distinctively Adlerian procedure. Since Adlerians believe that discouragement is the basic condition that prevents one from functioning, they see encouragement as the antidote. Encouragement is an essential part of each phase of the counseling relationship.

> Encouragement on the part of the counselor is comprised of both verbal and nonverbal procedures that enable a counselee to experience and become aware of his own worth. The counselor expresses faith in and total acceptance of the counselee as he is, not as he could or should be. Encouragement as defined here does not imply that the counselor rewards, bribes, or praises; it means rather that he places value on the counselee's uniqueness and humanness and indicates to him that because he is human he is of worth and value. Counselor encouragement helps to correct the counselee's mistaken assumption that he is inferior to or not as able as others. The counselor demonstrates encouragement with a strong, empathic attitude that emphasizes health rather than illness, strength rather than weakness, ability rather than inability. He completely accepts the counselee as a person of real value [Dinkmeyer, 1972, p. 177].

REFERENCES

Adler, A. *The practice and theory of Individual Psychology.* Patterson, N. J.: Littlefield, Adams, 1958.

Allen, T. W. Adlerian interview strategies for behavior change. *The Counseling Psychologist,* 1971, *3*(1), 40–48. (a)

Allen, T. W. The Individual Psychology of Alfred Adler: An item of history and a promise of a revolution. *The Counseling Psychologist,* 1971, *3*(1), 3–24. (b)

Dinkmeyer, D. Use of the encouragement process in Adlerian counseling. *Personnel and Guidance Journal*, 1972, *51*(3), 177–181.

Dinkmeyer, D., & McKay, G. D. *Systematic training for effective parenting*. Circle Pines, Minn.: American Guidance Service, 1976.

Dreikurs, R. A psychological interview in medicine. *Journal of Individual Psychology*, 1952–1953, *10*, 99–122.

Dreikurs, R. *Psychology in the classroom*. New York: Harper & Row, 1957.

Dreikurs, R. *Psychodynamics, psychotherapy, and counseling*. Chicago: Alfred Adler Institute, 1967.

Eckstein, D., Baruth, L., & Mahrer, D. *Life style: What it is and how to do it*. Chicago: Alfred Adler Institute, 1975.

Ellis, A. *Reason and emotion in psychotherapy*. New York: Lyle Stuart, 1962.

Gushurst, R. S. *The interpretation of early recollections*. Unpublished doctoral proposal, University of Chicago, 1970.

Gushurst, R. S. *The reliability and concurrent validity of an idiographic approach to the interpretation of early recollections*. Unpublished doctoral dissertation, University of Chicago, 1971. (a)

Gushurst, R. S. The technique, utility, and validity of life style analysis. *The Counseling Psychologist*, 1971, *3*(1), 30–40. (b)

Kefir, N. *Priorities*. Unpublished manuscript, 1972.

Kopp, R., & Dinkmeyer, D. Early recollections in life style assessment and counseling. *The School Counselor*, 1975, *23*(1), 22–27.

Mosak, H. H. Early recollections as a projective technique. *Journal of Projective Techniques*, 1958, *22*, 302–311.

Mosak, H. H. Life style. In A. G. Nikelly (Ed.), *Techniques for behavior change*. Springfield, Ill.: Charles C Thomas, 1971.

Mosak, H. H., & Dreikurs, R. Adlerian psychotherapy. In R. Corsini (Ed.), *Current psychotherapies*. Itasca, Ill.: Peacock, 1973.

Mosak, H. H., & Gushurst, R. S. What patients say and what they mean. In H. H. Mosak (Ed.), *On purpose*. Chicago: Alfred Adler Institute, 1977.

Nikelly, A. G., & Bostrom, J. A. Psychotherapy as reorientation and readjustment. In A. G. Nikelly (Ed.), *Techniques for behavior change*. Springfield, Ill.: Charles C Thomas, 1971.

Nikelly, A. G., & Verger, D. Early recollections. In A. G. Nikelly (Ed.), *Techniques for behavior change*. Springfield, Ill.: Charles C Thomas, 1971.

Shulman, B. H. The family constellation in personality diagnosis. *Journal of Individual Psychology*, 1962, *18*, 35–47.

Shulman, B. H. Psychological disturbances which interfere with the patient's cooperation. *Psychosomatics*, 1964, *5*, 213–220.

Shulman, B. H. Confrontation techniques in Adlerian psychotherapy. In B. H. Shulman (Ed.), *Contributions to Individual Psychology*. Chicago: Alfred Adler Institute, 1973.

Sweeney, T. J. *Adlerian counseling*. Boston: Houghton Mifflin, 1975.

CHAPTER 7

COUNSELING TECHNIQUES

In order to facilitate change, Adlerian counselors make use of a variety of procedures. For the purposes of this chapter, we shall present the techniques as they relate to three major facets of the counseling process:

1. Developing the relationship and exploring problems;
2. Assessing, understanding, diagnosing, and clarifying the problem;
3. Considering alternatives and choosing a course of action (reorientation).

Although the techniques may be used in any facet of the interview, we shall discuss them in the section that covers the stage at which they are most likely to occur. In order to help you identify with the counseling procedures discussed in this chapter, we address you, the reader, as if you were the counselor.

DEVELOPING THE RELATIONSHIP AND EXPLORING PROBLEMS

Attending Behavior and Attentive Listening

The effective therapeutic relationship begins with your focusing on the concerns as presented by the counselee. Such focus is facilitated if you initiate and maintain good eye contact with the client. Note that this visual contact is not a fixed stare. Your posture is relaxed but conveys interest and involvement through a slightly forward body position, which indicates that contact is being maintained and that you are completely available. Your comments follow directly from what the person is saying and reinforce the person's free expression, without adding new data. This helps the counselee express himself or herself spontaneously.

Establishing an effective counseling relationship requires that you be responsive to the client's communication and that you clearly communicate your attentiveness. In most of our everyday situations, we rarely encounter people who really listen and who can hear not just the words but the content, the feelings, and the intentions. Thus, coming in contact with someone who does listen is a powerful encouragement to keep talking.

> *Alan:* I feel badly about not being able to work up to my parents' expectations. I don't think I'll ever be able to meet their standards.
> *Counselor:* You feel it's pretty futile to try.
> *Alan:* I've tried, but, no matter what I do, it's not enough. This feeling I have all the time that I'm not making it really makes me very angry. For example, . . .

You hear the message, follow the content and the feelings, and seek verification about what you believe you heard. Especially during the first few minutes, it is useful to just indicate what you have heard and observed. This encourages the counselee to spontaneously tell more about how he or she feels. It is important to never let anything pass that is not fully understood.

Goal Alignment

Counseling is conversation with a purpose. The purpose is to increase the counselees' awareness of their feelings and beliefs and their understanding of how such feelings and beliefs may keep them from functioning more effectively. In a counseling interview, there are times when you become aware that the counselee is not working on the problem, is avoiding a topic, or is not following up on a comment you made. It is your role to reestablish the focus by commenting on what is happening in the here-and-now conversation. Refocusing on the task enables counselees to develop a better understanding of how they avoid certain issues. It also helps to reestablish the purpose of the contact and the implicit contract—to work on the concerns that keep the individual from effectively meeting the challenges of life.

In order to align goals, you may ask ''Is this the person you want to be? Can you think of a different way to act? What do you suspect will happen if you persist in this pattern?''

> *Claudia:* I'm very mad about the way Paul treats me, and I don't intend to stand for it.
> *Counselor:* You are angry and feel that you have to do something.
> *Claudia:* I get mad, but I get over it. Did you see that game on T.V. where the Bears lost? I was really upset.
> *Counselor:* I notice that, when we get to the point of discussing your anger and what to do, you usually talk about something else, as you are

now. I'm wondering whether you have noticed that, too. How do you feel we can deal most effectively with this problem?

You refuse to be sidetracked and talk about how this ploy by the counselee hinders the process.

Reflection of Feelings and Empathic Understanding

There is considerable evidence that the effects of counseling are related to the counselor's level of functioning on emotional and interpersonal dimensions such as empathic understanding (*The Counseling Psychologist,* 1972). For our purpose, empathy has been best defined by Carkhuff (1972): "Empathy involves experiencing another person's world as if you were he." Empathy is the communication of understanding. The counselor attempts to get into the counselee's world so that both counselor and counselee can get in better touch with the counselee's feelings, beliefs, and intentions.

Empathic understanding involves capturing the essence of the person's feelings and communicating such understanding to the person. Carkhuff indicates that we can be certain that we have responded to a person's feelings when we have made a response that is interchangeable with the feelings expressed by the individual.

Empathy also involves concentrating on the total message. Therefore, it involves both the feelings expressed by the message and the feelings elicited in the counselor by the transaction that is taking place. Reflection of feelings helps counselees become aware of and express the feelings they are experiencing. Responding to cognitive content deals basically with the literal meaning of a person's communication; it is somewhat like listening to the words of a song without the music. Instead, empathic understanding and reflection of feeling involve the whole message and permit both counselor and counselee to get in touch with the feelings and motives that influence the counselee's behavior. The process is crucial to the counseling relationship because it not only increases the counselee's awareness and self-understanding but makes it possible for the counselor to develop a situation in which change can be facilitated.

> *Robin:* I'm tired of being controlled by the group and forced to compromise. I can't function this way.
> *Counselor:* You are angry about the group's control and want to be free to make your own decisions.
> *Robin:* I know I can be happier without them, because then I'll be able to decide for myself.

Productive Use of Silence

It is not always easy to appreciate the meaning and value of silence. Too often the counselor feels impelled to say something to break the silence. Unfortunately, in some instances he or she does so with a "closed question''—a question that requires only a yes or no on the part of the client—which only compounds the problem.

Silence can and should be used productively. Letting the counselee assume responsibility for the choice of topics is one way of doing so. By accepting silence without becoming anxious, the counselee begins to recognize his or her responsibility for initiating topics and sharing his or her concerns. After accepting the silence for a time, you might ask ''What do you think is going on right now?'' Another approach is to explore with the client the hidden reason for the silence—for example, ''Could it be . . . ?''—and allude to a possible purpose. Is this a way for the counselee to control, get special service, retaliate, or perhaps show that nothing can be done about his or her situation?

In some instances, silence is an indication that the counselor and the client have not developed mutually acceptable goals. Goal alignment may not have been achieved, or there may be some false assumptions on the part of the client—for example, that it is the counselor's role to dispense advice and take full responsibility for the interview. In this situation, a reformulation of goals is necessary.

Counselee-initiated silence might mean that the individual is considering an idea, examining himself or herself, attempting to fully understand a new insight or awareness, or evaluating new directions. These are all good reasons for silence, and you need not intervene.

However, silence may also mean avoidance. Observation may produce a clue as to the purpose of the silence. For example, if the counselee's eyes appear to be fixed upon something but not focused, it is highly probable that the person is engaged in a productive silence. If, instead, he is tense and nervous and avoids eye contact, it is possible that he is avoiding the topic. By being in touch with your own feelings during the silence, you may also be able to understand the client's purpose. Anger may indicate that the client has a desire to control; confusion, instead, may indicate that the client feels that there is nothing you can do about the situation or himself.

Silence can also be used to slow the pace of the interview and permit the counselee to absorb understanding of his own feelings and purposes. Letting the client know that you, the counselor, are willing to wait without demanding that your needs be satisfied can be a very positive and reassuring way to communicate understanding and acceptance.

Nonverbal Communication

While most communication in counseling is verbal, its nonverbal components—such as facial expressions, body position, muscle tonus, voice tone, and breathing tempo—are also very important. Every time a person talks, all of the person talks. If you fail to comprehend this, you may miss the real message. For example, a double-level message is being sent when the voice says one thing and the body says something else (Satir, 1972).

Nonverbal communication can be examined in terms of its global interpersonal effect. Does an individual appear to be forceful and vibrant or subdued and restricted? Does he come through as feeling inadequate, fearful, cautious, and uninvolved or does he seem to only want to intellectualize?

Satir (1972) has characterized four types of dysfunctional nonverbal responses as *placating, blaming, computing,* and *distracting.* "Placaters" agree so the other person doesn't get mad. "Blamers" are aggressive and disagree to create an impression of strength. "Computers" talk as if they had no feelings and establish their self-worth by using big words. "Distractors" behave as though problem and people were not there. Your goal is to help the person's feelings and nonverbal behavior match the verbal message—that is, help the body message and the word message fit, be congruent.

You should also be aware of voice tone and eye contact. The individual's posture, muscle tonus, facial expressions, and gestures all emit continuous nonverbal signals. Some of the various possibilities to note include relaxed or stiff posture with hands clenched or relaxed. A client may sit in a posture that conveys defiance, distance, and control of herself, or her facial expression may reveal anger, confusion, or recognition. The recognition reflex is that characteristic grin that communicates instantly that your client understands, regardless of what she says.

If you observe a pattern in the counselee's nonverbal communication, it is often productive to interpret the message in the form of a tentative hypothesis. You might say "It seems this is very difficult for you to talk about. . . . Could it be that the thought of it makes you angry? . . . Is it possible you feel no one could understand? . . . " It is not necessary to inform the counselee of the source of your interpretation, unless your intent is to help the person become aware that he communicates as a whole person and you believe that he is ready for such awareness. This may improve the relationship, create insight, and facilitate change.

Obviously, you must also be aware of your own nonverbal behavior and how such behavior encourages or discourages a line of exploration and conveys approval or disapproval.

Counseling means total involvement, and total involvement is often accompanied by tears. It is handy to keep a box of tissues within reach. When the counselee shows signs that he is about to cry, nonchalantly give him the tissues or actually say "It's okay to cry." If the person is fighting back tears, you can discuss what this means or inquire if the person believes that crying is a sign of weakness.

ASSESSING, UNDERSTANDING, DIAGNOSING, AND CLARIFYING THE PROBLEM

Paraphrasing

Paraphrasing is the process of checking with the client to be certain that you understand his ideas as he intended them. Paraphrasing requires paying selective attention to content and feeding back the essence of what the person said. The process involves your mirroring the thoughts presented to see whether you are hearing accurately, as well as communicating your understanding. Thus, the task is twofold—listening intensively and accurately and expressing what you have heard so the person knows that he is understood.

Paraphrasing is not word swapping or parroting; it is communication of understanding. This may be achieved either by generalizing the counselee's message or by making it more specific. Because paraphrasing conveys the listener's interest, it, too, serves to enhance the relationship.

Claudia: I don't know about him. At times he's very nice, but then, again, he can be very nasty.
Counselor: You are not sure how he's going to act. He's hard to predict.

Paraphrasing may also allude to the goal or purpose implied in the client's communication. For example, ''It seems you want to get even'' or ''I get the impression you want to show they can't control you.''

Confrontation

Confrontation is a procedure by which the counselor, in a sensitive but perceptive manner, enables counselees to be aware of discrepancies between their behaviors and their intentions, their feelings and their messages, their insights and their actions, and so forth.

Shulman (1973) indicates that confrontation is the combination of a challenge and a question designed to evoke the feeling that an immediate response is required. Thus, it is used to stimulate therapeutic movement by mirroring to counselees their mistaken goals. Shulman (1973) suggests a number of techniques, whose use depends on the object of the confrontation.

Confronting clients with their subjective views. Dreikurs. refers to this confronting technique as ''revealing the hidden reason.'' That is, the counselor confronts the client with the private justification that the client gives to himself to make his behavior acceptable in his own eyes. For example: ''I'm acting this way just because I'm drunk,'' or ''I had so little sleep that, even if I went to work, I couldn't get anything done,'' or ''I'm too nervous'' (Shulman, 1973).

Dreikurs suggests that the confrontation be pursued by asking the person ''What were you thinking of at the moment?'' or ''What did you say to yourself then?'' He also suggests that, if the counselor wants to be understood and make the confrontation effective, he or she must put the hidden reason into the counselee's words.

Confronting clients with their mistaken beliefs and attitudes. The beliefs and attitudes to which this type of confrontation refers are the person's basic convictions about his own nature, the world, and the meaning and requirements of life. Shulman (1973) says "These basic convictions fill in the following blanks: I am . . . ; life is . . . ; therefore . . . . " (p. 201). For example, the person who complains that others pick on her might be confronted with "You look, talk, and behave like a pushover; so you invite people to pick on you. Don't blame others but yourself, since you invite them."

Confronting clients with their private goals. This confrontation may be used when the counselee attempts to deny a feeling that you suspect is there. The confrontation is brought about by offering a tentative hypothesis such as "Could it be that you wanted to get them upset?" or "Is it possible you thought this would be an excuse?" These statements may produce a recognition reflex or an acknowledgment that indicates acceptance of the confrontation.

Confronting clients with their destructive behavior. Here we deal with the counselor's here-and-now, immediate experiences. For example, "You just changed the subject. Were we getting too close to something?" or "I notice you are arguing about one word and ignoring the concept. How come?"

As Shulman (1973) states, "Confrontation techniques are intended to challenge the client to give an immediate response, make an immediate change or an immediate examination of some issue" (p. 205). Adlerian confrontation is intended to help counselees become immediately aware of their goals, private logic, and behavior, as well as ability to change.

Interpretation

Interpretation deals with the reasons why a person behaves in a certain manner—that is, with the purpose of the behavior, belief, or feeling. By bringing about a shift away from the counselee's internal frame of reference, interpretation provides a new perspective for understanding a situation. In other words, the counselor uses this technique to help the person consider and develop a new point of view, thus gaining access to a wider range of alternatives.

Interpretation is effective only if the counselee is receptive and can understand it and use it. In order to minimize resistance, interpretation is usually presented in a tentative format, such as "Could it be . . . ?" or "Is it possible . . . ?" and at a time when the counselor believes that the counselee is ready to hear and seriously consider the interpretation.

> *Alan:* I'm confused about how well I can do my work. I can do some of it. But, if I do well, they expect more of me, and I can't live up to their expectations.
> *Counselor:* You are not sure of your ability. Could it be that you don't do too well so they excuse you?

You hear the feelings and allude in a tentative manner to the purpose of displaying inadequacy.

"The Question"

This counseling technique, first developed by Adler, is used to determine whether a problem has an organic or a functional basis. If the person complains of a physical symptom, such as headache, difficulty in breathing, or heart tremors, you ask "What would be different if you were well?" If the basis of the condition is functional and, therefore, has a purpose, the person might say "I could meet girls," or "I could go back to work," or "I could study harder." This tells you what he is avoiding by having the physical symptom. However, if he does not indicate any such purpose, it is highly probable that there is a physical cause and that the condition is organic. It should be added that, while there may be a physical ailment without psychological etiology, the counselee may still use the ailment for a special purpose.

Perceiving and Responding with Concreteness

This is the procedure through which you encourage a high degree of specificity and concreteness on the part of counselees. You do so by responding with clear, concise statements that clarify the counselee's problem. Since the aim of counseling is to develop a concrete plan for action, a technique that promotes concreteness is quite useful. This approach also achieves the goal of assuring clients that you are ready to discuss concerns in detail. Finally, your concrete responses encourage clients to be concrete not only in the counseling interaction but in all of their interactions with others as well.

You begin by encouraging self-exploration and problem exploration in a very specific manner. Once the concern has been clarified, it is appropriate to encourage the counselee to consider and explore at a lower level of concreteness the purpose of his behavior. By offering tentative hypotheses and by mirroring the individual's self-defeating goal and mistaken ideas, you help the client see, in very concrete form, why he behaves as he does.

Concreteness is your guiding principle also when you help the counselee to choose specific alternatives and implement action.

> *Sandy:* Well, I know I should expect trouble with children. But I come from a big family and have read a lot. Still, it doesn't relieve the pressure of guiding my children.
>
> *Counselor:* You recognize that fights between children are normal, and you'd like to find ways to reduce the pressure.

Concreteness is especially important when the counselee tends to be vague and abstract, talks in generalities, or tends to intellectualize.

> *Julie:* You don't know how some husbands might react.
>
> *Counselor A:* Some are certainly unpredictable.

Counselor *A*'s response is not concrete and blocks progress.

> *Julie:* You don't know how some husbands might react.
> *Counselor B:* Tom was very quiet when you came home.

By using the indefinite *you* instead of *I,* Julie was attempting to be vague and not assume responsibility for her own statement. She referred to husbands in general, not to her husband, Tom. By being concrete and mentioning the name of her husband, Counselor *B* helps Julie assume responsibility for her actions and feelings.

CONSIDERING ALTERNATIVES AND CHOOSING A COURSE OF ACTION (REORIENTATION)

Problem Solving and Decision Making

Problem solving and decision making are basic skills in the action phase of the counseling process. They are employed to help the counselee to explore and understand the problem adequately, so that the goal can be defined precisely. The next step involves considering alternative courses of action and assisting the counselee to examine and order his values. Each course of action is considered in terms of how it helps the person realize his goals and values.

Carkhuff (1973) has schematized this phase in terms of the following steps:

1. Define problem: develop accurate grasp of situation.
2. Define goal: clearly determine task to be achieved.
3. Develop alternative courses of action: develop means to achieve goals.
4. Develop counselee's value hierarchy: describe things that matter to counselee.
5. Choose course of action: evaluate course in terms of value hierarchy.
6. Implement course of action: develop a way to act on a course of action.

In the Adlerian counseling process, counselor and counselee align their goals, consider possible alternatives and their consequences, evaluate how these alternatives will help the counselee meet his goals, and then reorient by taking a course of action. The counselor helps the counselee consider how his mistaken, self-defeating perceptions may keep him from making effective decisions.

> *Gina:* I'd like to go on to medical school, but I'm not sure if I could do as
> well as I should. So maybe I'll teach biology.
> *Counselor:* You are not sure of yourself. Your belief that you have to
> be first or you are nothing seems to keep you from deciding in favor
> of medicine.

Immediacy

Immediacy means expressing how you are experiencing the counselee in the here and now. Since the immediacy dimension has the potential to upset, as well as advance, the relationship, it is usually approached tentatively. If the counselee has progressed in self-awareness and self-understanding, the communication of immediacy can be more direct.

Immediacy is used to help clients become aware of what they are communicating both verbally and nonverbally. Healthy and mature persons communicate congruently. They say what they intend to say. In the immediacy aspect of the relationship, you make explicit the relationship between you and the counselee.

> *Peter:* I want to do something to help me get started; but it's no use. They are all ahead of me.
>
> *Counselor:* You say you want to get started, but I get the impression from your tone of voice that you have given up and are still concerned with how you compare with others.

You share your impression that the counselee is defeating himself.

Encouragement

Encouragement focuses on helping counselees become aware of their own worth. By encouraging them, you help your counselees recognize and own their strengths and assets, so they can become aware of the power they have to decide and make choices (Dinkmeyer, 1972).

One's identity is a product of interpersonal relationships, because the feedback one receives is internalized and creates identity. If the person feels discouraged and inadequate, the lack of self-esteem produces dysfunctional behavior and a failure to become involved in the tasks of life. Encouragement is the most powerful procedure available for changing the counselee's beliefs.

Encouragement focuses on the person's beliefs and self-perceptions. It searches intensely for assets and processes feedback so the person will become aware of his or her strengths. In a mistake-centered culture like ours, this approach violates the norms by ignoring deficits and stressing assets. The counselor is concerned with changing the person's negative self-concept and anticipations.

Encouragement can take many forms, depending on the phase of the counseling process. At the beginning, you let your clients know that you value them by really listening to their feelings and intentions, and you stimulate their confidence by accepting them as full and equal participants in the process. In the assessment phase of counseling, which is designed to illuminate strengths, you recognize and encourage the counselees' growing awareness of their power to choose and their attempts to change. In the reorientation phase, change is promoted by stimulating the individual's courage. Thus, encouragement is a vital element of every aspect of the counseling process.

> *Gina:* School grades have little meaning for me. I could do it; but my
> teachers demand too much and go too fast.
> *Counselor:* You feel you could do the work at a different pace.

You sense the discouragement and value the counselee's belief in her own ability. If she accepts her ability, then procedures for modifying the pace can be considered. You demonstrate that the person has resources.

Paradoxical Intention

Adler called the paradoxical intention "prescribing the symptom," and Dreikurs called it "antisuggestion." It is a technique in which clients are encouraged to emphasize or develop their symptoms even more. For example, if the child doesn't do her arithmetic homework, you might suggest that this is a good way to resist authority and encourage her not to do any schoolwork. If an individual bites his fingernails, you encourage him to bite even more and deeper.

Usually it is best to make the paradoxical recommendations for a specific period of time and treat them as an experiment. That is, you encourage counselees to see what they learn from the experience.

The paradoxical intention makes people dramatically aware of the reality of their situation and of the fact that they must accept the consequences of their behavior. When you confront a client with your paradoxical refusal to fight his behavior, the behavior becomes less attractive in the client's eyes. This procedure also implicitly indicates confidence that, when the individual sees the problem in a magnified perspective, he will choose to change his behavior. Also, this technique may make the symptoms appear so ridiculous that the counselee finally gives them up.

> *Terry:* Mr. Smith is very unfair. He bugs me all the time, and, when I talk
> back, he sends me to the principal.
> *Counselor:* You feel that Mr. Smith is unfair. But why do you cooperate
> with him?
> *Terry:* Cooperate? Ridiculous! I never do.
> *Counselor:* It seems to me that you play his game. You say he gets you in
> trouble; but you could really defeat him if you didn't go for the bait.
> Can you imagine how he'd look if you didn't respond?

You suggest doing exactly the opposite and "winning" by failing to cooperate with the teacher. Actually, both student and teacher win.

Adler and Dreikurs taught that a symptom must be fought against in order to be maintained. The paradox is often effective because, when the counselee comes for help, the counselor tells him to go back and do what he was doing. By no longer fighting it, the counselee may be free to choose.

Spitting in the Client's Soup

Adler's technique—which he also referred to as "besmirching a clean conscience"—comes from the boarding-school practice of getting someone's food by spitting on it. It is one application of the Adlerian strategy of modifying behavior by changing its meaning to the person who produces it. The counselor must determine the purpose and payoff of the behavior and spoil the game by reducing the pleasure or usefulness of the behavior in the counselee's eyes.

> *Alan:* You've said that I don't function unless I can be first or best. I suppose I should give that up.
> *Counselor:* You can continue.
> *Alan:* I'm confused.
> *Counselor:* All I'm saying is that you have to be always so careful about being first that you don't try a lot of things you'd enjoy. But you are entitled to miss them if you want to protect yourself.

You point out that the individual has a right to insist on being first, but you also clearly show how such approach restricts him. The choice is still with the counselee, but it is now less palatable.

Acting As If

This is an action-oriented procedure used with the counselee who pleads "If only I could . . . " and consists in suggesting to the person that, for the next week, he should "act as if"; that is, he should behave how he wishes he could behave but doesn't believe he can. The counselee will usually protest that it would be only an act and that, in essence, he would be the same person. This is how Mosak and Dreikurs (1973) suggest that you deal with such protestations: "We show him that all acting is not phony pretense, that he is being asked to try on a role as one might try on a suit. It doesn't change the person wearing the suit, but sometimes with a handsome suit of clothes, he may feel differently and perhaps behave differently, in which case he becomes a different person" (p. 60).

> *Marcos:* I just can't get acquainted with girls. If only I could be like Tom and walk up to a group and talk about the game . . . .
> *Counselor:* It's difficult for you to talk with girls. For this week, I'd like you to act as if you were Tom and just begin by talking about the game.

You suggest a limited task, such as acting as if Marcos had the courage to talk to girls. The expectation is that the plan will work. If it doesn't, you explore what kept it from being a good experience.

Catching Oneself

Through confrontation and interpretation, counselees become aware of their goals. Once they decide to change, the counselor suggests that they learn to "catch themselves" in any behavior that they want to change. At first, they will catch themselves too late and recognize that they have again fallen into the trap of seeking attention, trying to prove their power, or whatever. With awareness and practice, clients learn to anticipate the situation—that is, their self-defeating perceptions and the behavior that ensues. As a result, they can learn to avoid the situation or to change their behavior when they are in a situation that tends to stimulate the behavior in question. This approach necessitates having a sense of humor and being able to laugh at one's own ineffective behavior instead of becoming discouraged about it.

> *Robin:* I know I shouldn't, but I seem to keep getting trapped into power struggles with Jack.
> *Counselor:* You recognize that he stimulates you to prove you are right.
> *Robin:* Yes, we get into lots of quarrels mainly over who's right.
> *Counselor:* I suggest that, as you sense a struggle coming, you catch yourself—become aware that you're about to get involved in being right and more powerful—and just withdraw by refusing to get involved in the argument.

Creating Movement

The counseling process reorients clients toward a new perspective by helping them understand the purpose of their behavior. Often this movement occurs by mutual consent and interaction. When it does not, you have alternatives by which you can create movement.

No tactic, strategy, or other counselor intervention can succeed unless the client wishes to succeed. Utilization of strategies and tactics that can effectively move the client will depend on the quality of the counselor/client relationship, as it exists. The counselor needs to enlist the cooperation of the client, whatever his or her resistance to the reorientation process may be. Clients may lose faith in the therapist if they perceive any of the counseling techniques as threatening (Dreikurs, 1967, pp. 25–26). Movement tactics, such as surprise, should be used judiciously. The indiscriminate use of the following tactics—that is, a use that fails to consider the appropriateness of the tactic to each setting—would result in failure.

When you surprise a client, the client is hearing and seeing unexpected counselor behaviors. The purpose of surprise is to create movement by drawing dramatic attention to a specific behavior on the part of the counselee.

One form of surprise allows you to agree, for the moment, with the client's faulty belief.

> *Claudia:* Whenever I go out with boys, they always criticize me. I'll never date again!
>
> *Counselor:* Yes, I agree. Don't ever date critical men again. They can't possibly have anything valid to say.

You have adopted the client's point of view, advocating her despairing remark about dating. Since the client has dealt with the issue in absolute terms ("never"), you reflect her certainty ("Don't date critical men again"). By temporarily agreeing with the faulty belief, you have focused on the belief and you have diplomatically pointed to the problems inherent in that belief.

Avoiding the Tar Baby

Allen (1971) says that this procedure is based on the recognition that, no matter how self-defeating a person's perceptions and methods of operation may be, they still remain in that person's eyes as his or her most effective method. Hence, he or she defends them. The counselee's faulty assumptions and mistaken goals may be ineffective, but they make sense in terms of the counselee's biased perception and may yield some kind of payoff.

Thus, the counselee may attempt to fit you—and everybody else—into his or her perception of life. It is important that you elude the traps and avoid confirming the counselee's anticipations. For example, some counselees may try to provoke you in order to substantiate their assumption that they are unlovable. If you fall in their trap, they can point out that even those whose job it is to like all kinds of people dislike them. Other counselees may attempt to discourage you in order to show that nobody can help them. Still others may try to trap you into making a decision for them; carry out the decision poorly, and then put the blame on you.

As a counselor, you will attend to and encourage only those behaviors that help the counselee to mature psychologically and develop greater social interest. You will avoid power struggles, feeling hurt, or expressing discouragement about your attempts to help the counselee. This technique essentially requires altering the meaning of the behavior to the counselee. To do this, you respond in ways contrary to the person's expectations and perceptions, thus forcing him or her to give them up (Allen, 1971).

> *Terry:* I can never establish a friendship in a short time. They reject me. Even *you* are angry that I'm not making as much progress as I should.
>
> *Counselor:* You would like to have me feel discouraged, but I'm not. Tell me how things are going.

You refuse to be trapped into defending yourself and, instead, redirect the counselee to look at the positive.

Task Setting and Commitment

Task setting and commitment are the steps taken by counselees to do something specific about their problems. Thus, these steps take counselees beyond simply considering alternatives and lead them to actual implementation of change. To be effective, the task should be specific and chosen by the person being helped. You can, however, assist the counselee by creating an awareness of the various alternatives.

It is essential that the task be for a limited period of time. Counselees are more resistant if they think that they are signing up for life. When the counselee is successful at a specific task and within a limited period of time, you have something concrete to encourage.

The step of setting tasks and developing specific commitments helps the counselee translate new beliefs and feelings into action, generates energy for the process, and provides feedback by which progress can be evaluated. When the task is not accomplished, you help the counselee to evaluate the effectiveness of the plan. If the plan is not effective or appropriate, you revise it.

> *Terry:* I'm still having trouble making friends. People are so different here. I just can't get started. The popular kids all ignore me.
>
> *Counselor:* You're having trouble getting to know the popular kids. Whom would you like to know better?
>
> *Terry:* Well, I guess Jack. But I know he's too popular and too busy.
>
> *Counselor:* You recognize that your goals may be too ambitious. Who is someone else you feel you'd have a better chance to become friends with?
>
> *Terry:* Bill is somebody I'd like to know better, and he's not impossible. He's even talked to me.
>
> *Counselor:* What could you do this week to get to know Bill better?
>
> *Terry:* I'm not sure. That's the problem.
>
> *Counselor:* What's something he likes to do that you could do with him?
>
> *Terry:* He likes to play ball, and we could do that at my house or at the park.
>
> *Counselor:* You've decided to try to play ball together. When do you plan to ask him? What day or days are you hoping to play ball with him?
>
> *Terry:* I'll see him sometime, and we'll figure it out.
>
> *Counselor:* I think you'll accomplish more if you are specific. I would like you to set a day, even a time, to talk with Bill. Have in mind some days when you could play ball together.
>
> *Terry:* I'm not too sure, but I'll see him Friday morning, and I'll ask him about playing ball Saturday morning or Sunday afternoon.

As we said earlier, task setting involves helping the person establish a specific task—in this case, choosing a playmate. The goals of the tasks should be realistic, attainable, and measurable, so that, at the next meeting, progress can be discussed in terms of specifics.

Terminating and Summarizing the Interview

The effective closing of an interview is often a problem for the inexperienced counselor. You should have some idea of the minimum and maximum time the interview should last. Generally, 30 minutes with children and 45–50 minutes with adolescents and adults are sufficient periods of time. The counselee should know when the interview begins and when it will be over. It is important that you establish these limits not only for practical purposes (such as being available for the next client) but also because counselees will often postpone talking about their major concerns as long as possible. Being aware of time limitation, counselees will get to the important issues more readily.

The termination deals with what has been discussed, not with new material. If the counselee brings up a new topic, you can just suggest "That might be a good place to begin next week." Asking the counselee to summarize the interview helps you have a clear picture of the counselee's perceptions and intentions.

> *Counselor:* Our time is up. I'm wondering what you got out of our session. If you could summarize it, I believe it would help both of us.
> *Robin:* I recognize I do some things that bug the teacher, and I think I'll ask Marcia to help me with the homework.

In this chapter we have considered the basic elements of the helping relationship and the perceptual organization of effective helpers. Goals of counseling, a theory of change, and a number of counseling techniques have been described. The techniques must become a part of the counselor, not merely a professional procedure. They require a sensitive, empathic listener who uses active methods because he or she cares and because they are more likely to produce movement and change on the part of the counselee.

REFERENCES

Allen, T. Adlerian interview strategies for behavior change. *The Counseling Psychologist,* 1971, *3*(1), 40–48.

Carkhuff, R. R. *The art of helping.* Amherst, Mass.: Human Resource Development Press, 1972.

Carkhuff, R. R. *The art of problem solving.* Amherst, Mass.: Human Resource Development Press, 1973.

The Counseling Psychologist. New directions in training (Part 1). 1972, *3*(3), whole issue.

Dinkmeyer, D. Use of the encouragement process in Adlerian counseling. *Personnel and Guidance Journal,* 1972, *51*(3), 177–181.

Dreikurs, R. R. *Psychodynamics, psychotherapy, and counseling.* Chicago: Alfred Adler Institute, 1967.

Mosak, H. H., & Dreikurs, R. Adlerian psychotherapy. In R. Corsini (Ed.), *Current psychotherapies.* Itasca, Ill.: Peacock, 1973.

Satir, V. *Peoplemaking.* Palo Alto, Calif.: Science & Behavior Books, 1972.

Shulman, B. H., Confrontation techniques in Adlerian psychotherapy. In B. H. Shulman (Ed.), *Contributions to Individual Psychology.* Chicago: Alfred Adler Institute, 1973.

CHAPTER 8

COUNSELING CHILDREN AND ADOLESCENTS

The approach to counseling children and the approach to counseling adolescents differ enough to warrant treating them as two separate subjects. With young children, most of the counseling is with the parents, teachers, or parent surrogates. As children become more verbal, they can be counseled individually and in groups. Adolescents (12 years of age and older) present unique challenges to the counselor or therapist. These challenges involve decisions about emphasis in therapy—whether to strive toward stimulating more autonomy or whether to work at helping the young person function within the system (the school or the family). Naturally, it will never be an either/or decision.

The formal use of the life-style assessment is another element that differentiates child and adolescent counseling. In most instances, the use of Dreikurs' four mistaken goals and the knowledge of the child's family constellation make any formal type of life-style assessment unnecessary. "Maturing," however, involves increasing self-deception and sophistication in hiding one's goals and motivations from self and others. Mistaken behavior on the part of young children is for the most part directed toward adults, since young children seek belonging through their relationships with adults. Youths, however, become more and more concerned with pleasing peers and less and less concerned with pleasing adults. Peer pressure, the desire for excitement and experimentation, and the profound physical and psychological changes that are taking place are some of the elements that make the counseling of adolescents qualitatively different from the counseling of children.

COUNSELING VERY YOUNG CHILDREN

Many Adlerians believe that even preverbal toddlers can understand rather sophisticated psychological interpretations. To substantiate this rather startling view, its proponents point to the fact that, when the recognition reflex is elicited in a demonstration setting, toddlers clearly show that they understand the counselor's recommendations to their parents. These children indicate that they realize that the behavior in question is no longer going to "work," and they change, often rather strikingly, their way of acting. The following case, not unusual in family-education centers,[1] clearly illustrates the situation.

Cynthia, age 19 months, was described by her mother as a destructive terror. She was constantly into everything, emptying drawers, tearing things apart, and creating a ruckus. Her mother was at her wit's end. Having been one of the eldest of a family of 12 children, she had considered herself competent as a parent until she began to deal with Cynthia. The fact that she could elicit no cooperation from her daughter was particularly galling since her profession was that of a labor mediator. She was deeply hurt by Cynthia's behavior and stated that she vigorously disliked her daughter.

The counselor postulated that Cynthia's goal was revenge and asked the mother if she would be willing for one week to go immediately to the bathroom, without any comment, each time Cynthia began tearing the house apart. In her desperation, the mother agreed but predicted that she would be forced to retire to the bathroom at least ten times a day before Cynthia would believe that her mother meant business. But she agreed to keep a chart.

The mother was dismissed from the stage, and Cynthia entered. She was an attractive toddler who didn't say a word during the interview but listened attentively. She had a marked recognition reflex when the goal of revenge was presented. Apparently, she felt that in some way she had been mistreated; so her feelings were hurt and she wanted to get even. The counselor then told her that her mother would go to the bathroom each time she began destroying something and asked her if she thought that this arrangement was fair. Cynthia shook her head negatively. Finally, when the counselor asked Cynthia if she believed that her mother would actually carry through such a recommendation, the child looked pensive.

One week later, Cynthia's mother returned to the family-education center and reported that the relationship between herself and her daughter

---

[1]Family-education centers (which are discussed in detail in Chapter 13) are community resources in which children, adolescents, parents, teachers, and other interested adults can learn more cooperative ways of living together in harmony, whether it be in the home or in the classroom. Counseling is done in public, in front of an audience. Mental-health principles are taught to the audience by interviewing volunteer families who have in the past been themselves a part of the audience (*International Encyclopedia of Psychiatry, Psychology, Psychoanalysis, and Neurology*, 1977).

had undergone a dramatic change and that she enjoyed her daughter and was having fun with her for the first time since Cynthia was born. She also reported that on the first day she had retired to the bathroom six times, on the second day twice, and, except for one flurry the night before, she hadn't found it necessary to use the "bathroom treatment" again.

Probably the mother would have been fairly successful even without Cynthia's being involved in the counseling process. It is our impression, however, that Cynthia's new awareness of the goal of her misbehavior, coupled with the knowledge that her mother was going to deal with her differently, contributed significantly to a change that appeared almost miraculous.

In our experience, interviewing very young children is useful primarily for diagnostic purposes. As children become more verbal, they can be drawn into the counseling process itself, their cooperation can be enlisted, and their involvement and participation can be promoted. Furthermore, since Adlerians believe that every misbehaving child is a discouraged child, specific encouragement of the child by the counselor and, in the case of the family-education centers, by members of the audience, is a significant part of the counseling process. In the centers, the younger children are often interviewed separately from their parents. Many of them enjoy being in front of the audience, particularly when audience members are asked to give feedback on what they sincerely appreciate about the child or children who have been interviewed.

We often have to see with our own eyes just how actively very young children influence those around them and, consequently, what an important role they play in the counseling process involving other members of their family.

> Tina, 8 months, was the youngest of five children. The older four had all gone through periods of minor behavioral disturbances, and now the parents returned complaining about Tina. When, at the family-education center, the entire family was interviewed together, it became very clear that this 8-month-old was tyrannizing the rest of the family by merely sucking on her lower lip. Throughout the entire session, Tina would periodically suck on her lip, and one of the parents or one of the children would get up, walk across the room, and pull her lip out.

As children get older and more verbal, individual therapy is often the best way to deal with their problems.

> John, age 4, was badly bitten by a neighbor's dog. At the time of his referral, he had become enuretic, asthmatic, plagued with nightmares, and extremely fearful. In other words, he was behaving like a typical adult neurotic. Since litigation was involved, the child was interviewed by his attorney, who asked him to describe the incident. John did so by drawing pictures and writing under them "Bowser bit John," followed by the date. In John's case, although the parents needed help in understanding

how to deal with the child, the therapists at the center elected to work directly with John in talking therapy.[2] John was certainly an exception, since the youngest child with whom talking therapy had been used at the center was 8 years old.

However, some nursery-school teachers, kindergarten teachers, and teachers of primary-grade children are reporting success in their regular classroom group discussions, in which children are encouraged to discuss the affairs of the classroom as well as their own personal feelings and concerns. One of the most exciting therapy groups conducted at one of the family-education centers was a group of 9- to 12-year-olds. Anyone who has seen a movie like Truffaut's *Small Change* or has seriously observed small children at work and at play will not find it hard to believe that young children think deeply and are very candid and perceptive in discussing their thoughts and feelings with other children. Unfortunately, most adults are so prejudiced about what young children can and cannot do that they overlook children's capability to participate in the counseling process.

A counselor who works with young children needs to be familiar with the normal developmental process and its many variations. At the same time, the counselor must not misuse "developmental stages" and the like as a means of labeling children and failing to see them and respect them as unique individuals. Every infant is born a full-fledged human being, and all infants very quickly become actors as well as reactors, learning precisely how to influence adults.

The primary goal of counseling with families is to help the parents become a match for their children. The primary goal of counseling with children is to win the children's cooperation and help them see that it is to their benefit to operate with, rather than against, their parents. If a child is seen separately from his or her parents, it is essential that the counselor inform the child as fully as possible of what was discussed with the parents.

COUNSELING OLDER CHILDREN

What we just said about counseling young children also applies to older children, except that children who are 6 or 7 (or older) can be counseled individually, in peer groups, or in family groups. It is important that counselors treat children of all ages with the utmost respect and courtesy, just as they would treat adult counselees. It is not necessary to change vocabulary or tone of voice, nor is it necessary to "get down to the child's level." Immature people are delightful with their creativity, imagination, intelligence, and spontaneity. Unfortunately, these characteristics are drilled out of most of our children.

[2]Talking therapy means just that—sitting down with the child and talking with him or her for a part of the session, establishing a warm and trusting relationship, and, from time to time, gently challenging the child's mistaken views about himself or herself and the world.

The counselors who are most successful with children are those who feel comfortable with childlike behavior on the part of the children as well as on their own part. There are not many children who are mentally ill, as we would use the term with adolescents or adults. But children may not be skilled in communicating verbally; activating personality patterns through other media may help them communicate. Dance, music, psychodrama, movement, and art—all represent nonverbal channels that many children will find quite comfortable.

Much of the so-called "play therapy" is not therapeutic at all, except perhaps for the therapist who doesn't know what else to do with children. Naturally, it is fun to play with children, but for the most part this is an unnecessary luxury, although in special situations the child at play will reveal things about himself or herself that do not come out in any other way. Therefore, play therapy—if it is to be used—is probably more meaningful from a diagnostic standpoint, since it provides the therapist with a good opportunity to learn how a child communicates, how he relates to another his willingness to cooperate, how he uses his hands and small muscles, and how well he can see and hear. The need for the counselor to be as keen an observer of human behavior as children are is of paramount importance. Children grow up in what often appears to them as an enemy camp. Thus, astute observation is often practically a matter of life and death for the child.

Children don't have the experience necessary to be good interpreters; so, although they are astute observers, they often come up with very poor and mistaken interpretations. But most children seem to be able to change their views very easily and very quickly. It is easy to establish rapport with children almost instantly, as the following example illustrates. The speaker is one of the authors.

> I am asked to see a 4-year-old for psychiatric evaluation. I go to the waiting room and escort the child to my office. I close the door and sit down. The child remains standing, and I ask him "Are you used to having people tell you what to do?" He may respond either verbally or nonverbally in an affirmative manner. Using the "goal-disclosure" method described by Dreikurs, I say "Perhaps I can guess why you don't do what people ask you to do." The child will usually give me some encouragement. I then ask him "Could it be that you don't do what you're asked to do so you keep people busy, thus letting them know that you're around?" I seldom get a response to this.
>
> However, I frequently get a response to the presentation of the second goal: "Could it be that you want to show people that you are big and strong and that they can't make you do what they want you to do?" The child may respond with what Dreikurs referred to as the "recognition reflex." Even though he shakes his head negatively, there is a twinkle in his eyes and a roguish smile on his face. He may blush, and he may even attempt to hide his face. When I obtain this type of response, I know I am on the right track. I then assure the child in a variety of ways that he is in

fact stronger than me and that I have no intention whatsoever of attempting to overpower him or force him to do things that he doesn't want to do. The most common response at this point is for the child to very neatly sit down, and from that time on we are friends [Pew, 1969, p. 67].

Sometimes, the children's relief in discovering that some adult understands them is so great that it finds rather touching expression, often after relatively short interviews. For example, the child may shyly offer the therapist a piece of candy, shake his/her hand, or even give him/her a hug.

This kind of instant rapport is, of course, easier to obtain with small children. We repeat: it is a rapport that necessitates a basic respect for the child on the part of the adult. When interview techniques have been demonstrated publicly at family-education centers, observers have often remarked that the counselors there don't talk with children any differently than they talk with adults. The reason is simply that children respond very quickly to any adult who treats them with respect and doesn't talk down to them. Also, small children respond well to a fair, firm, and friendly attitude on the part of the adult and to the early demonstration that their behavior makes sense.

Usually, there is no need for a very extensive evaluation of the child. Much of the testing that children are subjected to is conducted by people who don't understand children or know what to do with them. The results of the tests when fed back to teachers and parents are seldom very helpful and often contribute to the child's being pigeonholed and consequently limited in his or her opportunity to grow and develop. A good example is that of intelligence testing, which is often used to justify the failure of the teacher or to qualify the school system for some kind of state or federal aid. IQ tests have been so badly misused in this country that many observers question seriously whether they should be used at all. How children perform on intelligence testing merely describes what they are doing at the moment and doesn't in any way tell us what the children's upper limits are. Unfortunately, testing often merely provides deeply discouraged children with further ammunition for their cold war with adults.

Whenever adults don't know what to do with children, they call them names—lazy, fearful, or aggressive—or use more sophisticated terms such as *minimally brain damaged* or *dyslexic*. Adlerian counselors are not satisfied with dealing with the observed behavior alone; they will try to understand the purpose of the child's fear or aggression or incapacity to read. Only if we can understand the goal of the child's mistaken behavior are we able to plan *with* the child approaches that will be helpful to him or her.

Ideally, the counselor working with school-age children will try to bring about a general agreement among the parents, the school personnel, and the child concerning the best possible course of action. Frequently, the parents blame the school, the school blames the parents, and the child goes off scot-free. The counselor must avoid getting into this kind of situation. Since counselors are often misquoted, a meeting of all parties concerned, *including the child,* is most helpful in order to achieve common purposes and goals. The counselor must recognize that most teachers are well qualified to teach children who want to learn or children who want to behave but that frequently teachers don't have the slightest clue as to what they should do with children who don't want to learn or don't want to behave. Therefore, the counselor must be willing and able to teach the teachers, as well as the parents, the basic principles of child rearing.

COUNSELING ADOLESCENTS

Adolescence is a recent invention and a product of Western, consumer-oriented, industrialized society. Adolescence, as we talk about it, is not recognized in many cultures. In some families and in some communities, adolescence is now so prolonged that the term may include people up to age 25 (the age when some males have finally completed their growth). This creates a rather peculiar situation, since today many young people are maturing earlier, at least from the physical and physiological points of view; that is, puberty is occurring earlier, and full adult size is achieved earlier. Furthermore, today's adolescents are generally taller and heavier than their counterparts of even ten years ago.

The phenomenon of earlier physical development does seem to be leveling off, but the counselor must be aware of it, nevertheless. If for girls puberty is defined as the onset of menstruation, some girls reach puberty as early as 10 years of age—that is, when they are in fourth or fifth grade. On the other hand, it is normal for some girls to begin menstruating as late as age 15 or 16. Although the onset of puberty in boys cannot be as clearly defined, there is still a wide range of what is considered normal. For example, a young man recently reported to the counselor that he did not develop secondary sex characteristics until he was 18 years old and a member of the armed forces. These normal variations in physical development make generalizations about young people at a particular chronological age virtually impossible, thus complicating the task of counseling.

Another factor that contributes to the difficulty of counseling adolescents is the variety of views of a given young person on the part of his/her parents, teachers, peers, and the community at large. With the exception of some rural towns, today it is very difficult for an adolescent to find useful ways of contributing to the community. Many adolescents react to this situation by neglecting some of the standard role expectations and by emphasizing the social aspects of their development, particularly as far as peers are concerned. This behavior leads many parents and teachers to see adolescents almost as members of a different culture. The tendency of young people to adopt fads in clothing, language, music, and dance—among other things—contributes to the adolescents' isolation from the general community. It is interesting to note, however, that many of these fads are later taken up by young, and not so young, adults. In a social sense, therefore, adolescents are often cultural pioneers.

Overcoming loneliness and achieving intimacy are major concerns for most adolescents, as is the more general goal of finding belonging in the human community. Since useful avenues are frequently blocked, there is a strong tendency for adolescents to find belonging in ways that many adults find objectionable. Today, adolescence is characterized by an ever-increasing disregard for the opinions of adults and by an ever-increasing concern for the recognition and acceptance of peers. Since many adolescents view themselves as outside the mainstream of social and cultural expectations, it is not surprising that they tend to band together with other similarly isolated youths, seemingly at war with adult authority as represented by parents and school. We said "seemingly," but in many ways there *is* a war between the generations, and this fact must be recognized if one expects to intervene in any kind of constructive manner.

However, it is often difficult to decide which generation we are dealing with. For example, by age 16, some adolescents are buying into the values of the adult society and, within a year or so, clearly see themselves as members of a different generation with regard to those who are two or three years younger. Adolescence is a period of examination of values, and young people find much to be skeptical of in society's values. But, in spite of their apparent isolation from the adult community, the vast majority of adolescents really want to know what adults think, particularly the adults close to them and especially parents. This tremendously important fact, established by several national studies, is often overlooked by the adults.

Counselors are always faced with a difficult dilemma. Should they put their efforts in helping adolescents accept what is frequently a very faulty system? Or should they concentrate, instead, on helping adolescents develop a constructively critical attitude that, if coupled with sense of responsibility and leadership, can bring about much needed change in the system? Unfortunately, many of our most imaginative adolescents are seen as troublemakers by both the school and society at large. The result is that the contributions these young people could make are lost.

All the psychopathological conditions described in Chapter 4 can be found in adolescents. However, the adolescent's ability to change rapidly often astounds his or her therapist. Florid psychiatric disturbances that in adults would often necessitate relatively long-term therapy can change in adolescents within three or four counseling sessions. On the other hand, although nowhere is an attitude of optimism more important, the counselor must be aware of the frequency and depth of depression in many adolescents and the serious potentiality for suicide. For the most troubled or troublesome adolescents, a trusting relationship with one adult may literally mean the difference between life and death.

Life Tasks

In working with adolescents, either individually or in groups, it is helpful to keep in mind the life-task areas of work, friendship, love, getting along with oneself, search for meaning, leisure and recreation, and parenting. As we indicated in Chapter 4, each of these areas may be an important source of information for the counselor. A simple self-rating process is useful in understanding how adolescents view themselves. The self-rating can be expanded to take into consideration how the adolescents predict that their parents will rate them and then, if the parents are involved in the counseling process, to check with the parents how in fact they do rate their son or daughter (Pew, 1974). If very extensive therapy or counseling is anticipated, a personal life-style assessment is indicated.

According to a general rule of thumb, most adolescents make better and more rapid progress in groups than in individual counseling. However, there are certain sensitive subjects that may, at least initially, be best dealt with on an individual basis—for example, incest. It is our experience that incestual behavior or other seductive behavior on the part of adults is a relatively common experience in adolescence. We also note that the actual experiencing of the sexual behavior is often not as difficult for the adolescent to deal with as the dishonest relationship that exists when a parent is overtly seductive while, at the same time, denying it in one way or another.

Symptom Bearers

Many of the adolescents we see in counseling have in some way been elected "symptom bearers" for their family. What we mean by "symptom bearers" is illustrated in the following case.

> Eleanor, age 15, a very talented musician, superb athlete, and good student, kept running away from home. She told the counselor that she would even take heroin in order to get herself into a drug-treatment center, so that she wouldn't have to be at home with her family. Her parents, ostensibly solid citizens, turned out to have a very unfulfilling marriage. The father dealt with the marital conflict by going out and getting drunk. But, when his daughter saw him intoxicated, her mother would deny the obvious by simply stating "Father doesn't drink." The father also seemed unusually interested in seeing his daughter nude or partially clothed, although he never made any overt sexual overtures. The more Eleanor ran away, the more controlling her father became, insisting that she must stay within the family to "help get the family together."
>
> As the family dynamics became clear, the counselor realized that Eleanor was the best adjusted member of her family—the one who could see clearly what was going on—and, yet, she didn't know what to do about it. Once an informal foster-home placement was arranged, Eleanor

made great personal strides, while the rest of the family required extensive therapy.

Eleanor was one of the lucky ones. Many young people faced with this kind of situation deal with it by engaging in drug abuse, juvenile delinquency, sexual misbehavior, or academic failure or even by attempting to commit suicide.

Drug Use

Adolescence is a time for experimentation, and many youths become involved, to a lesser or greater extent, with consciousness-altering drugs. In counseling, we see three groups of these young people: (1) those who are merely experimenting, looking for kicks and peer approval, (2) those who are looking for a new personality, and (3) those whose discouragement is so profound that they are seeking oblivion. The drug scene is constantly changing and may be decidedly different from one school district to another. In the same community, the students in one high school may be using primarily alcohol and tobacco. Only a few miles away, the students of another high school may be deeply involved in experimenting with all kinds of legal and illegal chemicals.

Although there is no solid evidence that marijuana in itself is particularly hazardous, one would question why a young person—or an older person, for that matter—would choose to get "high" several times a week, just as one would question why a person would choose to get drunk several times a week. What is missing in such a person's life? What is he/she trying to avoid? Also, we have noticed that, when young people who had reported smoking several marijuana cigarettes every day stopped using the drug, their behavior showed profound changes. While using marijuana, these youths were failing to function effectively in any of the life-task areas. When they stopped using the drug, they made great academic progress, became gainfully employed, and found a place in their family, with their friends, and in their community.

The use of chemicals is so widespread among adolescents that any counseling should include an exploration of this area. Counseling with anyone who is under the influence of a chemical is not likely to be very effective. Some youngsters are so heavily into drugs of one kind or another that only a residential-treatment approach is effective. We are seeing alcoholism even in grade schoolers, and alcoholism has certainly become a significant problem among adolescents. The use of tobacco is a major health hazard, and it doesn't seem to be influenced by adult efforts to control it, partly, of course, because many adults indicate through their own behavior that they either are unaware of or do not accept the facts concerning the dangers of tobacco use.

The major hazard posed by street chemicals is the fact that most young people don't know what they are buying. Marijuana, for example, is often laced with a variety of other chemicals, including animal tranquilizers and so-called "safe" downers (central-nervous-system depressants or sedatives), which are often seriously addicting. The combination of downers and alcohol can be fatal. There is no doubt that a massive educational effort is needed in this area. But the bankruptcy of our educational system offers little reason for optimism.

What is the prognosis for those adolescents who have been deeply involved with drugs? As clinicians, we have seen many young people come through rather extreme and bizarre uses of chemicals and end up as fully constructive and unaffected young adults. We have also seen others—for example, those who have injected amphetamines intraveneously—who have never returned to their prechemical state and who have never really recovered. Their history has been one of repeated hospitalizations, institutionalization, and therapy of all sorts.

Delinquency

Delinquency is a major problem among adolescents. One large study a few years ago indicated that one out of every four adolescent males would appear in juvenile court sometime during the teenage years and that the incidence of delinquency is ever increasing among girls. The problem is compounded by the fact that there is considerable confusion in the criminal-justice system, which results in many so-called "status offenders" (persons in need of supervision) being introduced to criminality through institutionaliza-tion. Their only legal offense is being below the legal age. The same behavior by an adult would not be characterized as criminal or even delinquent. Fortunately, some communities have begun to develop treatment and counsel-ing programs aimed at keeping the adolescent out of the criminal-justice system. Since much of the delinquency is group related, generally the most effective counseling work is that done in groups. The unfortunate aspect of this need for group counseling is that most of those who are hired to work with delinquent adolescents have no background in group leadership or group dynamics.

Sex

Sexual experimentation results in a number of problems in our society. Venereal disease is pandemic. It has been estimated that, in the immediate future, the vast majority of adolescents will have experienced intercourse by age 17 and that one out of five babies will be born to unwed teenage mothers. In this area, too, there is a profound difference between the values of many adolescents and those of adult society. Our educational system, with few exceptions, does a very poor job of dealing with the whole area of human sexuality, particularly as it relates to interpersonal relationships. Since the counselor of an adolescent can be almost certain that the youth will pose some questions or express some concerns about sexuality, it is most important that the counselor think through his or her own values in this area. Although the willingness on the part of many adolescents to talk very openly about sexuality is a positive element for the counseling process, such frankness may represent a problem for the counselor who is not prepared to deal with it.

School-Related Problems

Many adolescents express their rebellion against adult society and values by failing to conform to academic expectations. Since this is a complex area, we are reluctant to make sweeping statements. But one thing we can say with confidence: adolescents, like children, are not—for the most part—full-fledged partners in the educational system. Therefore, many of them feel justified to exclude themselves from the process. They fail to see a meaningful relationship between what goes on in the school and what they see going on in society at large. In one rural Midwestern community, a hulking farm boy signed up for a class in knitting to express his frustration at the school system's refusal to provide courses in animal husbandry, agriculture, and other areas relevant to him and other future farmers.

The conflict that often exists between the demands of the school system and the requirements of the adolescent for healthy growth and development poses a serious problem for the counselor. The unfortunate fact is that many school workers have no idea of how to deal with troubled or troublesome adolescents. Frequently, a telephone call by the counselor in the presence of the adolescent—and with his or her permission—to the appropriate person in the school will be all that is necessary to win the cooperation of the school personnel. In other instances, by the time an adolescent has got into counseling, his or her reputation in a given school is so damaged that transfer to another system is indicated.

> Harold and John were the oldest in their senior class. They were both star football players as well as successful students. In the middle of the football season, Harold abruptly left the game, avowing that he would never play football again. He found himself under a lot of pressure both at home and at school, and, as a reaction, he began using alcohol and engaging in violent behavior against fellow students, teachers, and other members of the community. He was soon in trouble with the law, but, despite his ever-deteriorating relationship with the school, he was kept on the roll and even urged to participate in graduation exercises. By that time, however, he was in such bad graces with both students and faculty that he himself recognized that he was likely to get in further difficulty by showing up at commencement, so he refused to go. At the same time, John was elected outstanding young man of the year.

In our opinion, Harold never received proper treatment. His case was so complicated that no one at his school was qualified to deal with it. Yet, the school was unwilling to take a strong stand and insist that Harold get appropriate therapy.

Too many public schools find themselves all too often in a situation similar to the one we just described. Some enlightened private schools do exercise the option of refusing to accept a student who, in their opinion, is heading for serious difficulty, unless certain conditions are met. The school must be assured that proper treatment is available for the student and his or her family, if indicated, then that such treatment is underway, and, finally, that it is continued appropriately.

The Adolescent's Parents

The adolescent's parents are often a great source of difficulty for the counselor. The more the adolescent displays autonomy, the more resentful some parents become. And their resentment is frequently directed at the counselor. Counselors must be willing to maintain the strictest confidence with regard to their counselees while, at the same time, walking a tightrope with the parents, who often demand to know what their child is thinking or doing or feeling. When this kind of situation occurs, family therapy is indicated, unless the adolescent is old enough to decide to work toward personal emancipation from the family. In many communities, parents maintain some legal responsibility and hold onto their adolescent children until they are 18 years of age. Sometimes counseling is primarily a holding action until the adolescent can strike out on his or her own. At the other end of the spectrum are those adolescents who are so close to their families that they reach adulthood without having made a successful separation from their families. In these cases, too, the most hopeful approach is family therapy. Here is an example of one such case.

George, 17 years old and a high-school junior, had never had a date with a girl, preferring to spend his spare time at home tinkering with gadgets. His mother, a widow, greatly enjoyed George's company. They were good friends and shared many common interests. Mother didn't date or engage in other activities outside the home. Toward the end of his junior year, George began developing symptoms in the form of anxiety attacks with chest pains. Initially seen individually, he was then introduced to group therapy. In both individual and group therapy, he gained a lot of insight, but there was no change in his behavior or any reduction in his symptoms.

Only after a number of joint counseling sessions did George and his mother begin to see how important it was that they developed their own lives, independent of each other. In the next several years, although George continued to live at home, he completed his schooling, became a pilot, and used his interest in gadgetry to make several inventions on the job. His mother, a school teacher, became very active in local politics and in various activities within her church. The previously pathological symbiotic relationship between mother and son developed into a cooperative, interdependent relationship that allowed each party to move out and become a person in his or her own right.

COUNSELING COLLEGE STUDENTS

Many college students are still adolescents by most definitions. It is estimated that one out of five college students will seek some kind of psychiatric service during his or her college career. For the most part, college mental-health services are essentially adolescent counseling. To be effective, however, a counselor must know something about the system in which the college student must operate, how decisions are made, who wields the power on the campus, and so forth. The high-achieving college students seem to be particularly susceptible to some sort of breakdown. If they were successful in high school but for the wrong reasons—that is, in order to be better than others—on the college campus they often show a dramatic flip-flop. Students who were the best at being "good" become the best at being "bad," and this reversal may be seen in the form of academic failure, sexual misbehavior, crime and delinquency, drug abuse, and all of the classical psychiatric syndromes, such as psychoses and neuroses. For most college students, group therapy is undoubtedly the treatment of choice. However, individual sessions may be necessary to build trust and allay fears before involving the student in a therapy group.

> Diane was a junior in an excellent liberal-arts college, and, yet, she had never learned to read properly. She had become skillful at gleaning information by talking with other people and was achieving good grades despite the fact that she had never completely read through an assignment. She had difficulties in her relationships with boys as well as with her elderly parents (she was an only child). Diane came to the psychiatric clinic looking for help in these areas but was so embarrassed about her reading disability that she staunchly refused to consider group therapy. The life-style assessment was completed, and she was seen approximately ten times individually. During this period, Diane developed a trusting relationship with her therapist, who was also the cotherapist of an ongoing open-ended group, The next quarter, she joined that group and had a very positive experience.

Diane's case is unusual in that most young people don't need so many individual sessions before joining a therapy group.

Summary

Adolescence is a period in life fraught with difficulties. The successful counselor is one who can accept each adolescent as he or she is at the moment, who is nonjudgmental and flexible, and who can approach counseling with adolescents as a learning experience, for adolescents have much to teach counselors. Since adolescents develop most of their difficulties in group interactions, working out their problems in groups is generally the most effective form of therapy. Many of the problems that adolescents face are related to the way they are treated by society and at home. Therefore, in order to be effective, the counselor must remain somewhat detached. If he or she becomes too involved as an advocate for the adolescent against the family, school, or community, the effectiveness of the counseling is likely to be significantly reduced.

REFERENCES

International Encyclopedia of Psychiatry, Psychology, Psychoanalysis, and Neurology, 1977, s.v. "Family therapy: Adlerian," by W. L. Pew.

Pew, W. L. Instant rapport with children. *Elementary School Guidance and Counseling,* 1969, *4* (1), 67–68.

Pew, W. L. Taking your own psychological temperature. *Single Parent,* April 1974, 5–7.

CHAPTER 9

GROUP COUNSELING AND GROUP PSYCHOTHERAPY

Human behavior can be best understood in its social context, since it is the social context that explains the purpose of the behavior. For example, a child's behavior on the playground might be considered totally out of order if it occurred in a structured classroom. Children's temper tantrums may be effective with the children's parents but not with their teachers. Children learn that it is so and will have temper tantrums only in the "appropriate" social settings.

The counselor or therapist who believes in the holistic, social, purposive, and decision-making nature of human behavior recognizes that groups are a most effective resource for influencing attitudes and behavior. Group counseling and group psychotherapy are an interpersonal process led by a professional trained in group procedures. Group counseling usually focuses on exploring typical developmental problems—for example, getting along with peers, being acceptable to members of the opposite sex, or becoming involved with school tasks. Group therapy, instead, is more concerned with the correction of mistaken assumptions about life or faulty approaches to the basic tasks of life. In the following discussion, we use the terms *group* and *therapeutic group* to refer to both group counseling and group therapy.

HISTORY

Group therapy has an interesting history. Although Dreikurs (1952) indicated that the origins of formal group therapy can be traced back to Franz Anton Mesmer's hypnotic sessions in Paris two centuries ago, group psychotherapy, as we know it, is basically a product of the 20th century. J. H. Pratt, a Boston internist, is credited with having been the first to apply group psychotherapy. In the early 1900s, he was using an educational group approach to treat tuberculosis patients.

> The early period of group psychotherapy may be dated from 1900 to 1930. During this time the major steps toward a systematic use of the group method, called at that time "collective counselling," were made in Europe. Dreikurs (1952) reports the early efforts of collective therapy by Wetterstrand with hypnosis, Schubert with stammerers, Hirschfeld with sexual disturbances, Stransky with neurotic patients, and Metzl (1937) with alcoholics. In Russia, Rosenstein, Guilarowsky, and Ozertovsky (Ozertovsky, 1927) used the group method. In Denmark, Joergeson used action methods with psychotics (Harms, 1945) [Dreikurs & Corsini, 1960, p. 22].

There is some question concerning the relationship between "collective counselling" and our current forms of group therapy. It is clear that the early efforts mentioned above never reached a degree of organization comparable to group therapy as we know it today and that the psychiatrists who used the group method worked independently of one another. With the advent of totalitarianism in both Germany and Russia, these psychiatrists were forced to abandon group methods.

In 1928, Dreikurs published "The Development of Mental Hygiene in Vienna." In this historically important paper, he described in detail, possibly for the first time anywhere, the dynamic differences between individual and group therapy, which he called "collective therapy."

> Alfred Adler (1931), in his child guidance clinics, was probably the first psychiatrist to use the group method systematically and formally. Moreno (1953) started group therapy around 1910, using techniques completely unrelated to the concepts and practices of individual therapy. He later developed a theoretical framework, sociometry, for the group approach [Dreikurs & Corsini, 1960, p. 22].

In 1931, Moreno coined the term *group psychotherapy,* which became the formal name of the new method.

The literature of group psychotherapy and group counseling developed slowly. From 1900 to 1929, only 31 papers on group psychotherapy were published in this country. The literature has expanded greatly in recent times. Articles can be found in *Small Group Behavior* (Beverly Hills, Calif.: Sage Publications), *International Journal of Group Psychotherapy* (New York: International Universities Press), *Group Organization Studies* (La Jolla, Calif.: University Associates), and *Together* (Washington, D.C.: Association for Specialists in Group Work, American Personnel and Guidance Association).

THE NATURE OF THE GROUP PROCESS

The group process focuses on the beliefs, attitudes, values, feelings, purposes, and behavior of the members of the group. The unique nature of the interpersonal relationships that develop within the group makes it possible for the members to become aware of their mistaken and self-defeating beliefs and actions and to feel encouraged to change them.

The requirements for membership are unique. People don't belong because of their status. They belong because they have problems and are ready to acknowledge them and work on them. The focus is on helping the members establish personal goals and, by challenging their perceptions, enabling them to cope more effectively with the tasks of life.

Group Interaction

By their very nature, humans live in continuous social interaction and are inevitably involved in the dilemma between serving their own interests and meeting the needs of those of the groups to which they belong. It is within the group interaction that one can observe how the individual decides to belong to the group. Some believe "I belong only if I can please," while others believe "I belong only if they give me my way." It is the Adlerian bias that one's social interest and, eventually, self-interest can often be best served through involvement in the give and take of cooperative endeavor with the group. This type of involvement creates a communal feeling and enhances one's feeling of belonging. We are social beings who live in and are influenced by the social system and who behave in a manner designed to attain the approval of others. Our basic striving is to belong and to be accepted and valued. The methods we use to search for significance and recognition indicate how we decide to belong.

Psychological problems result from disturbed interpersonal relationships, reduced courage, and insufficient social interest. Yalom (1970) did a study of 20 successful group-therapy patients to determine the critical incident, or most helpful single event, for the members of the group. He found that, almost invariably, the incident involved some other group member and rarely the therapist. Yalom (1970) lists the components of the corrective emotional experience in group therapy:

1. A strong expression of emotion which is interpersonally directed and which represents a risk taking on the part of the patient;
2. A group supportive enough to permit this risk taking;
3. Reality testing, which allows the patient to examine the incident with the aid of consensual validation from others;
4. A recognition of the inappropriateness of certain interpersonal feelings and behavior or of the inappropriateness of certain avoided interpersonal behaviors;

5. The ultimate facilitation of the individual's ability to interact with others more deeply and honestly [p. 23].

The therapeutic group will invariably move toward becoming a social microcosm of the members' experiences. All participants begin to interact in the group as they do in their real-life interpersonal relationships. In some instances, the members may seek the same position they held in their childhood family. Members also display in the group their faulty beliefs and ineffective approaches to the tasks of life. The participants don't need to describe their problems; their behavior reveals their life style and assumptions about human relationships. The therapist, instead of hearing about how the members behave, observes and experiences the participants and their behavior, since each member's style of life eventually emerges in the various transactions among the members of the group.

Interpersonal Learning

Interpersonal learning becomes impetus for change through the following process:

1. The group becomes a social microcosm, representing each member's social world.

2. The group members, through feedback and self-awareness, become aware of the purpose and consequences of their interpersonal behavior. Through feedback, which is congruent and caring, one's strengths and limitations are discussed. Unlike the typical social situation, in which one may not be able to communicate honestly, the group values openness and congruence—saying what one feels and means. Feedback permits one to learn from the transaction, because the message is not perceived as threatening and, therefore, can be accepted and internalized. This phenomenon occurs because feedback does not demand change but, instead, the sharing of what one is experiencing and perceiving. The receiver of feedback is free to decide his or her own course of action.

3. For communication in the group to be effective, the transaction must be real and genuine. The participants must communicate their involvement and feelings about what they are experiencing, as well as the feelings that the communication of others provokes.

4. Change occurs as a result of (a) awareness, (b) involvement and commitment to make specific changes, (c) the amount of belonging to the group that the member feels and the resultant importance of being accepted and valued by the other members, and (d) encouragement by members and by the group leader.

5. Through the process of trying on new behaviors and beliefs and learning that it is safe to change, the person gains the courage to continue making positive movement.

6. The whole process can be described as a cycle that is being set in motion and in which (a) perceptions and beliefs change, (b) courage and belonging enable one to try on new behaviors, (c) involvement and risking are rewarded by acceptance and belonging, (d) fear of making a mistake is replaced by the courage to be imperfect, which reduces anxiety and insecurity, and (e) as self-esteem and feelings of worth develop, the person is able to try additional change.

RATIONALE

The Adlerian view that humans are indivisible, social, and decision-making beings whose actions have a social purpose adds value and meaning to groups. Verbal and nonverbal transactions acquire new significance when the members are understood as social beings. In the group, the individual's private logic, priorities, and the way in which he or she seeks to be known are revealed.

The group has some unique diagnostic and therapeutic qualities. In terms of assessment, the therapist or counselor doesn't have to conduct extensive interviews, because, by observing and understanding the social meaning of behavior of the group members, he or she becomes aware of each member's assumptions about life and human relationships. The group can also provide the therapeutic advantages that come from belonging. The corrective influences and encouragement of the peers—that is, the members of the group—is often more potent than that available from any one individual. It has been demonstrated through our personal experience and research that peers may have a strong influence on behavior. Most problems are interpersonal, and, for most individuals, alternatives or solutions are best developed in a social setting. Discouragement often begins in group interaction and can best be dealt with in a group situation.

The measuring stick for someone's progress is the person's increased capacity to meet the tasks of life, to give and take, and to cooperate—what Adlerians call social interest. An individual's capacity to interact effectively with the other members of the group is a measure of the person's social growth, which is one of the goals of the group experience.

The following opportunities are offered by an effective group:

- The opportunity to belong and be accepted;
- The opportunity to receive and give love and the unique opportunity to have a therapeutic effect on others;
- The opportunity to see that one's problems are not unique but are often experienced universally;
- The opportunity to develop one's identity and to try on new approaches to the various social tasks of life.

THE SOCIAL CLIMATE OF THERAPEUTIC GROUPS

The therapeutic group provides a unique social climate and an atmosphere in which the individual's psychological movement can be observed and, at the same time, corrected. The group setting also offers members the opportunity to develop new perceptions of their approach to the basic tasks of life.

Therapeutic groups are agents that promote values. A group accepts certain values and influences the members of the group in terms of those values. The group therapy setting requires the following conditions:

1. Members have their place regardless of deficits or assets. They are not judged in terms of any position or status they hold outside the group. They establish their own position inside the group and are accepted on that basis. The full worth of each member is taken for granted simply because he or she is a part of the group.

2. The members' capacity to reveal themselves honestly and openly is valued. Failing to reveal one's feelings, putting up a front, disguising hidden agendas, and covering up one's intentions—all things that are accepted and even valued in certain other social situations—are challenged in the group. The group values congruence, or the capacity to honestly reveal and share what one is experiencing.

3. Members learn not merely by verbal understanding. They are expected to put their insights into action as they transact with the other members of the group. Insight is not valued unless it produces "outsights"—that is, some action or reality testing.

4. The leader models attentive listening, caring, congruence, confrontation, and interpretation to help the the participants acquire these interpersonal skills. Members learn what behavior is expected and are encouraged when they produce the desired behaviors.

5. Members can express their true feelings without fear of permanently disrupting relationships. Interpersonal conflict between members is dialogued and worked through, so that members learn that conflict, when dealt with honestly, can produce improved relationships. The norms of the therapeutic group prescribe that participants continue to communicate despite intensive negative feelings they may have developed toward one another.

CONCEPTUAL FOUNDATIONS OF THERAPEUTIC GROUPS

The Adlerian approach to therapeutic groups recognizes the following conceptual foundations of the nature of behavior:

1. All behavior has social meaning. Each transaction between and among members of the group has a social direction and a social intention. Members are encouraged to understand the meaning of the transaction in terms of such direction and intention.

2. Behavior can be best understood in terms of holistic patterns. Early in

the transactions with one another, group participants are encouraged to become aware of the consistent pattern that an individual is revealing by his or her behavior within the group. Thus, the life style, which includes the characteristic pattern of responding and behaving, is exposed, understood, and dealt with in the group setting. The group is organized so that the life style of each member is revealed. The participants learn to understand one another in terms of each person's unique style of living. They facilitate one another's development in various ways. One is becoming aware of the faulty or mistaken assumptions that may keep a person from developing effective approaches to the tasks of life. Another is a willingness to process feedback about what one is experiencing.

3. Behavior in the group, like all behavior, is goal directed and purposive. The members become aware of their own purposes and intentions and seek to understand the behavior of the other members in terms of its purpose. Participants learn to confront one another not only with the expressed beliefs, attitudes, and values but with the purpose of the overall psychological movement. They soon learn that, while words may deceive, the psychological movement always clearly reveals directions and intentions. A person may say that he or she intends to change, but the members of the group give more credence to what the person does.

4. Members are encouraged to become aware of their own motives and methods for finding a place in this and other group situations. The group transactions help to reveal the way in which the members seek to find their place.

5. The group has specific hopes for the positive psychological development of each member. More importantly, there is also a criterion for determining such development. The criterion is the individual's capacity to belong to the group, to make a commitment, to engage in the give and take of life, and to extend his or her social interest.

6. Members are understood in terms of how they see themselves and their situation—that is, in terms of their phenomenological field. They are actively encouraged to help one another to understand how their perceptions influence their feelings and their behavior.

These basic concepts about human behavior provide guidelines and structure for the social climate of the group—a climate in which members look at the transactions in terms of their patterns, social meaning, and purpose. The hypothesis is that, as members increase their social interest, feel belonging, and make a commitment to others, their emerging social interest becomes a major factor in their psychological growth.

THE THERAPEUTIC FORCES OF THE
GROUP SETTING

The therapeutic forces that develop in a group setting are responsible for stimulating changes in the members' behavior. Thus, if a leader is to effectively influence development, he or she must be aware of the potential mechanisms that operate in the group and of their effect on the participants. Also, the leader must be aware of how he or she can facilitate the potential therapeutic effect of such mechanisms. The leader must accept responsibility for stimulating a climate that will promote growth, self-understanding, and commitment to change. The group mechanisms are the dynamic processes that occur in any therapeutic group. However, they don't occur automatically as a concomitant of the group meeting. The leader consciously creates situations in which the mechanisms are likely to operate. When these processes do occur spontaneously, they must be recognized and encouraged. The mechanisms are catalysts for individual as well as group development.

The following mechanisms are particularly significant as therapeutic forces.

Acceptance. Acceptance refers to the respect and empathy that each individual in the group receives simply because he or she is a member. When acceptance has developed, group members come to identify with one another and to have a strong communal feeling. Such feeling is expressed in the belief that "this is where I belong, and I can trust the members of the group to be concerned, caring, and congruent." These strong feelings of acceptance and belonging are an essential undergirding of the growth process. Acceptance is fostered as the leader not only models empathy but, when necessary, intervenes to help participants learn how to be more empathic with one another. Each member of the group has a need to belong, and the therapeutic group provides the unique opportunity to find one's place and be accepted without having to undergo instant change.

Altruism. We recognize that there is a positive desire in people, no matter how discouraged by our current climate of competitiveness, to be of direct service and assistance to others. The group provides a situation in which altruism is valued. To stimulate altruism in the group, the leader models and demonstrates it and encourages any attempt on the part of the members to express altruistic feelings. The group is organized in such a way that opportunities to exert and utilize altruism are systematically included in the group experience.

Transference. The term refers to the strong emotional attachment that members of the group develop as a result of their intensive experience with one another. Transference may be originally directed to the leader but eventually is manifested toward members of the group and even toward the group as a whole. Transference may involve both positive and negative feelings. The group provides the opportunity to give as well as receive love. It is transference and the identification the members feel for one another that form the glue holding the group together. Transference is experienced as a continuous flow of emotional support. Unless transference, as we have described it, develops, the group doesn't have enough strong emotional feelings, positive and negative, to make the group a therapeutic experience.

Spectator therapy. This technique permits the group members to achieve some understanding of their own concerns by hearing the concerns of others. If a member of the group has a problem and another member brings up a similar problem, the person has an opportunity to recognize that his or her situation is not unique. The person can also develop solutions by considering the suggestions that are being made in the group. The behavior of the other member may represent a mirror in which the person learns about himself or herself. It is important for the group leader to recognize that members can and do benefit from the ongoing interaction even when they don't participate verbally. Through spectator therapy, one observes others, learns more effective interpersonal skills, and benefits from the transactions that occur in the group.

Universalization. Universalization is the recognition that one's problems are not unique. The more one recognizes universalization, the more one becomes aware that others share the same problems and the less one feels lonely and alienated from the rest of humanity. Recognizing the commonality of problems makes the communication of one's own problems easier. The leader intentionally stimulates universalization by creating a conducive climate and by asking "Have any of you experienced that or felt that way?" An effective leader will underline similarities in thoughts, feelings, and actions by pointing them out clearly as they occur.

Feedback. This term refers to the learning process that the members of the group undergo by sharing their reactions to one another. Psychological feedback is the process whereby we receive information concerning how we are experienced by others. The purpose of feedback is to enable us to develop some insight about our own interpersonal relationships and to make us see how we are being experienced by others. Feedback enables us to explore our feelings, values, and attitudes, and reevaluate our faulty assumptions or mistaken perceptions. Providing authentic feedback requires that the group members be truly concerned and care about one another. It also requires that the participants recognize that feedback is an honest sharing of impressions and does not necessitate a change of behavior. Feedback, then, becomes a strong source for creating psychological movement. If the members truly feel a part of the group and if they are concerned about peer evaluation, feedback can be a strong motivational force for change.

Ventilation. The group setting provides an opportunity for the members to express a number of emotions that they may have inhibited or repressed. This emotional release often reduces internal pressures. Through ventilation, the participants learn to expose and explore their inner feelings, both positive and negative, and to recognize that the concerns they have about how they will be received are often just fantasies. By verbalizing their strong feelings, the members of the group develop new insights that enable them to make therapeutic changes.

Reality testing. In the group setting, the participants can not only test certain concepts but work through actual relationships. This gives them the opportunity to see their behavior more accurately as it is experienced by others. For example, if a woman has problems relating to men, she can experiment in the group with new methods of relating to men. Thus, she doesn't have to wait until she is outside the group to get some real-life experience in dealing with her new insights. The group provides an opportunity to practice a new life style and new perceptions in a social setting that is accepting and nonthreatening and that, at the same time, provides open and honest feedback.

Interaction. The interactions that take place within the group make visible to the group the goals and purposes of each member. We said "make visible" because leader and peers don't have to depend on what the individual says but, instead, can observe the person's behavior. Words may deceive, but behavior seldom lies in its direction and intent. An individual may protest that he intends to help or cooperate, but, unless he does it, his words are just words. The group interaction moves the participants beyond the words into action.

GROUP COHESIVENESS

In the previous chapters, we have stressed the importance of the relationship in individual therapy. Yalom has indicated that cohesiveness in group therapy is the analogue of the "relationship" in individual therapy (Yalom, 1970). The term *cohesiveness* refers to the positive pull, or attraction, that the members of the group feel for one another. It refers to the forces that enable the members to experience a feeling of belonging, a solidarity, and a common bond. This cohesiveness creates conditions whereby the individual feels not only understood, accepted, and valued but also free both to reveal himself or herself and to accept feedback from the members of the group. A cohesive group is one in which members have a high level of mutual understanding and acceptance. Cohesiveness helps to supply the feeling of belonging that is essential to all of the other therapeutic forces.

Dickoff and Lakin (1963) found that members who perceived their group as cohesive attended more sessions, experienced more social contact with other participants, and judged the group as offering a therapeutic experience. Yalom (1970) indicates: "We have cited evidence that patients in group therapy consider group cohesiveness to be a prime mode of help in their therapy experience. There is tentative evidence that self-perceived positive therapy outcome is related to individual attraction to the group and to total group cohesiveness. Individuals with positive outcome have had more mutually satisfying intermember relationships'' (p. 43). Cohesiveness is a crucial factor because, as we said earlier, understanding and acceptance by peers often have greater power and meaning for the individual than acceptance by the leader.

The significance of cohesiveness is best understood when we recognize that most persons who come to the group for assistance have problems in establishing and maintaining meaningful interpersonal relationships, in developing and maintaining a sense of personal worth and self-esteem, and in experiencing what it means to be an equal member of an equalitarian group. The group, because of its unique social climate, develops cohesiveness and provides an excellent corrective experience for these specific problems.

THE ROLE OF THE GROUP LEADER

The leader is responsible for forming, establishing, and keeping the group going. In the early stages, the leader is the only person with whom all the members in the group are familiar. Members expect the leader to assume responsibility for the group's growth.

The group leader must be very sensitive to the forces that make the group a therapeutic experience for the members. He or she is a facilitator who both creates and encourages situations in which participants provide emotional support, universalization, feedback, and opportunities to try on new behavior. These processes promote learning, personal growth, and cohesiveness.

The leader must participate actively in the development of norms that facilitate growth and interpersonal learning. He or she intentionally and planfully establishes a structure for the group and indicates guidelines for behavior in the group, such as congruence, open interaction, involvement, nonjudgmental acceptance, confrontation, and commitment. Much of our social behavior is characterized by facades, surface interactions, inhibited expression of feelings, and other modes that are destructive to the development of a productive group. It is crucial to understand that the norms that govern the group don't come about automatically as a result of forming a group. Their development requires an intensive effort on the part of the leader.

The therapist or counselor must recognize that, as leader, he or she must provide a model as well as technical expertise, so the group can move. In the formative stages of the group, the leader may need to utilize exercises that create productive interaction. He or she may explicitly point out interactions that don't implement therapeutic goals and reinforce and encourage any attempt on the part of the members to effectively utilize the group's therapeutic forces. Some leaders like to believe that productive groups emerge from their inactivity and even consider the kind of intervention we have discussed as manipulation. Yalom (1970) deals with the issue directly: "The manipulation in therapy is often covert, implicit, and unplanned; however, it may be overt, explicit, and planned without sacrificing therapeutic effectiveness" (p. 88).

Spontaneity is an important factor in effective group work. It enables the leader to pick up on what is happening in the here and now and turn the interaction into a growth-promoting experience. Leaders must utilize all of their creativity and spontaneity, since both accelerate the progress of the group and provide a valuable model for the participants.

GROUP-LEADERSHIP COMPETENCIES

The group leader must be able to function in a continuously flowing process with all members, no matter how different their beliefs, feelings, and intentions may be. He or she must be able to create an atmosphere in which the members can achieve their goals and learn to help one another grow.

The leader pays attention not only to the content of the members' messages but to the method, setting, and timing of such messages. How are the feelings conveyed—with considerable involvement or apathetically? Does the message indicate that the person is trying to focus the interaction on himself or that he wants to stay with the here-and-now transaction? The leader is always aware of the purpose of the communication, and, when it is appropriate, he or she confronts the participants with their beliefs, feelings, and intentions.

Thus, while leadership requires a person who is open, honest, accepting, spontaneous, understanding, and congruent, these personality traits alone are not enough. The leader must be trained and skilled in all of the following competencies:

- Structuring the group and communicating its purpose
- Utilizing interaction exercises and programs effectively
- Universalizing
- Dealing with the here-and-now interaction
- Linking
- Confronting
- Blocking
- Encouraging and focusing on assets and positive feedback
- Facilitating participation by confronting nonverbal clues
- Facilitating I-messages
- Paraphrasing and clarifying to stimulate reality testing
- Offering feedback
- Formulating tentative hypotheses
- Setting tasks and getting commitment
- Capping and summarizing

In order to make the meaning of these competencies and skills clearer, we shall describe each of them and explain the rationale for using it in the group setting.

Structuring the Group and Communicating Its Purpose

Definition. Structuring the group and communicating its purpose are essential for effective therapeutic groups. Defining goals and setting limits give the group a purpose and direct its activity. Structuring involves helping the group to understand the purpose of the sessions. For example, the leader may indicate that each person in the group is there to work on a specific concern, that they will all be sharing that concern, and that they will help one another. More specifically, the leader may structure by indicating that members are to speak directly to the other members about their feelings and use I-messages, which express what the person is experiencing but don't mandate change in others. Structuring may also encourage members to focus on the here and now—that is, on what is being dialogued between persons in the group, in contrast to a discussion of events that happened outside the group.

Rationale. By structuring the group, the leader helps the members to focus their discussions on matters that are meaningful and purposeful. Structuring enables the leader and the group to set limits and to focus on tasks. Structuring is a demanding job, because the leader must be continually aware of what is currently happening and determine whether it is within the structure, goals, and purposes of the group. Once the members are ready to stay within the structure, more productive group work is accomplished.

The following dialogues contrast ineffective and effective use of the competency.

Ineffective use

David: I can never be on time. This makes my girlfriend really mad.
Joan: David, tell us about your girlfriend.
Frank: What kind of girls do you consider attractive, David?
Leader: We are concerned about how you get along with girls.

Comment: If the group agreed and structured itself not to discuss personal problems unless the counselee volunteered such information, this dialogue is beyond the structure. Furthermore, David's personal goal is solving the problem he has in being punctual. Therefore, the above comments violate group structure. The leader should have interrupted the interaction to indicate a violation of contract.

Effective use

Lynn: Well, why are we here?
Ramon: Yes, silence makes me nervous (looking at the leader).
Leader: You have all met with me individually, but let's review our goals.

Our purpose is to share our concerns and to help one another by relating honestly and by providing feedback.

Utilizing Interaction Exercises and Programs Effectively

Definition. To program a group, the leader chooses to initiate specific group behaviors at a specific point in order to create an experience for the members. Programming is in contrast with permitting the interaction to be spontaneous and following whatever course of interaction happens to occur. Programs are usually utilized to achieve specific goals. They are structured experiences that may be used to get people acquainted, build cohesiveness, help members understand certain phenomena by experiencing them, increase feedback, and create an awareness of various group dynamics and processes.

Programs or exercises that are generally productive include:

- Get-Acquainted Activity, in which people learn one another's name and some information about the various members' interests;
- Depth Unfoldment Experience (DUE), in which members share their most important experiences—those that they feel made them the persons they are;
- Strength Recognition, in which members are asked to recognize, acknowledge, and state their own strengths;
- Multiple-Strength Perception, in which a member, after listing his own strengths, has the group present to him their perceptions of his strengths;
- Paraphrasing, in which a member can talk only after he has paraphrased what the person who preceded him in the conversation has said;
- Learning to Link, in which members are asked to show how previous statements by different persons are similar or different;
- Having the members present their position in the family constellation and indicate the ways in which they are most like, or different from, their siblings;
- Having the members indicate their number-one priority and have the group give a feedback on the priorities they have observed.

Rationale. Although some leaders are philosophically opposed to exercises and are uncomfortable in using programs, it is important to understand the rationale and timing of programs. Programs are usually most effective early in group life, since they tend to improve communication, increase cohesiveness, and reduce anxiety when new members and inexperienced leaders are uncertain about what is expected. Although some object that programs are anxiety provoking, it must be recognized that the novel, unstructured situation of open-ended group life can itself generate considerable anxiety. The leader who understands the use of programs, is familiar with a variety of structured experiences, and knows how to use them appropriately can facilitate group movement. The programs and exercises have as their basic purpose the promotion of the members' growth and the communication within the group. The following dialogue shows an ineffective use of this competency.

> *Anne:* Well, what should we do?
> *Laura:* I don't know what is expected of us.
> *Anne:* It seems so pointless without a topic.
> *Leader:* Now I'm going to show you how to become more involved with one another. Here is an experience . . .
>
> *Comment:* The leader waited until the group was in a state of confusion and now, instead of working through it, proposes a solution. The leader should sense when there is a lack of understanding of purpose and a lack of skills and provide them in a more timely manner.

Universalizing

Definition. Universalization is the process by which a group leader makes group members aware that their concerns are shared by others. The leader elicits responses that will make it clear to group members that there are elements of similarity in their thoughts, feelings, or actions. This is accomplished by asking questions that will reveal whether others have similar concerns: "Has anyone ever had that problem or felt that way?" In other instances, the leader may show how certain ideas and feelings are related. This requires listening for some common themes and, by making the members aware of those themes, help them see that they have similar problems. By easing or, at times, even removing the feeling of isolation, universalization permits the participants to realize that they all share similar human concerns.

Rationale. Universalization is basic to the cohesion of the group. For cohesion to take place, the group members must have positive feelings about one another and see one another as equals. By helping the members to see similarities in one another, the leader increases the group's cohesion. The leader encourages the sharing of concerns, because such sharing creates a bond among group members and promotes growth. This awareness of the commonality of problems also provides reassurance and gives the participants the courage to learn ways of becoming more effective.

The following dialogues contrast ineffective and effective use of this competency.

Ineffective use

> *George:* I take after my father—the bad side of him. When he asks for juice and someone brings him water, he gets real mad. I'm like that. If I don't get my way, I feel like hitting.
> *David:* Yeah, when my sister gets to hog the TV every Friday night, I get angry and pick a fight with her. She always gets what she wants.
> *Leader:* Why do you think she gets what she wants?

Comment: The leader could have pointed out the similarity of George's and David's problems. By asking the reason for someone else's behavior, the leader is taking the group out of the here and now and is missing an opportunity to show George and David that their feelings are similar.

Effective use

Marianne: I really like science books, and I want to read them. But I always have to ask somebody to explain what some words mean. They're too hard.

Leader: Is anyone else experiencing this problem?

Dealing with the Here-and-Now Interaction

Definition. This competency refers to the ability to deal with what is happening now, as it is experienced by the entire group as well as by the individual members. It means moving away from the memories of the past and from the plans for the future to the awareness of the present moment. What is important now is *now.* To be concrete, specific, and in touch with one's sensitivities now; to refer only to those past events that are affecting one in the present moment; to be conscious of what is happening in this session rather than in the last session of the group—all this is a part of the here-and-now focus in group work.

Rationale. The here-and-now interaction, as opposed to the there-and-then interaction, is essential to the spontaneity, growth, and effectiveness of the group process. Dealing at length with distant concerns is like cutting off the oxygen supply of the group. It is present worries and concerns, not past ones, that the members are trying to reduce or satisfy. Excessive lingering on past feelings, without reference to the now, is a distraction that affects the growth of the group. Behavior is not caused by something that occurred in the past; behavior has a current purpose. If the group fails to deal with the here and now, it forfeits the opportunity of working through problems and eventually resolving them. Members may attempt to avoid the here and now by trying to talk about the past or about events outside the group. By talking about the there and then, participants may give the impression that they are confronting themselves honestly and thoroughly. If the counselor is aware of this tendency, he or she will try to lead the group members to discuss here-and-now behavior.

The following dialogues contrast ineffective and effective use of the competency.

Ineffective use

Tom: I've never been very confident of myself. When I was a little kid, I used to hide behind the furniture when my mother had company.

Leader: Has this pattern continued?

Tom: Well, when I was in high school, I took as many babysitting jobs as I
could on weekends so I could avoid going to dances and parties.
Leader: Avoiding people made you feel secure.
Laura: Gee, I used to feel the same way . . .

Comment: The group leader has failed to recognize what was happening. By not shifting the conversation to Tom's feelings now, rather
than then, he or she has set a tone for the group to ineffectively wallow in
what has happened.

Effective use

Tom: I'm not very sure of myself, and I don't know how to talk about
myself.
Leader: You are not sure of what is expected of you here.

Linking

Definition. The leader tries to point out to members of the group the
similarities and differences he or she detects in what the members are saying,
from the point of view of both content and feelings. Linking necessitates being
aware of meanings. A person's comment may often have hidden meanings.
The leader makes it clear to the group how a member's statement is related
to the comments of another member. Linking can also be used to link an
individual's verbal and nonverbal messages.

Rationale. Linking is very important because it allows the leader to show
to group members that their problems, although stated in different terms, are
basically similar. This applies to feelings too; that is, the members are made
aware of the relationship between their feelings and those of others, even if
verbalized differently. The assumption is that linking promotes interaction.
At the beginning, interaction in a group is often minimal and at a superficial
level. The interaction produced through linking helps promote cohesion. The
person perceiving these linkages and realizing that his or her problems and
feelings are shared develops a greater understanding of human behavior and
becomes more willing and able to contribute to the group. The members
are more willing and free to interact, because they perceive that the members
are interested in understanding one another.

The following dialogues contrast ineffective and effective use of
the competency.

Ineffective use

Ramon: Mom and Dad always call my friends' homes when I'm a minute
late getting home. All of the guys rib me about it the next day and call
me "Mama's little boy."
Tony: When I get home from school and just begin to relax, both my
parents come at me and demand to see what I have for homework. If

I don't have any—wow! The war starts! Sometimes they even call the teacher to check my story.

Leader: Have you ever thought of having your teacher sign a no-homework slip for you?

Comment: The leader has offered a possible alternative to Tony and left Ramon hanging all alone. This procedure limits interaction in the group. Ramon probably feels that he was not heard and must wonder what this group has to offer. He will probably be less willing and able to contribute the next time. The leader should have tried to link the feelings of anger at not being trusted that both Ramon and Tony expressed. This would have made both of them aware of the likeness of their situations and feelings and enabled them to contribute more appropriately to the present situation.

Effective use

Sally: I like to go to the show on Sunday afternoon. Every time I suggest it to my friends, they want to do something else, so I just go along with them.

Marianne: When we break up into small groups in class to do a project, I get a good idea, but, before I have a chance to say it, someone else talks about his idea first. Most of the time, I just let mine go, and follow theirs.

Leader: I hear both of you saying that you get mad at yourselves when you let your ideas drop and just do what the group wants to do? How do you feel about that?

Comment: Here the leader links both the feelings and the problem of the two persons, thus helping Sally and Marianne realize that they are not alone.

Confronting

Definition. The leader, in a sensitive and perceptive manner, enables the members to become aware of discrepancies between their behavior and their intentions. The disclosure focuses on the purpose of the behavior. Disclosure is done through tentative hypotheses—for example, "Could it be?" or "I have an idea that perhaps . . . " and deals explicitly with the discrepancy between what one says and what one does or between the behavior and its purpose.

Rationale. The goal of confrontation is not catharsis or challenge. Confrontation is aimed at making the person aware of his or her effect on others. It helps the members of the group to view more clearly their behavior and to be more congruent and more sharing.

Confrontation should be offered with empathy. By caring and being congruent and authentic, the confronter offers a gift of great value. Hill

Interaction Matrix (Hill, 1965), which is a method of evaluating the group interaction, has assigned the highest level of productivity to some aspects of the confrontation process. Hill (1965) believes that it is at this level that individuals go beyond superficial human contacts and become productive.

If the leader operates with high empathy and regard, confrontation is facilitating and moves individual and group to new levels. The leader who confronts takes a risk by sharing with the members how they are perceived by others.

It can be helpful to make participants aware of how they may be subtly provoking other members of the group. This confrontation, as developed by Shulman (1962), is based on the hypothesis that each person's behavior in the group can be seen in light of the person's psychological movement in relation to other group members and that this movement reveals the member's intentions (Shulman, 1962).

Once the purpose of the behavior is ascertained, the group, with the member's consent, responds to the member's behavior by complying in an exaggerated manner with the person's mistaken demands. For example, if the person wants to be special, extensive time in the session is spent in treating the person as *very* special. In other words, the procedure consists in acting out the type of world the member wants. Thus, the member's purpose is exposed and, through the group's focusing on the mistaken demands, the behavior tends to be inhibited. This procedure is similar to the paradoxical intention, which we discussed in Chapter 7, since it exaggerates the behavior and thereby makes it less satisfying. Adler called this technique "prescribing the symptom."

The following dialogues contrast ineffective and effective use of the competency.

Ineffective use

Wayne: I have had lots of problems in Mrs. Kasey's class. She picks on me.

Joan: Yeah, she really is on you. I try to cooperate, but I won't let her treat me that way.

Leader: Tell me what you do.

Effective use

Wayne: I have had lots of problems in Mrs. Kasey's class. She picks on me.

Joan: Yeah, she really is on you. I try to cooperate, but I won't let her treat me that way.

Leader: Could it be you want to show Mrs. Kasey that you can't be controlled?

Comment: The leader takes the dialogue to another level by focusing on the purpose of Joan's resistance. However, the leader does this in a tentative manner that permits Joan to consider the purpose of her behavior.

Blocking

Definition. Blocking involves intervening in communication destructive to the group as a whole or to individual members. Since the leader's goal is the progress of the group, he or she tries to check communication that hinders such progress. For example, one of the participants may try to manipulate the leader into expressing his or her feelings toward other members. The person fears a direct confrontation and wants the leader to do his work for him.

Rationale. Through the blocking technique, the leader encourages members to express their inner feelings. Members are pressed to come out in the open with a clear statement of "where they are," manifesting openly their beliefs and feelings. The blocking technique must be handled effectively and gently, so that it doesn't come across as rejection of the person.

Blocking may take several forms. It can be used to block questions and make members come out with a clear-cut comment on their own feelings and beliefs. It can be used to block gossip, by intervening and directing a member to speak directly *to* the person he or she is talking about and not *about* the person with the group. Blocking can also be used to help members focus on the here and now of group life instead of the there and then. This kind of blocking directs attention to the interpersonal experiences and internal feelings as they are currently being experienced in the group. The tendency to smooth something over with a soothing comment needs to be blocked when the intensity of the confrontation needs to be continued to its resolution. By continuing certain types of honest confrontation, growth is produced. However, blocking may be used to stop the invasion of a person's privacy on the part of someone else who is trying to guess that person's thoughts.

The technique of blocking is like a traffic signal. If handled improperly, it causes a traffic jam; if, handled correctly, it results in smooth-flowing traffic. The true test of whether the competency of blocking has been well mastered is to note whether or not the group can fulfill its purposes. Blocking prevents being sidetracked by insignificant and harmful tactics.

The following dialogues contrast ineffective and effective use of the competency.

Ineffective use

Lisa: I don't like the way John always sits with his arms folded.
Lynn: Yeah, that bugs me too!
Leader: He's just not a part of the group.

Comment: The leader has failed to have Lisa direct her remarks to

John. Lisa wanted the leader to say something to John that she didn't dare to say herself, because she feared the confrontation.

Effective use

Frank (to the leader): I wish you would say something to Carol. She doesn't contribute anything to the group.
Anne: We all feel that you should say something to her.
Leader: You would like me to speak for you? But I feel it would be more helpful for Carol if you spoke directly to her.
Frank: Carol, how do you feel about my difficulties with my mother?
Carol: I was afraid to say something because I thought you would laugh at me. To me, it seems as though you . . .

Comment: The leader effectively blocks the attempted gossiping of the group. The comments are redirected to the member concerned. Her feelings are brought into the open, and a constructive suggestion is made.

Encouraging and Focusing on Assets and Positive Feedback

Definition. The leader is aware of the powerful effect of making assets and positive feelings explicit. Positive feedback from peers has considerable influence on our attitudes and feelings of self-esteem. The leader finds opportunities to focus on assets and to supply positive feedback. This encourages the members of the group to do the same by offering encouragement to one another.

Rationale. The individual is often concerned about his or her place in the group and generally is much more susceptible to the suggestions and pressure that come from peers than to those that come from the leader. The group is a value-forming agent.

The leader can help the group to encourage the development of the participants. As the group sees and accentuates the positive, social interest is stimulated and members grow by their opportunities to interact positively. As genuine encouragement is fostered and practiced, the group becomes more integrated and cohesive.

The following dialogues contrast ineffective and effective use of the competency.

Ineffective use

Tom: I don't seem to be able to get acquainted with girls easily.
Laurie: Yes, you do seem very shy.
Tom: I guess that's it; I'm just shy.
Leader: Let's talk about your shyness.

Comment: Here the leader falls into the trap of discussing an assumed deficit.

Effective use

Tom: I don't seem to be able to get acquainted with girls easily.
Laurie: Yes, you do seem very shy.
Tom: I guess that's it; I'm just shy.
Leader: I've noticed that you seem relaxed when you talk with the boys in our group. Why are you at ease with boys?

Comment: The leader is attempting to use the person's stengths and transfer them to the area in which the person doesn't function as well.

Facilitating Participation by Confronting Nonverbal Clues

Definition. "The facilitator is one who is concerned about having contact with the whole person—his thoughts, feelings, purposes and actions" (Dinkmeyer & Muro, 1971). In order to understand the language of behavior, the leader begins by noting if the person's basic organic, emotional, and safety needs are being met. The group member's set of assumptions about self and others is constantly being confirmed and occasionally rejected through reality testing in the group. The leader helps the group members become aware of the language of nonverbal behavior and of nonverbal behaviors that open or close communication channels.

The leader should know when to look directly at a member and when to sweep the whole group with his or her gaze. The leader should also note overt blushing, tension, excitement, weeping, and laughter and be able to detect them in their incipient stages.

Rationale. The group leader, by helping members become aware of nonverbal behaviors that open or close communication channels, adds another dimension to the group communication. The members become aware of their own messages and learn to read the messages of others. They also learn to point out and deal with incongruencies in themselves and others.

The following dialogues contrast ineffective and effective use of the competency.

Ineffective use

Gary (at the first meeting of the group, seats himself all the way in the back, away from the group).
Leader: I often feel that, when people hang back there, they really don't want to be in the group. Gary, is there somebody here you don't like?

Comment: The leader's comment is a direct attack on Gary's position. It could have been made more general by saying "Let's all move in more closely."

Effective use

Lisa (intellectualizes about herself and dominates the group with her reflections and recollections).

Wayne (begins to twist and stretch in his chair).
Leader: You seem awfully agitated, Wayne. What's going on with you?

   Comment: The leader is commenting only on Wayne's actions. It is up to Wayne, if he wants to and if he can, to make a connection between his own and Lisa's actions.

Facilitating I-Messages

   Definition. The I-message is the message that is clearly directed to someone and concerns the sender's feelings and attitudes. The group leader's task is to facilitate the exchange of I-messages by modeling, by providing examples, and by intervening when indirect messages (you-messages) are being sent. The task also involves intervening when someone asks questions instead of making a statement about his or her own feelings. The leader will then ask the person to make the statement instead of asking the question—for example, instead of asking "Why are you doing that?" stating "I'm very bothered when you do that."

   Rationale. The I-message, as opposed to the you-message, is much less apt to provoke resistance and rebellion. When people send I-messages, their awareness increases, because they become aware that they are responsible for themselves and only for themselves and because they are forced to identify with, clarify, and become honest about the messages they send. The senders of honest I-messages risk revealing themselves to others as they really are. It takes courage and inner security for a person to do so. It should be noted, however, that I-messages state only what the person's feelings are and don't demand a change in the other person because of the statement.

   A direct I-message in the group process eliminates the need for a third member to interpret and send the message to the member it was intended for. The rationale is that, when the members learn to deal directly with each other, more feedback and honest communication are developed. When members are not communicating with each other or are using dysfunctional communication, the group becomes ineffective.

   The following dialogues contrast ineffective and effective use of the competency.

Ineffective use

Jerry: Jack keeps saying he can't help laughing at me, and I'm tired of it.
Leader: You'd like to punch him in the nose.

   Comment: The leader's comment is ineffective because all it does is to pick up Jerry's feeling instead of suggesting that Jerry address his feeling of anger directly to Jack.

Effective use

Jerry: Jack keeps saying he can't help laughing at me, and I'm tired of it.

Leader: Jerry, I'd like you to speak directly to Jack and tell him how you feel about it.

Comment: Encouraging members to face each other concerning their feelings is much more effective. Such an approach helps the participants face up to their feelings and get them out into the open in order to deal with them. As a consequence, the members of the group are able to explore insights directly and not feel as though they are dealing with someone not in the group.

Paraphrasing and Clarifying to Stimulate Reality Testing

Definition. In paraphrasing, the leader selectively focuses on content and feedback—that is, on the essence of what has been said. The leader mirrors the thoughts to make sure that he or she has heard them accurately. The leader then encourages the members to clarify their assumptions, values, attitudes, and behavior through interaction in the group. The group provides a unique setting for going beyond the verbal and trying on behavior to study its appropriateness and effect.

Rationale. Paraphrasing helps members find out whether they are being understood. Through reality testing, the person tries on a certain behavior, learns from it, and evaluates its effects. The group then can help him "see himself in action."

The following dialogues contrast ineffective and effective use of the competency.

Ineffective use

Sally: I've been having lots of problems with my mother.
Anne: I'm getting tired of your always bringing up your mother in this group.
Leader: Each person has a right to discuss what he wants. Let's be patient.

Comment: The leader fails to hear Anne's message.

Effective use

Sally: I've been having lots of problems with my mother.
Anne: I'm getting tired of your always bringing up your mother in this group.
Leader: You are pretty angry that Sally always talks about her mother. Could you tell us what you are experiencing when that happens?

Comment: The leader helps Anne to be heard and to clarify what she believes and feels.

Offering Feedback

Definition. The term *feedback,* first applied to the behavioral sciences by Kurt Lewin, relates to the process whereby we learn how we are perceived by others, so we can modify our behavior accordingly. In everyday life, the opportunities to obtain accurate feedback are quite limited. The group, instead, provides the psychological safety that makes it possible for people to give and receive true and valuable feedback.

Rationale. Feedback serves two distinguishable functions: (1) providing information about the effects of one's behavior on others, and (2) providing positive or negative reinforcement.

The more clearly the feedback is related to specific responses, the better. Feedback about each response is better than information about overall progress, and precise information at the time the response is made is better than general advice about a sequence of responses. Feedback in the group seems most effective when it stems from here-and-now observations and when it follows the generating event as closely as possible.

In the process of feedback, individuals rapidly acquire a great deal of data concerning how they appear to others. The overly friendly type finds that others in the group resent her exaggerated friendliness. The man who weighs his words carefully and speaks with heavy precision may discover for the first time that others regard him as stuffy. A woman who shows a somewhat excessive desire to be of help to others is told in no uncertain terms that some group members don't want her for a mother. Genuine feedback can be extremely upsetting, but, as long as the various bits of information are offered in the context of caring that is characteristic of groups, they can be highly constructive.

The following dialogues contrast ineffective and effective use of the competency.

Ineffective use

Emily: I somehow feel that it's so easy for me to put myself inside another
    person, and I guess I feel that . . .
Leader: Why is it so easy for you?
Emily: Probably, I'm just sensitive.
Leader: You're really lucky to be like that. How about you, Al?

    Comment: In this example, the leader doesn't give feedback about how Emily's comments strike him or her but simply accepts and reassures.

Effective use

Greg: What I meant by being careful is that, if I'm not careful about how I
    say something, it's twisted on me.
Leader: I have the impression we can tell when you're being careful.
Greg: I guess so, but it's my way. That's when I get into arguments.
Leader: I have the feeling that being honest is very hard for you.

Formulating Tentative Hypotheses

Definition. Tentative hypotheses are the hypotheses the group leader makes concerning the purpose of a member's behavior in the present group situation. Such hypotheses help the group consider the purpose of behavior and become aware of the here and now by investigating what is happening in the moment.

Rationale. The leader offers a tentative hypothesis of behavior (that is, makes a disclosure) in an attempt to help the individual develop insight into his or her own behavior by understanding its purpose. Since the group is in itself a social setting, it affords the members a situation in which they can observe the purpose and the consequences of their social behavior. Although tentative hypotheses are directed to one person, they are valuable for the entire group, because there is often considerable similarity in various people's mistaken perceptions and self-defeating patterns. Feedback from peers in the group may make the hypothesis more valid and provide additional insights.

Tentative hypotheses are most effective when they are offered at the right time—that is, when the person is ready for them—and in the right way. The leader's attitude when he or she makes a disclosure is crucial, and so is the manner in which the disclosure is made.

Disclosure is concerned not with the causes of the behavior but with its purpose. The leader avoids making assertions about the person's behavior, which may be discouraging, but makes the person aware of what the purpose of the behavior may be. Such revelations may evoke an immediate recognition reflex. The disclosure is made by approaching the subject in a friendly atmosphere of mutual respect. The leader asks the individual if he would like to know why he behaves in a certain way and offers the hypothesis tentatively, in terms of "I wonder," "Could it be," "I have the impression," and so forth.

The following dialogues contrast ineffective and effective use of the competency.

Ineffective use

Wayne: If the subject we're discussing in the group doesn't interest me, I sometimes yawn out loud.

Leader: You're obviously trying to draw attention to yourself and keep us busy with you.

Comment: The leader has offered a hypothesis in the form of a blunt statement, *telling* Wayne what his goals *are* rather than *hypothesizing* about what his goals *may be*. Confronted with this attitude on the part of the leader, Wayne is likely to become defensive and deny the possibility that this is the true purpose of his behavior. He may also resent the leader for making such an "accusation." He will certainly feel trapped.

Effective use

Wayne: If the subject we're discussing in the group doesn't interest me, I sometimes yawn out loud.

Leader: Is it possible that, because you are bored with what is happening, you yawn to keep us busy with you?

Comment: Here the leader has offered the same hypothesis to the person but in a much less assertive and abrasive manner. Wayne can consider the possibility that the leader's hypothesis truly reflects his own intention, without feeling trapped. And he can accept the leader's insight as a helpful suggestion rather than as an accusation.

Setting Tasks and Getting Commitment

Definition. The leader sets tasks by helping the members verbalize the job or task that they have set for themselves in the group. The members clearly state what they hope to accomplish through their interaction with the other members of the group in an individual session or—as is more often the case—in the entire series of sessions. The more specific the statement of the task is, the easier it will be to accomplish it. The group leader promotes specificity by first hearing what an individual is attempting to say and then encouraging him to verbalize his ideas and to commit himself to doing the job. Encouragement may come in the form of helping the individual see the value of accomplishing the task. The member makes a specific contract and is expected to report back on his progress at the next meeting.

Once the task has been specified, the leader should try to help the person say exactly how he feels he can best accomplish the task. Here, too, specificity is very important. However, the leader may allow the individual to change the method to which he has committed himself, if it is not effective. The essential thing is that the individual make some kind of commitment to accomplish the task that he has taken upon himself.

Rationale. Task setting and commitment are both very important to the group process because, without them, very little would be accomplished. It is important that the leader help all members become aware of some area at which they need to work in the group. It is equally important that all members make some kind of definite commitment to follow through with the job or task that they have set for themselves. Task setting and commitments usually occur early in the group, but they may be developed as new perceptions and situations arise.

The following dialogues contrast ineffective and effective use of the competency.

Ineffective use

Maureen: I'm not sure what the purpose of this group is. I know I'm not perfect, but I don't know what the group can do for me.
Leader: Well, there must be something! With that attitude, nothing will be accomplished.
Maureen: I already did say what I feel. I don't know what the group can do for me.

Leader: You can't really mean that.

Comment: The leader is trying too hard to get Maureen to react. This kind of strong-arm tactics doesn't work, because Maureen feels far away from where the leader is. Force will not get people to participate.

Effective use

Maureen: I'm not sure what the purpose of this group is. I know I'm not perfect, but I don't know what the group can do for me.
Leader: I think we all share some of these feelings. The purpose of the group is to help us understand ourselves and relate more effectively with others. Is there something in that area you'd like to discuss?
Maureen: Well, I feel uneasy in large groups of people. Perhaps we could talk about that.
Leader: Would you want to discuss with the group this uncomfortable feeling?
Maureen: Yes, I think I would.
Leader: Can you tell us how you feel in large groups and how you would like to change?
Maureen: Well, I just can't get my thoughts out, and I'd like to feel more free and relaxed.

Comment: Here the leader does not try to force anything. Instead, he or she tries to get the person to decide on a task for the group. The leader doesn't give Maureen a task but lets her find one. Then he or she guides Maureen to explore the situation.

Capping and Summarizing

Definition: Capping. Capping takes place near the end of a session, when the leader helps the group ease up on the emotional side of the interaction and focus, instead, on its cognitive aspects. Thus, the group leaves behind deep emotional explorations and prepares to function in the typical life spaces of the world of social reality. The leader does this consciously by responding to content rather than to feelings—that is, by looking at ideas instead of picking up on feelings. When an emotional point is raised, the leader uses capping techniques to change the subject to something less intense. The subject can be changed back to a topic previously discussed or to a new and less loaded topic. In using capping techniques, the leader must make sure that no member is left in a state of crisis. The participants should not leave the session feeling that they cannot cope with their feelings. At the end of the session, the leader may want to "go around" and give each member an opportunity to make a final comment.

Definition: Summarizing. Summarizing is a way of looking at the themes that are coming through in the session. This can be done by the leader, by the members of the group, or as a collective act. It may occur during the session when the leader wants to pull together what has been happening and look at the meaning of the interaction. It can be stimulated by questions such as "What's happening here now?" or "Where are we?" In other instances, the leader will choose to cap and summarize to the group what he or she has been experiencing and what he or she believes is the emotional level of the group. The leader may choose to identify where various members of the group appear to be on certain issues. This can also be accomplished by asking members to indicate what they have learned and how they feel about what they are experiencing.

Rationale. Probably the most basic reason for capping is that it allows time for all members to get themselves together and back in touch with reality. By summarizing, the session closes on a note of positive planning, since the members become aware of where they are. Summarizing lends a cognitive element to the interaction and enables the group to tie structure and purpose to what has really been happening. Summarizing also provides all members with access to one another's perceptions and can generate new data for the group. Finally, it provides the leader with an accurate reading of what is being experienced by the members of the group.

The following dialogues contrast ineffective and effective use of the competency.

Ineffective use

Jerry: I'm really uptight.
Leader: Well, it's about time to close, so let's leave that for next time.

Comment: Perhaps Jerry is in crisis, and he is abruptly put off.

Effective use

Jack: I'm not really sure whether we have solved our problem or not.
Leader: What do you think you've learned so far?

Comment: The leader caps the discussion and requests a response to what has been learned to this point. This provides an opportunity to assess what development has occurred for Jack so far.

REFERENCES

Adler, A. *Guiding the child.* New York: Greenberg, 1931.

Dickoff, H., & Lakin, M. Patients' views of group psychotherapy: Retrospection and interpretation. *International Journal of Group Psychotherapy, 1963, 13,* 61–73.

Dinkmeyer, D., & Muro, J. J. *Group counseling: Theory and practice.* Itasca, Ill.: Peacock, 1971.

Dreikurs, R. The development of mental hygiene in Vienna. *Allg. Zeitsch. Psychiat., 1928, 88,* 469–489.

Dreikurs, R. Group psychotherapy: General review. *Proceedings of the First International Congress of Psychiatry, Paris, 1950.* Paris: Hermann, 1952.

Dreikurs, R., & Corsini, R. Twenty years of group psychotherapy. In R. Dreikurs

(Ed.), *Group psychotherapy and group approaches*. Chicago: Alfred Adler Institute, 1960.

Harms, E. *Nervous child,* 1945, 4:186.

Hill, W. F. *Him, Hill interaction matrix*. Los Angeles: University of Southern California, Youth Studies Center, 1965.

Metzl, J. Die Arbeitzmethoden der Trinkerfuersorgestelle Brigittenau. *Int. Zeits. gegen den Alcohol*, 1937, *35*.

Moreno, J. L. *Who shall survive?* New York: Beacon House, 1953.

Ozertovsky, D. S. *Zhurn. Neuropath. i. Psichiat.*, 20:587, 1927.

Shulman, B. H. The use of dramatic confrontation in group psychotherapy. *Psychiatric Quarterly,* 1962, *36,* 93–99.

Yalom, I. D. *The theory and practice of group psychotherapy*. New York: Basic Books, 1970.

CHAPTER 10

ADLERIAN GROUP METHODS

Adlerians place great emphasis on the social meaning of behavior. Recognizing that, basically, most problems are social and interpersonal, they believe in the necessity of understanding behavior in its social context. This approach, common to all Adlerian therapists and counselors, allows, however, some differences in group procedures. The following are some special group methods used by Adlerians.

LIFE-STYLE GROUPS

Adlerian groups often employ the life style to develop self-awareness and understanding. Usually, the members of these groups present enough information about themselves to compile a mini-life style, which covers the individual's relationship with the parents, rating and trait comparison with the siblings, and some early recollections. The leader provides a brief summary of the individual's mistaken perceptions, assets, and goals. In some groups, the members indicate how successful they are in the various tasks of life.

The members' life styles and the way in which each participant copes with the life tasks are all ''grist for the mill,'' since they enable the members of the group to understand the perceptions, beliefs, goals, and values of the other members. The equalitarian nature of the group relationship is emphasized as the members get to know one another, participate in the diagnosis, and learn to guess or formulate tentative hypotheses about the purpose of each person's psychological movement.

Robert Powers, an Adlerian affiliated with the Alfred Adler Institute of Chicago, uses an educational approach to group therapy. All participants actually keep some notes regarding the life styles in the group. The fact that leader and members of the group have access to the same information about life style and interaction makes it possible for members and leader to treat one another as equals sharing in a learning experience.

The following is Frank Walton's excellent guide, based on Powers' format.

Part I: A Guide for Presenting Yourself to the Seminar
A. You have ten minutes, uninterrupted, in which to tell us who you are.
B. Stay, as much as possible, in the *present tense*. Later on you will have an opportunity to tell us about your childhood.
C. Life challenges each of us, and each person is now approaching its challenges in a way unique to himself. Tell us about your responses to these challenges:
    1. What kind of friends have you made? What kind of friend are you? How do you get along with strangers in chance meetings? How do people treat you generally? How do you feel about other people, most of the time?
    2. What kind of work do you do? What kind of worker are you? Do you enjoy what you are doing? Do those with whom or for whom you work appreciate your contributions?
    3. Whom do you love? What kinds of problems have you had over loving and being loved? Do sex, closeness, and intimacy have a comfortable place in your life or not? What does masculinity mean to you? What does femininity mean to you? How do you measure up to whatever you expect of yourself as a man or a woman?

Part II: A Guide for Sharing in Responses
A. Someone has just spent ten minutes presenting himself. How did you receive what he presented?
B. Did you *recognize* things in yourself that he mentioned about himself? Was it easy to understand him or difficult? Did he sound strange or familiar?
C. How do you *feel* toward him? Did your feelings toward him change as a result of his presenting himself as he did? How?
D. Do you feel invited to *act* any particular way toward him? Did you welcome that invitation or resent it? What would you like to do *for* this person? What would you like to do *with* this person? What would you like to do *to* this person?

Part III: A Guide for Drawing Your Family Constellation
A. In childhood each of us learned how to define the *place* he had amongst others. Help the members of the seminar to see the kind of place you had as a pre-adolescent child in your family.

B. How many children were there in your family, and where did you fit in amongst them? How were you different from the others, and how were you like them? Which of the others was most nearly like you, and which was most different? What were you "good at"? What was hard for you?

C. What was father like? Who was his favorite? What did he expect from you? How did you feel about his expectations?

D. What was mother like? Who was her favorite? What did she expect from you? How did you feel about her expectations?

E. How did your parents get along with each other? What were their differences/arguments/fights about? To which parent did you feel closer? Why?

F. Were grandparents or other relatives important to you? How?

G. Did anything change at adolescence? How? What did puberty, physical development, and dating mean to you?

    1. For boys: What did "being a man" mean to you? Did you think you would have been happier, luckier, better off if you had been born a girl?

    2. For girls: What did "being a woman" mean to you? Did you think you would have been happier, luckier, better off if you had been born a boy?

Part IV: A Guide for Discussing a Family Constellation

A. Can you share any feelings about yourself in your family with the person who just told you about his childhood?

B. Can you understand this person better? How?

C. Can you see something in the way he presented himself initially which didn't make sense to you at the time?

D. What more do you want to know about this person?

E. Can you see a relationship between the *role* he played as a child, in his family and among other children, and the way in which he has tried to find a place in this seminar?

F. Each of us has the *private goal* of playing a certain kind of *social role*.

Parts I and II are repeated for each member of the group before the group moves on to Parts III and IV, which are also repeated for each member of the group. A fifth and sixth part can be added at the option of the leader. Part V would consist of obtaining two or three early memories, while Part VI would be devoted to the interpretation of the memories by the leader and participants. These additional segments are limited to ten minutes each in the fashion of Parts I through IV.

A group may terminate at the conclusion of Part IV or Part VI, or it may continue to meet periodically in order to help group members work at relating the increased awareness of the purposes and patterns of their behavior to the challenges of social living.*

*From "Group Workshop with Adolescents," by F. Walton, *The Individual Psychologist*, 1975, *12* (1), 26–28. Reprinted by permission of *The Individual Psychologist*.

ACTION THERAPY

Action Therapy is a group procedure developed by Walter O'Connell (1972, 1975). The format is similar to psychodrama, but the spontaneous release of emotions is not an end in itself but a move toward honesty with self and others. People are understood as decision-making beings who seek to enhance their self-esteem; their mistaken perceptions and faulty methods are highlighted in the group process. The hidden purposes of behavior are revealed, and the individual is encouraged to develop more socially responsible motivations and purposes.

Although the techniques of Jacob Moreno, the originator of psychodrama, helped generate Action Therapy, O'Connell (1975) indicates that his own system is Adlerian because of the following elements:

1. Man is not viewed as a mechanistic system powered by a closed source of energy. Feedback and resultant fluctuations in self-esteem better fit our world-view (Frankl, 1963; Mowrer, 1963) and seem capable of explaining our behavior, a necessary segment of the total treatment field (Oliver & Landfield, 1962).
2. We have worked ourselves free of intrapsychic overemphasis with its accentuation of infantile and pathological determinism in favor of behavioral responses amenable to change in the here-and-now.
3. The preference is for a diagnosis which attends to self-esteem, compensatory fantasy and extent of humanistic identification abstracted from behavior over time and changing external conditions.
4. Treatment is a process for correction of mistakes and stupidities instead of eliminating impersonal disease processes, and is carried out in a group setting which highlights the creative hypothetico-deductive life style of the individual (e.g., experiences lead to cognitions which are self-reinforced and call forth strong expectations and demands toward others) [p. 63].

Basic Concepts and Tactics

The following is a brief summary of the basic principles and tactics of Action Therapy, as described by O'Connell (1975, pp. 64–66).

1. *Guardian principle.* Every member of the group should have a "guardian," who shows understanding and acceptance and treats the person with dignity.
2. *Responsibility.* The goal is to educate each person to be responsible for his or her own behavior. Although feelings of anxiety and guilt are uncomfortable, the use of illness as an explanation for goal-directed behaviors is discouraged.
3. *Outsight.* If self-esteem is low, acceptance and belonging must be increased. This is accomplished by getting outsight into the motives and feelings of others.

4. *Awareness.* This is the concept of the Internalized Sentences and Negative Nonsense. Action Therapy avoids pointing to the past and, instead, highlights the individual's immediate, automatic reactions to internalized sentences.

5. *Self-disclosure.* The leader's stimulus value as a positive-identification model is emphasized. The members will more often do as the leader does than as the leader says.

Techniques

"The number of techniques employable in action therapy seem infinite" (Moreno, 1959). Our five-year experience has taught us the recurrent utility of the mirror, double, role reversal, aside and dialogue techniques. The reluctant patient has always, in our experience, become involved in acting upon his problems when a staff member has temporarily enacted his kinetic and verbal reactions through the mirror play. The patient is generally quite astounded that someone seems to know him so well (without retaliating) and is willing to expend time and effort toward one who basically feels so unworthy. The double technique also provides for staff participation, with the protagonist standing behind the patient while verbalizing feelings and "automatic" reactions (e.g., "I feel that I'll be punished for whatever I think or say. I'll try to wriggle my way out by saying something strange. I don't dare try anything more . . ."). Role reversal has remained an excellent vehicle for introducing anyone to his unfruitful arbitrary demands on others then launching the discussion and practice of attending to the needs of others as a means of cementing friendship bonds. In the aside the real feelings and hidden manipulatory games (Watzlawick, 1964) are verbalized although the patient or staff protagonist might be behaving in a defensive self-defeating style. Rather than aim an interpretation toward an uneasy avoiding patient and thereby compounding his lack of self-disclosure, staff or patients may debate the particular patient's motives and goals among themselves. Such an interchange (dialogue) is usually tempered with such overt themes as "We know you've learned this in the past . . . but you can change, if you want to and think it's possible. . . . If you think we're wrong, tell us." [O'Connell, 1975, p. 67].

As O'Connell indicates, "Action therapy is a form of group therapy which is focused on what the patient can do for others, rather than on the patient as such" (O'Connell, 1975, p. 36).

Action Therapy includes "lecturettes" on Adlerian theory, which explain in common language the participants' mistaken concepts and self-defeating beliefs and how these errors in living can be overcome. The need for self-esteem (significance or worth) and social interest are emphasized. The liabilities of low self-esteem are illustrated through examples of members' misbehavior, such as oversensitiveness, feelings of worthlessness, and unwillingness to risk imperfection. The courage to be imperfect is discussed. Also discussed is the consequence of a lack of self-esteem—restricted social interest, which creates distance and either overdependency or active or passive competitiveness and aggressiveness.

> A part of the lecturette is concerned with topics which help the director to get the group going, avoiding abstractions and past histories. One such topic is the specific error of lowering self-esteem and narrowing social interest in this present encounter. "We all do this. Why? And how? Why are you doing it right now?" Another topic is anxiety, feeling "certain" that something catastrophic is going to happen to one, beyond one's control. "What do you fear will happen? Tell the group in a fit of openness and honesty. Is it a fear of loneliness, of humiliation, of others detecting imperfections?" Still another topic is knowing another, i.e., understanding how he lowers his self-esteem and social interest in terms of outer and inner (cognitive) movements; knowing his hidden anxieties; understanding the nature of his habitual relationships (hyperdependent, cooperative, or competitive); lastly, knowing how he wants to be confirmed, as "what," and by what types of reinforcements, e.g., as the best speaker, by constant nodding and smiling of others. Ideally, all members know this information about all other members and are willing to share themselves, and confirm others. This builds authentic "community," and each member is able to mirror or double for every other [O'Connell, 1975, pp. 38–39].

In Action Therapy, the members of the group, one at a time, volunteer to be the protagonist and contribute their concerns and challenges of living to the group. The protagonist's low self-esteem and negative nonsense are explored.

> While working with the protagonist the director inquires from other members for similarities and understanding. "Why don't you understand Joe?" "What information do you need? What movements does he have to make before you understand him?" "What do you tell yourself about Joe to keep distance from him?" "What have you said or done to Joe to help him tell himself that he is (or you are) inferior as a person?"
>
> The director might ask if others have had similar problems. "Let's see the hands of those who have had sex problems" (two hands up, ten arms motionless). "I see we have two guys with guts and ten liars (laughter). I've had sex problems too. What do you think of that?"
>
> The director can play upon competition itself to precipitate insight into the goals of competition on the useless side and develop group cohesion. One statement might be, "The group's task is to find the most depressed guys. Who is the sickest?"
>
> The director can capitalize upon competitive power struggles to stimulate sharing and practice of openness. When Harry, a sullen, violently-passive alcoholic, steadfastly refused to play the son who infuriated Harry and led him to drinking behavior, a bet was made with Joe. Joe, also on the stage because the director called for the group to select

people with the "best tempers," was told by the director, "I'll bet you two bits you can't get Harry to play his son." Almost immediately the director lost his quarter and the group had a hearty laugh over their power to "defeat" authority. But authority in this case was not defeated since it also laughed and was pleased at the creativity of the group in demonstrating power struggles and provoking movement.

Guessing at another's constricting cognitions highlights the other's "creativity" (albeit of an unexpected negative kind) and focuses on the possibility of his making alternative choices. Guessing in itself is stressed because it is encouraging to realize that no one of us has absolute certainty and guessing is what we are all doing. Guessing at another's creativity also helps to show him a developmental route to the sense of humor through experiencing the tragicomic paradox, e.g., knocking oneself down while crying for help. The humor of unloving the self while demanding pampering from others, the humor of being the best or most perfect self-devaluator, can also be brought out through mirroring and doubling in action therapy [O'Connell, 1975, pp. 39–40].

Emphasis may be placed on the paradox of having the participants strive harder to accomplish their "symptoms." The lesson is "either stop your negative nonsense, or immediately increase it and learn to enjoy your misery more fully" (O'Connell, 1975, p. 41).

The leader or director moves to develop peer support, acceptance, and especially encouragement. It is stressed that self-esteem comes from positive reinforcement of self and others, from courage, and from social interest.

THE ENCOURAGEMENT LABS

O'Connell is also the founder of the Encouragement Labs. He developed them because his concept of humanistic identification "conceives of man as having both a relatively stable inner core (life style or existential-humanistic attitudes) and an innate potential for social intercourse (the need for power, seen as the ability to stimulate or resist interpersonal change)" (O'Connell, 1975, p. 52).

The goal of the Encouragement Labs is to teach the participants, through lecturettes and experiences, that they are not passive victims of their environments. "The principal lab premise is that social interest does not emerge full-blown in the absence of psychological complaints (symptoms), but needs to be explicitly taught, especially in a competitive society like ours where there are no institutionalized efforts to teach the movements and responsibilities of love" (O'Connell, 1975, p. 53).

Encouragement includes in its progressive repertoire of social skills the art of courage: giving and asking for feedback about peoples' reactions to one's behaviors and guessing at the goals of misbehavior (self and others). Encouragement in its most advanced state includes recognizing the importance of being open and self-disclosing and not provoking and reinforcing inequality (e.g., feelings of insignificance *or* feelings of significance in narrow noncontributory social roles). Encouragement labs point toward knowledge and practice of the humorous attitude, for there is no more encouraging or growth-precipitating person than one with a humorous attitude. Contrary to popular practice, encouragement is definitely not pampering. Yet almost one hundred students, asked to write on how they would encourage authority figures in their lives, gave examples more appropriate to pampering. In these examples, students behaved as if they had no right to give feedback, or if they did it would be ignored or retaliated against: so they made themselves discouraged. Encouragement is not such destructive pampering as telling a person what he wants to hear about how wonderful he is, completely ignoring his motivated mistakes. Encouragement is a process of getting the message across, loudly and clearly, that one is responsible for constricting or expanding his feelings of self-esteem and belonging [O'Connell, 1975, pp. 53–54].

The Encouragement Lab includes lecturettes and exercises aimed at developing encouragement skills. The members of the group are taught to produce natural highs by increasing their self-esteem and social interest. Opportunities to encourage various kinds of constricted individuals are presented, and success bombardment (finding something good) is utilized. Participants learn to even congratulate creatively arranged rejection and other forms of negative nonsense and misbehavior. They learn to give encouraging feedback, instead of reinforcing negative nonsense and negative behaviors.

The following are some of the essential elements for practicing the encouragement process in dyads:

1. Attend through eye contact and attentive listening.
2. Paraphrase your partner's message and feelings.
3. Identify similarities between yourself and your partner, since acceptance encourages belonging.
4. Share yourself through authentic self-disclosure of your feelings.
5. Give each other feedback, sharing the impressions that have been developed.
6. Find something good about everyone in the group—even how creatively a person arranges for reinforcement of his or her behavior.
7. Tell how your partner has encouraged you.
8. Make guesses concerning how you have helped the group.

SOCIAL THERAPY

Toni and Theo Schoenaker originated Social Therapy at the Rudolf Dreikurs Institute for Social Equality in Zuntersbach, Germany. The process is called Social Therapy because all humans are understood as social beings and all problems as social problems.

People are accepted in the group with all of their strengths and weaknesses. The basic assumption is that all neurotic disturbances and personality problems are not illnesses but exaggerations of problems we all hold in common. The change comes by making progress toward courage, affirmation of self, and social interest.

Social-Therapy groups are composed of 20 participants who meet seven hours a day for five days. Members are encouraged to familiarize themselves with the principles of Adlerian psychology before joining a group.

Like all Adlerian groups, Social-Therapy groups function in an atmosphere of equality. Efforts are made to foster feelings of belonging and acceptance on the part of the group members, and there is an emphasis on the positive use of constructive feedback to promote self-confidence and change. As the Schoenakers (1976) state, "In Social Therapy, one expands usual behavior in a positive direction and dares to act on suggestions for behavioral change. We hope that self-confidence will be strengthened, that social interest and courage will increase" (p. 16).

Belonging and acceptance are created by an emphasis on the participants' mutual respect and responsibility for self and others. Disparagement and attack, as well as useless feedback, are, therefore, avoided. The goal is to experience equality and humanness instead of competition and rivalry. A basic rule is that nobody talks about the group members outside of the group sessions. Social-Therapy exercises are organized and guided so that each person is aware that he or she is not there to fulfill another's expectations and that others are not there to fulfill his or her own expectations.

Exercises include relaxation to become aware of the body and its functions, respiration and movement exercises to help members regulate their rhythm of respiration so it matches the rhythm of the group, and sound exercises to learn how to express oneself.

Each participant creates his or her own emotions and seeks to belong according to his or her life style. Mistaken ideas of belonging—such as "getter," "driver," "controller," "pleaser," and "morally superior"—are discussed. Behavior is seen and discussed as useful and useless and as active and passive.

The ultimate goal is to help members believe that they are good as they are and reduce their drive for self-elevation. In a meditative atmosphere, the person comes to state "I am I, and I accept myself as I am," "You are you, and I accept you as you are," and "You are you, and you are not here to live up to my expectations."

Each participant comes to understand some aspects of his or her life style. Because of the unity of the personality, the overall psychological movement in the group helps each member understand his or her own behavior. As Adler indicated, "An individual's every slightest action, every behavior symptom is characteristic of the whole individual, and, like a stone from the mosaic, it indicates the style of the whole. From the way a person talks, moves, reacts to certain events, the traits and characteristics of his life style can be more or less easily recognized'' (quoted in Schoenaker & Schoenaker, 1976, p. 46).

To promote understanding of the life style, the group leader may suggest that the group move around in the room without speaking, taking interest in one another. As the participants move about, the leader may ask questions, in the first person, such as:

- Am I interested in the other person or am I occupied with the question "What does the other think of me?"
- Do I seek contacts or do I just wait?
- Do I go where the most contacts can be made, or do I move where I can only meet a few people?
- Am I friendly for fear of not being accepted?
- Am I afraid not to meet enough people and to leave one out?
- Am I so active in contacting because I want to control the situation? [Schoenaker & Schoenaker, 1976, p. 40].

After the activity, the discussion focuses on what one has learned from the activity.

With the help of other group members, each participant tries to determine his or her number-one priority, the methods he or she uses to maintain the priority, and the price he or she pays for it (see Table 10–1). "Try on a behavior"—that is, criticize while looking a person directly in the face, ask a person of the opposite sex out to lunch, or experiment with any other thing they

Table 10–1. Number-one priorities.

Number-one priority	How the other may feel	The price you pay for your priority	What you want to avoid with your priority
Comfort	irritated or annoyed	reduced productivity	stress
Pleasing	accepting	stunted growth	rejection
Control	challenged	social distance and/or reduced spontaneity	unexpected humiliation
Superiority	inadequate	overburdened	meaninglessness

From *Adlerian Social Therapy,* a monograph by T. Schoenaker and T. Schoenaker. Copyright 1976 by Green Bough Publications, St. Paul, Minnesota. Reprinted by permission.

find difficult to do. Therefore, the focus is not merely on insight but on outsight and action as well. Role playing, psychodrama, self-observation, relaxation, movement, and expression exercises are all used to help the individual understand his or her mistaken beliefs and faulty approaches to the challenges of living and to see alternative, more viable beliefs and approaches.

TELEOANALYSIS: UNDERSTANDING SELF, OTHERS, AND THE PURPOSES OF BEHAVIOR

The Teleoanalytic Workshop, developed by Don Dinkmeyer, is designed to help participants become aware of their beliefs, values, goals, and style of life and to move toward more effective relationships with others by shifting from self-awareness (insight) to activated social interest (outsight).

The workshop is based on the following Adlerian premises:

1. People are social, decision-making beings, whose actions have a purpose. All behavior has social meaning.

2. The members' life style is expressed in their transactions with the group.

3. People's behavior is best understood by a holistic approach, which recognizes that psychological movement reveals the person's life style and unitary striving toward a goal. To understand the person or a specific behavior, one should seek to understand the purpose.

4. Social interest and courage are criteria for mental health.

5. Individuals are understood in terms of their perceptions, or phenomenological field. The subjective factors of biased interpretations and perceptions influence people's decisions.

The workshop is didactic (it includes lecturettes to provide information) and experiential (it engages the participants in experiences that bring into play their feelings, beliefs, and values).

The topics discussed might include:

- Self-esteem, self-image, self-acceptance;
- Social interest;
- Purpose and finalistic causality, goal striving, fictional goals;
- Search for significance, power (active and passive);
- Understanding life style: family atmosphere, family constellation and psychological position, methods of training, early recollections, creative capacity to decide and private logic;
- Priorities and the triangle;
- Life tasks and challenges;
- Discouragement, failure to function, courage to be imperfect;
- Encouragement and courage;
- Unity of personality, holism, pattern;
- Social equality: horizontal versus vertical communication;
- Understanding and deciding feelings;

- Commonly observed life styles: driver, controller, getter, self-elevator, righter, pleaser, morally superior, aginner, victim, martyr, inadequate, excitement seeker;
- Mistaken ideas about self: I am special, entitled, something only if first, must be perfect;
- Self-acceptance, self-encouragement, being a winner.

Exercises and experiences are carried out in a manner aimed at developing feelings of belonging in the participants. This is done through improved communication first in dyads, then in groups of four, then eight, and so on. Through this process, all the members become more visible, more transparent, and more congruent to one another. The exercises involve presenting oneself to the group in terms of one's strengths, priorities, self-esteem, family atmosphere, family constellation, and assets. A variety of Adlerian techniques are used, including Corsini's Behind-the-Back Technique, Multiple-Strength Perception, Role Playing, Action Therapy, Relaxation and Centering, Fantasy, Psychodrama, and Analysis of Psychological Movement and Purpose.

PSYCHODRAMA-ORIENTED ACTION TECHNIQUES

Insight can be gained by showing the group members the underlying purpose of their behavior and their biased perceptions. The method developed by Shulman and one of his cotherapists, A. Starr, focuses on moving from words to action (Shulman, 1973). Since members may refuse to accept the group's interpretation of their behavior, this method helps them attain insight by letting them experience the group's reactions to the underlying purpose of their behavior. The group is directed to react in an exaggerated manner to a member's neurotic goals, thus communicating the message in a dramatic and forceful way.

> Instead of only using words, action was employed. This is close to the approach of Moreno. . . .
> The plan was discussed during a group session. It was agreed that the group would try to discover the purpose of the irritating and provocative behavior and would then, in an exaggerated way, respond to the behavior, in line with the provocateur's neurotic demands. "If he wants to be a baby, let's treat him like a baby and see if he likes it" [Shulman, 1973, p. 181].

Here is an example of the procedure, which involves selecting one of a member's outstanding faulty goals and the way in which the person achieves it in the group and dramatizing them.

> John, a 26-year-old male, an only child, continually apologized for

his behavior, remarks and appearance. He insisted that he was the most poorly endowed in the group, was stupid, unattractive, unmanly and that he felt inferior to all the others. The group first tried to help him by denying his self-description and pointing out his assets, but had become discouraged and antagonistic toward him.

His early recollection was: "I was running alongside a low (un-fenced) porch, screaming with fright. My parents, sitting on the porch, saw me run but didn't see anything chasing me. They got up to look and saw that I was being chased by a tiny gosling, so small they couldn't even see its head from where they were sitting."

The patient thus tells us through his memory that he is absolutely inadequate. He has to run from something so small that no one else would be afraid of it. How can anyone expect him to face adult tasks? He cannot take care of himself, others must protect him and care for him.

The group decided to respond to John as if he actually were inade-quate and worthless. They began to ignore him or to deride his remarks. They told him that he couldn't possibly have anything worthwhile to offer but that they suffered his presence because they were too kind to throw him out of the group. A common response when John spoke was, "There you go making stupid remarks again. You are just inadequate, nothing you say is worthwhile," or "If you say it, it must be wrong."

The procedure was used in one session only. John became very angry but did not show it. At the ensuing session he spoke of his anger and was surprised at how the group accepted his anger. Once he began to apologize and caught himself, saying, "There I go again," the group offered warm feelings and John felt he didn't have to display his inade-quacy any longer. Surprisingly, the provocative behavior returned only at long separated intervals, and a simple reminder from another group member was enough for him to catch himself [Shulman, 1973, pp. 181–182].

In his article, Shulman gives three more examples of how to apply the psychodramatic procedure—a procedure that is closely related to the paradox-ical intention. He points out that being confronted with one's mistaken goals and suddenly becoming aware of them often lead to an immediate feeling of release of tension and may result in spontaneity of behavior. "At the moment when the person catches himself, which is a process of insight and re-evaluation, the goals can change, and the defensive distance-keeping opera-tions are, for the moment, at least, suspended" (Shulman, 1973, p. 186). The group setting stimulates cooperation and insights, which, together with the stressful experience, tend to move the person emotionally closer to the group.

The psychodramatic technique is based on the hypotheses that (1) all behavior is goal directed, (2) each member's behavior in the group shows the person's psychic movement in relation to the other group members, and (3) this movement reveals the person's secret intentions—his or her pri-vate goals.

THE MIDAS TECHNIQUE

A variation of Shulman's procedure is the "auxiliary-world" technique of Z. T. Moreno (1959), which Shulman called the Midas Technique. In this type of dramatic confrontation, the group member and/or leader acts out roles that create for the individual the kind of world and relationships he or she would like to have (Shulman, 1973).

Confronting a patient with his mistaken goals not only leads to greater spontaneity of behavior, insight, and re-evaluation, but also promotes insight and re-evaluation in certain specific ways:
1. The patient is shown what his secret goal is.
2. He is shown that others are aware of his secret.
3. He is shown that it is acceptable to others and that they are even willing to help him achieve it.
4. However, by doing so, they indicate that what the patient has so greatly prized is not at all prized by the others. A thing that no one else wants tends to lose some of its value (as described by Papanek, 1958).
5. The exposé spoils the "ploy." The group is "spitting in the patient's soup" by behaving in an unexpected way.
6. The ensuing acute awareness of the patient's behavior and the knowledge that the group is focused on it tend to inhibit such behavior.
7. The invitation to perform takes the steam out of the patient and further inhibits the behavior.
8. Unless the group can be seen as refusing the neurotic demand, it seems unimportant to work so hard for it. If it is so easily had, why worry about it? If the group is willing to give in, why fight for it? [Shulman, 1973, pp. 192–193].

The following general principles apply to the Midas Technique:

a. The technique and its purpose must be freely discussed and understood by the group members.
b. The purpose must be to help a member, not to discipline or humiliate him.
c. The atmosphere must be friendly. The group is engaged in giving a member something he secretly and/or unconsciously wants. It is not denying him or prohibiting him.
d. Consequently, the patient must not be made to do something he doesn't want to do [Shulman, 1973, p. 193].

TAYLOR'S GROWTH GROUP EXERCISES

John Taylor, a clinical psychologist in Salem, Oregon, has led some effective growth group exercises based on Adlerian principles. Here are some of them.

The Marshmallow

The Marshmallow teaches that withdrawal is an effective countermeasure to a power struggle. It begins with the leader and one participant facing each other and conversing for about one minute.

> *Procedure:* Select a volunteer participant. Give instructions: Tell the volunteer to lock his/her hands together in front of his/her chin, palms facing away from his/her body, with the elbows at shoulder height and the forearms horizontal. Tell the volunteer that, as soon as he/she hears you make a statement, he/she is to say "I will not clean up my room!" Immediately after making the statement, he/she is to make a quick, forceful thrust of the locked hands straight out away from his/her body. He/she is to try to experience the strength in his/her arms and shoulders during the thrust.

Part I: "Standoff"
1. Place the palm of one of your hands against the volunteer's locked hands and say "Clean up your room!"
2. Keep your palm steady, opposing the volunteer's force, so that the two of you are pressing against each other's hands. Make statements that symbolize this mock parent/child power struggle. For example:
   "Oh, yes you will!"
   "You will do as I say!"
   "You obey me this instant because I am your parent!"
   "You can't do this to me!"
   "Get your room cleaned up this instant!"
(Allow about 15 seconds.)

Part I: Discussion
1. Why did the volunteer seem to enjoy this experience, even though he/she was being attacked by the "parent"?
2. Could the volunteer experience the strength in his/her arms and shoulders?
3. Can children experience strength when parents oppose them in power struggles?
4. In what situation do I get caught up in power struggles?

Part II: Solution
1. Have the volunteer get into the starting position, and tell him/her that the same procedure applies this time.
2. Place the palm of one of your hands against the volunteer's locked hands and, in a gentle but firm voice, say "Please clean up your room."
3. Withdraw your palm from the volunteer's hands when he/she thrusts outward, so that you exert no opposing pressure. Say "O.K., you're the one who has to sleep in it!"

Part II: Discussion

1. Why did the volunteer seem to have less joy this time, even though he/she was being dealt with in a kind and courteous fashion?
2. Could the volunteer experience the strength in his/her arms and shoulders?
3. Why is being like a "marshmallow" in response to a child's attempt to power struggle not equivalent to "giving in" or "surrendering" to the child?
4. Who had more power?
5. In what ways can I withdraw from potential power struggles?

The Shoo Fly

The Shoo Fly illustrates attention-getting behavior and the typical ineffective responses to such behavior.

Description: The participants form dyads (Participant A and Participant B), stand near their dyad partners, and read aloud while being pestered by their partners for about 3 minutes.

Materials: One book for each pair of participants, preferably the same book for all.

Procedure

1. Have participants form dyads.
2. Have each B obtain a book (preferably the same book for all).
3. Accompany all As to another room.
4. Give instructions to A: Tell A that B will be reading aloud from a book. A's job is to pester and annoy B in childlike fashion by tugging, tickling, asking questions, having tantrums, and so on. The goal of the pestering is to force B to pay attention to A rather than to the book.
5. Return the As to their partners.
6. Give instructions to B: If all Bs have the same book, select a certain passage and have all Bs turn to that passage. If Bs have different books, tell B to find a page with lots of words on it. B is to read the passage aloud slowly and distinctly. (Allow about 90 seconds.)

Discussion

1. What did B feel like doing to A?
2. Why is the "shoo" reaction an inefficient response to children's attention-getting misbehavior?
3. What was A's goal?
4. Who had more power?
5. What constructive responses can parents make to this type of misbehavior?

The Inferiority Complex

The Inferiority Complex illustrates the mechanism of the display of inadequacy.

Description: The participants converse with their partners, while holding heavy objects, for about 3 minutes.

Materials: One object (such as chair, purse, or book) for each pair of participants.

Procedure

1. Have participants form dyads.
2. Have *A*s go to another room.
3. Give instructions to *B*: Tell *B* to hold the object in one hand at arm's length. If heavy objects such as chairs are used, *B* may use a shoulder or both hands. *B* is to continue to hold the object off the floor without help while you go to talk with *A*.
4. Give instructions to *A*: Tell *A* that *B* will ask *A*'s help in holding the object. *A* is to refuse to help, making self-critical statements that indicate *A*'s desire to avoid participation and responsibility in helping *B*. For example:
   "I could never do that!"
   "My mom told me I'm not strong enough."
   "I have sore muscles today."
   "Don't even ask me!"
5. Return *A*s to their partners.
6. Tell *B* to ask *A* whether *A* would be willing to help *B* hold the object. (Allow about 2 minutes.)

Discussion

1. What did *B* want to do to *A*?
2. In what ways did *B* experience power? and *A*?
3. Who had more power?
4. What are some constructive responses that parents could make to the child who has an inferiority complex?

REFERENCES

Frankl, J. *Man's search for meaning.* New York: Washington Square Press, 1963.

Moreno, Z. T. A survey of psychodramatic techniques. *Group Psychotherapy,* 1959, *12,* 5–14.

Mowrer, O. *The new group therapy.* New York: Van Nostrand, 1963.

O'Connell, W. E. Adlerian Action Therapy techniques. *Journal of Individual Psychology,* 1972, *28,* 184–191.

O'Connell, W. E. *Action Therapy and Adlerian theory.* Chicago: Alfred Adler Institute, 1975.

Oliver, W., & Landfield, A. Reflexibility: An unfaced issue in psychology. *Journal of Individual Psychology,* 1962, *18,* 114–124.

Papanek, H. Change of ethical values in group psychotherapy. *International Journal of Group Psychotherapy,* 1958, *13,* 435–444.

Schoenaker, T., & Schoenaker, T. *Adlerian Social Therapy.* St. Paul, Minn.: Green Bough Publications, 1976. (Monograph)

Shulman, B. H. A psychodramatically oriented action technique in group psychotherapy. In B. H. Shulman (Ed.), *Contributions to Individual Psychology.* Chicago: Alfred Adler Institute, 1973.

Walton, F. Group workshop with adolescents. *The Individual Psychologist,* 1975, *12*(1), 26–28.

Watzlawick, P. *An anthology of human communication.* Palo Alto, Calif.: Science & Behavior Books, 1964.

CHAPTER 11

INDIVIDUAL AND GROUP CONSULTATION WITH TEACHERS

The education process concerns not solely the students but the teachers, the administrators, and the parents as well. We have dealt with the counseling of students throughout this book. In this and the next chapter, we turn our attention to teachers and parents. Chapter 12 deals with the unique and highly successful strategy that Adlerians use for parent education, whether it be implemented in schools, agencies, or other institutions. This chapter focuses on the counselor's relationship with the teacher.

American education operated without counselors for many years. After school counseling was established, it experienced a period of growing popularity. Recently, financial pressures, demands for a return to "basics," and the requirements of educational priorities have placed the counselor near the top of the list of "expendable" personnel in the school system. When the situation is such that the ratio of counselor to students is often 1 to 400 (or more), the question "Since counselors cannot possibly be effective, why have them at all?" becomes less than rhetorical. The fact that the U.S. Office of Education no longer has a guidance section is indicative of the state of affairs in school counseling.

Counselors have few chances of being effective, or even to merely survive, if their job is narrowly defined as counselor/student interaction. There is much more to student counseling than working with students alone. For school counselors to be effective, they must be able to work with all facets of the education process. For example, in an effort to help students become self-actualized, counselors will schedule classroom affective-education programs and activities. But their sphere of influence doesn't touch the teacher, who may operate that same classroom autocratically and demand that the children be dependent on his or her instructions, demands, and needs. In such extreme situations, the counselor's efforts have no chance of overcoming the teacher's more pervasive influence.

We (the authors), therefore, suggest that school counselors must have skills that will not only allow them to work with individual teachers on a request basis but permit them to initiate group education and problem-solving experiences for teachers. The latter is preferable, since groups can be more productive and successful than individual consultation. Dinkmeyer and Carlson (1973) indicate four reasons that militate in favor of the group model:

1. Individual consulting with teachers often forces the counselor to become an "answer man," in response to the teacher's problem.
2. It is important that counselors be aware of the teachers' internal frame of reference. What do teachers believe about human behavior, and how do these beliefs shape their behavior?
3. Individual consultation may allow the teacher to formulate excuses and defenses more easily than in a peer group of teachers. "I've tried that" or "There are too many kids in my classroom to change" carries less weight when the peer group can defuse these faulty beliefs. Were the counselor to make similar statements, they might be interpreted by the teacher as advice giving or critical and unsympathetic judgment.
4. When counselors work with a group, instead of an individual, they have instantly multiplied resources for the problem-solving needs of each teacher [pp. 201–202].

THEORETICAL FOUNDATIONS

Whether in groups or individually, consultation with teachers must be supported by a theoretical framework for understanding human behavior. Adlerian psychology readily offers such framework, as our discussion will indicate. But, first, let's examine some of the principles that are often used by teachers to understand behavior.

Common Mistaken Assumptions about Human Behavior

Behavior is a product of environmental factors. Suzy is a problem child because she comes from a poor home—from the other side of the tracks, so to speak. In other words, where you live determines how you behave. It seems almost unnecessary to answer the advocates of this theory by pointing to the countless cases of exceptional achievement and motivation among ghetto children and to the equally countless cases of apathy and failure among children who "benefit" from middle- and upper-class environments.

Behavior is a product of heredity. This view, expressed by the catchall phrase "The genes did it!" is more prevalent among parents than among teachers. The reason is simply that teachers have ample opportunity to make comparisons among their students and see quite clearly that heredity is only a small factor in the makeup of a child.

Behavior is a product of age and stage of development. Those who hold this view see behavior as a function of chronological age—the terrible 2s, the troubled teens, and so forth. Like the environmental view, this opinion ignores the wide variability of individuals—in this case, of individuals at the same age or "stage." It forgets the mature 12-year-old and the immature adult.

Behavior is a product of sex. Sex-role stereotyping is perhaps the view that, because of women's liberation, is dying quickest. It accounts for differences in behavior by focusing on the sex of the child. Although not too many people today would say that girls are made of "sugar and spice" and that "boys will always be boys," these stereotypes still influence our children's choices. For example, boys still take more high-school math courses than girls do—at least in North America. In other cultures, in which sex stereotyping doesn't exist or exists to a much smaller degree, these differences in the educational choices made by boys and girls are unknown.

All four of these minitheories of human behavior explain away, rather than understand, behavior. What can a counselor do when confronted with a teacher who subscribes to one or more or these "theories"? Short of having children change home, genes, age, or sex, there is not much the counselor can do in such a situation.

Applicable Adlerian Principles

In earlier chapters, we have outlined the Adlerian theory of personality. It is by introducing the teacher to the cardinal concepts of this theory that the Adlerian counselor can reach with the teacher a feasible understanding of the students' behavior. Here are these cardinal concepts.

Behavior must be seen holistically. The individual is a whole, not a conglomeration of diverse and often conflicting parts. We cannot understand behavior if we focus on small fragments of a person—for instance, certain confusing behaviors—ignoring the overall pattern. Each bit of information is indeed correct, but it performs a very limited, often useless, function in our effort to understand the structure of the entire person. For example, if we focus exclusively on a student's extremely high IQ score, we cannot explain that student's low grades. The two elements appear inconsistent until we recognize another factor—motivation. It is only through the broader picture of the person's overall psychological movement that we can understand the person's behavior.

All behavior has a purpose. When a child misbehaves, instead of asking "Why?" we Adlerians ask "What is the purpose of that behavior?" Our question, too, is aimed at understanding the behavior, but we use a more viable framework for inquiry. When we start from the premise that all behavior has a goal, whether we like the goal or not, all behavior makes sense—children's behavior as well. As you may remember, Dreikurs saw children's misbehavior as the result of one of four goals: attention, power, revenge, or display of inadequacy. These goals can be more easily recognized if the teacher identifies first the feelings that a misbehavior provokes in him or her—a concept that is discussed in detail in Chapter 12.

All behavior has social meaning. All individuals—adults and children alike—seek to become part of the group. It is, therefore, especially important that the teacher understand the social environment and the interpersonal relationships that a child chooses. When children don't succeed in their quest for belonging, they will often resort to antisocial behavior if such behavior gives them the uniqueness they have been unable to achieve otherwise. The class clown, for example, feels that to be noticed by others is so important that he will risk being punished by the teacher if that is the price he must pay to achieve his goal.

Each individual must cope with the life tasks of work, friendship, and love. How each child approaches these tasks gives us an understanding of the child's life style and willingness to cooperate with others. In school, the success at these tasks is indicated by the ability to function in schoolwork, by the capacity to get along with others, and by the playing of a sex role appropriate to the culture.

Each person operates on the basis of his/her own private logic. The overwhelming majority of students (and teachers) are in agreement with regard to the logic of appropriate classroom behavior. And, yet, the private logic plays an important role in classroom behavior, as in all behavior. Until we understand the child's private logic, we are unable to effectively change the child's undesirable behavior. The fact is—as we said earlier—that all behavior has a goal, whether we like the goal or not, and all behavior makes sense in light of its goal. Therefore, the class clown feels that it is logical to disrupt the work of the class, no matter what the teacher's logic may be.

The bias of our private logic colors our interpretation of the world and results in the tremendous variety of our behaviors. These behaviors are all "logical," whether they be political or religious preferences, styles of dress, or choices of words.

Behavior is always consistent with the individual's self-concept and life style. This principle enables us to distinguish patterns and themes in each person—for example, "I count only when I'm being noticed; therefore, I must attract attention at all costs," "I must be in control; therefore, I will challenge the teacher's authority," "getting even is very important; therefore, I won't hesitate to hurt or embarrass others," "I am incapable; therefore, I will not try." When we don't understand a certain behavior, we cannot invalidate it. Instead, we must seek to understand the private logic and the self-concept that make the behavior meaningful and reasonable from the person's point of view.

All behavior reflects the person's degree of encouragement or discouragement. When children tackle a new task, they have certain expectations about their probability of success in that endeavor. Encouraged, or courageous, children feel adequate and capable of coping with the task.

Discouraged children feel that they cannot succeed; therefore, they will not try. Overambition, inadequacy, and high standards are all affected by the level of encouragement or discouragement that the child experiences.

Adlerian psychology states that we choose our life style and determine our own behavior. We are both the products and the determinants of our behavior; each of us is at the same time the artist and the painting. The teacher and the counselor who share this view and wish to change the child's behavior have the advantage of knowing that an undesirable behavior can be changed because it is chosen. By offering the child the encouragement he or she needs, the counselor or teacher will have a profound influence on the child's behavior.

SOME COMMON ELEMENTS OF
LEARNING THEORIES

Dinkmeyer and Carlson (1973, pp. 69–83) examined the learning theories of Piaget, Skinner, Gagné, and Montessori, as well as the phenomenological theory, the field theory (Bruner and Lewin), and the social-learning theory. They found in these diverse theories of learning the following common elements, which echo some of the Adlerian concepts we have discussed throughout this book.

1. Each individual has a uniqueness that is basic to the structure of his or her personality.

2. Consequences are part of learning; reinforcement is one such consequence.

3. Motivation results from a state of disequilibrium. This disequilib-

rium may be internally perceived, may be imposed by external elements, or may be a combination of these two conditions.

4. It is important to understand the total situation, not just some components of it.

5. One must try to identify with others, demonstrate empathy, and understand others' points of view.

6. When dealing with children, one must take into account individual differences and begin where the child is ready to begin. This implies a need to be conscious of the child's degree of readiness and a willingness to cooperate with the child.

7. When examining heredity and environment as components of behavior, environment should be given more weight than heredity.

8. Learning occurs when behavior changes.

Implications

While numerous implications can be drawn from these common elements of learning theories, four specific points are especially relevant if one wants to challenge what should be considered as true misconceptions about teachers. These four implications represent essential elements of the successful teacher/counselor relationship.

A. Teachers cannot be responsible for their students' behaviors. It is often assumed that the teacher must change the child; in fact, teachers must first change themselves. If the counselor allows teachers to realize this point themselves rather than offer it as a fact, the concept will meet with less resistance in the teacher's process of self-discovery.

B. Teachers must be more involved with encouraging the discouraged child than with praising the good or accomplished student. This point implies a need to reexamine the use of grades in the classroom. Being a form of external evaluation, grades often become an unnecessary reinforcer for the "A" student and a potent discourager for the "D" student. The counselor can facilitate teacher growth in this area by explaining the differences between praise and encouragement and by discussing with the teachers some ways in which they may implement encouragement more frequently with their discouraged students.

C. Teachers cannot always protect their students from experiencing failure, whether in the classroom or on the playground. At first, this point may seem in contradiction with point A above, but the underlying concept is not. Teachers are not responsible for their students' behaviors; therefore, they should not feel compelled to shield the children from unpleasant experiences.

D. Teachers should attempt to provide more of a balance between the cognitive and the affective needs of their students. Our education system concentrates on the cognitive "three R's" and ignores another, very important, set of R's: responsibility, resourcefulness, and respect. This is an area in which the counselor can concretely aid the teacher by sharing value exercises, by teaching reflective listening and other communication skills, and by providing effective resources that the teacher can use in the classroom and share with the children.

We have identified the underlying theoretical assumptions in the successful teacher/counselor relationship. There are two basic formats for implementing this relationship: on a one-to-one basis and in small groups.

CONSULTING WITH THE INDIVIDUAL TEACHER

The counseling relationship with a teacher can take many different forms, depending on the teacher's expectations. Some teachers expect "expert" advice from the counselor—an attitude that reflects an unhealthy dependence on the counselor.

> Mrs. Smith teaches a third-grade class. One of her students, Wanda, doesn't like to do arithmetic. Wanda spends most of math time daydreaming, doodling on the margins, and talking with other children. It is the talking with the others that really upsets Mrs. Smith. On one particularly talkative day, Wanda simply ignores the teacher's pleas for cooperation as well as her threats. Mrs. Smith, "at the end or her rope," decides to see the counselor.
>
> As Mrs. Smith approaches the counselor's office, she entertains several thoughts about the problem and its possible solutions. These thoughts, which are sure to get in the way of a successful resolution of the situation, are likely to be "I can't do anything anymore about this," "The problem is with Wanda," or "Our counselor will give me some good ideas on how to get Wanda to be quiet."

But the counselor must share more than ideas with the teacher. A counselor/teacher relationship is a collaborative one. If the counselor deals only with the crisis between Wanda and Mrs. Smith, he or she can give advice only on how to improve things in this specific instance. Predictably, this will insure one of two things: if the crisis is solved, the counselor gets the reputation of being a "crisis fixer" and can count on a mounting number of crises that need fixing; if, instead, the counselor's advice fails, Mrs. Smith will be firmly convinced that the counselor has nothing useful to share.

The collaborative nature of the counselor/teacher relationship calls for the counselor to "give his or her skills away" so that the teacher will be able to solve this crisis and the next crisis to come along, which will surely be different. This expertise is represented by the understanding of behavior (especially group behavior), by communication skills, and by problem-solving skills. Counselors must avoid becoming "answer men." Counselors must examine their own personal values and life style, so that they will not fall into a trap they have set for themselves. For example, a counselor who seeks excitement will not want to give up many crises. A counselor who needs to be in charge will not easily give up an opportunity to be an expert and may try to place teachers in a dependent and inferior position.

The teacher seeking help is a critical resource in the consultation procedure. Does the teacher have certain beliefs or a life style that will impede a collaborative effort? Just as the counselor as expert may cause problems, the teacher as advice seeker may interfere with the effort. This situation often occurs with those teachers who don't see themselves as part of the problem they take to the counselor. The teacher is the client with whom the counselor must work. Thus, the relationship between counselor and teacher is similar to the counseling relationship. There must be mutual trust and respect as well as mutual goal alignment.

But there are, of course, those counselors who do structure their job so that teachers will indeed see them as experts who have all the answers. When counselors offer quick solutions off the top of their heads in the hall, teachers lounge, or office, they create the image of the "medicine man." The result is that teachers, instead of focusing on their own behavior as contributing to the problem, will go to the counselor to obtain a "prescription."

Teachers may tend to see counselors as special individuals who hold a privileged position in the school system. And often this perception is not entirely the product of a fanciful imagination. Counselors tend to have more freedom and unstructured time than teachers, and they frequently see students on an individual basis—a luxury that classroom teachers rarely experience. Thus, counselors must take several active steps to offset this view, which may well be true of traditional (and ineffective) counselor job descriptions.

Counselors must seek to avoid crisis intervention, and they must understand when a crisis is being used to manipulate their time. Crisis intervention is frequently an unproductive effort. By making themselves available to teachers in noncrisis situations, counselors can transmit totally different ideas about their skills and avoid appearing as "medicine men." It is imperative that the counselor spend the first month of the school year getting to know the teachers on a friendly and nonthreatening basis. The counselor must not come across as the "big person who stands up for the little people." By simply spending time with the teachers in their own environment, whether it be the teachers lounge or their classrooms after school, the counselor has immediate access to the teachers' points of view.

Dinkmeyer and Carlson (1973, p. 177) say that, to increase the chances of self-referral on the part of the teachers, counselors must seek to achieve the following three conditions:

1. Through presentations at faculty meetings, newsletters, and personal contact, the school staff needs to be made aware of the full services that the counselor offers.

2. The counselor cannot "hide in the office," seeing people by ap-

pointment only and being so inflexible as to greet a request for consultation with ''I can't get to you until Thursday.''

3. The school administration must see consultation with teachers as a valid counselor activity and actively direct teachers to the counselor for this purpose. Many administrators don't see consultation as valid and consider the counselor as a crisis resolver, as a bookkeeper, or as an affective-education specialist.

A counselor's concern with the school environment, with the image he or she projects, and with the services he or she provides is best summed up in a single question: ''If the counselor is missing from the the building for one day, who notices and why?''

Systematic Procedure for Collecting Data

A systematic procedure for collecting the necessary information from a self-referred teacher helps to structure the initial meeting between counselor and teacher and provides an opportunity to skillfully listen to the teacher's problem (Dinkmeyer & Carlson, 1973, p. 179). Figure 11-1 shows an example of the consultant referral form used to collect the necessary data.

Anecdotes. A vital technique in data collection is the anecdote. The anecdote is the recollection of an interaction between child and teacher that specifically demonstrates the dynamics of the relationship. Returning to Mrs. Smith and Wanda, if Mrs. Smith were to respond to the counselor's request for an anecdote with ''Today Wanda just didn't listen to me; she was so stubborn,'' her answer would be insufficient. The counselor helps the teacher to reconstruct a situation, so that specific behavioral evidence is available. For example,

> For the past two weeks, I haven't been getting any cooperation from Wanda at math time. She doodles and daydreams, but what really bothers the class is that she talks with others all the time. I tell her to be quiet, and she will just for a while. But then she starts up again.

Exploring beliefs. At this point, the counselor should ask Mrs. Smith for a tentative hypothesis concerning the purpose of Wanda's psychological movement and ensuing behavior. This allows the teacher to share some of her beliefs about child behavior—that is, her frame of reference. (From the example above, we already have a clue that Mrs. Smith feels that she must act ''for the best interests of the class'' rather than in response to whatever needs she may be experiencing herself.) Whether agreeing or disagreeing with the teacher's ideas (hypothesis), the counselor must at this point accept the teacher's knowledge and beliefs. Now counselor and teacher can begin to list the child's assets and strengths.

This tactic may seem strange to the teacher, who probably feels that it is irrelevant or useless to dwell on the good, when it is the bad that is the problem. But, by becoming aware of how Mrs. Smith perceives Wanda as being adequate, the counselor can help the teacher pursue an avenue that may lead to a successful interaction with Wanda. What has been tried in the past and worked? What has been tried and didn't work? This procedure, included in the referral form (see Figure 11-1), allows Mrs. Smith to become aware of her own effectiveness and permits teacher and counselor to move immediately from the specific problem into possible resources for solving the problem.

Child's name _____ Grade _____ Age _____

Teacher _____ Time available for consultation _____

Family constellation (by age) _____

Family atmosphere _____

Specific description of learning difficulty or behavioral difficulty:

Is the problem you are concerned with focused primarily on one of the following 5 areas? Please circle. These areas are listed only to suggest classifications at the moment. Obviously many problems will overlap.

1. Intellectual deficiency
2. Learning problems, educational adjustment, questions regarding placement
3. Emotional problem, personality maladjustment, social adjustment
4. Discipline
5. Delinquent tendencies

Please describe the problem briefly. Anecdotal observations would be particularly appropriate. The anecdotes should include the child's behavior, your response or reaction, and his response to corrective efforts (antecedent event, behavior, consequence).

Tentative ideas regarding reasons for the behavior: _____

Child's assets, strengths: _____

Corrective actions utilized to this point: _____

Procedures which work with this child: _____

Mutually acceptable recommendations: _____

Figure 11–1. Consultant referral form. (From *Counseling: Facilitating Human Potential and Change Processes,* by D. Dinkmeyer and J. Carlson. Copyright 1973 by Charles E. Merrill Publishing Company. Reprinted by permission.)

Tuning in to feelings. The counselor has established a cooperative relationship with the teacher and has obtained specific behavioral incidents. The next step is to assist the teacher in tuning in to his or her own feelings about and reactions to the problem situation(s), so that corrective actions may be formulated. The process must move into the teacher's affective domain, so that the goal(s) of the child's misbehavior may be correctly identified. The consultation process is deprived of an invaluable asset when the counselor omits this step or allows the teacher to deny any negative emotion that necessarily existed.

Recognizing and identifying negative feelings may present the first major roadblock. A "good" teacher may feel that it is important not to admit that a student can "get to me." Allowing the teacher to ventilate any feelings that may becloud his or her point of view, especially in the crisis situation, will be of tremendous help. (It is assumed that the consultation meeting is conducted in as private an environment as the circumstances allow.)

By indicating to the teacher that behavior can be best understood in an *ABC* format (similar to that used in Ellis' Rational Emotive Therapy), the counselor deals with the specific problem and shares skills that the teacher can use in future problem situations.

This is how the *ABC* format works. *A* is the antecedent behavior that starts the problem. It may be a behavior from either the teacher or the child, but, in either case, it produces a response from the other. *B* is the response from the other person. *C* is the action that the person who emitted behavior *A* takes in response to *B*.

The feelings that accompany each of these steps must be identified. The *ABC* method makes use of anecdotes, which are recorded in the shortest and most economical fashion. The following is an example of the *ABC* method, as used by the teacher above.

A: Wanda was not doing her math.
B: I went over to her desk and said "Please stop talking. You haven't even finished the first page!"
C: Wanda stopped talking for a while, but I had to come over to her again. It seems that she will work only when I stand over her.

    The feelings I had during all of this were, first, annoyance—"Nothing works short of personal attention"—and, later, frustration, even anger—"I have better things to do."

Finding alternatives. Counselor and teacher may now make a tentative hypothesis about Wanda's misbehavior. The child may be seeking attention, since she stops misbehaving as soon as the teacher pays special attention to her. Another possibility is power, since Mrs. Smith experiences anger at her failure with Wanda.

The teacher must then examine the alternatives to her own behavior. She may, for example, decide to ignore Wanda and let her bear the consequences of her own choice of behavior. Such consequences may entail having to do at home the work she didn't do in class or being the object of pressure from her schoolmates, who also object to her talking but, so far, have not had an opportunity to express their annoyance, since Mrs. Smith was sure to step in. By seeking alternatives and recognizing their consequences, the teacher will find more functional and less conflictual behaviors on her own part. All viable alternatives demand that the teacher change first.

RECOMMENDATIONS FOR CHANGES
IN THE CLASSROOM

This book cannot make specific suggestions for change in any particular setting. To do so would run counter to the Adlerian view that specific solutions can come only from applying to a specific situation principles based on a solid theoretical framework, lest one slide into the expert/problem-solver role. The following general recommendations are offered to be tailor-fitted to specific situations.

1. Encouragement is the significant element in the change process. When teachers want children to stop certain behaviors, they should ignore those behaviors and fill the void by encouraging and reinforcing other, more acceptable behaviors. The relationship between child and teacher is a result of how the teacher chooses to influence the child, whether it is nagging, demanding, praising, encouraging, ignoring, or any one of the myriad of other alternatives open to teachers (Dinkmeyer & Dreikurs, 1963).

2. The logical consequences of the misbehavior are more effective than punishment. Consequences are a natural outcome of the misdeed, while punishment is often arbitrary and unrelated to the change that the teacher hopes to induce. The child who chooses to come to class late will have to take on the responsibility of finding out what happened while he was not there, instead of being scolded or punished by the teacher. Punishment tends to obscure the punisher's intended message, whereas consequences allow the child to experience the results of his own choice of behavior. It removes the teacher as a potential butt of anger and resentment and allows the child to learn from his own actions (Dreikurs & Grey, 1968).

3. The teacher should be made aware of any behaviors that will unintentionally reinforce, rather than diminish, misbehavior. A child who seeks attention and stops misbehaving when asked to do so by the teacher has in fact heard "I am paying attention to you" rather than "Please stop that." Also, power struggles may often occur when the teacher is determined to prove to the child that certain misbehaviors will not take place. Often the teacher's feeling in this situation is "Who is in charge here, you or me?" (Dreikurs, 1957).

4. Counselors can provide teachers with an objective viewpoint of the teachers' relationship with their students. Effective teachers are both kind and firm; but many teachers are one or the other, and conflict results. "Tough-

ness" promotes rebellion, resentment, and noncooperation; "softness" induces the children to run all over their teachers. Kindness, instead, conveys the teachers' respect for the children, while firmness conveys the teachers' respect for themselves, which, in turn, encourages the children's respect. This task is perhaps more easily accomplished in C-groups (discussed later in this chapter and in Chapter 12), where the teachers themselves can tell to one another how they come across in the group itself or in the classroom. This avoids the problem, common among teachers, of responding to the counselors' suggestions with the attitude of "What do they know? They don't spend any time in a classroom."

5. Teachers should be encouraged to use the powerful forces of the group atmosphere that already exist in the classroom. One way to utilize these forces is to ask the class to make a tentative hypothesis about a certain misbehavior. When the teacher asks "Why do you think Bill is acting that way?" he or she may be quite surprised to discover that the students know as well as the teacher the purpose of the misbehavior.

6. Teachers can facilitate change in behavior by approaching children from a holistic perspective rather than concentrating on the specific irritating behaviors. By understanding both the positive and the negative ways in which children seek to become significant in the group, teachers gain access to new strategies that they can fruitfully employ.

7. Responsibility can be used as a powerful tool to promote change in the misbehaving child. Teachers often assign classroom chores or other responsibilities to those children who have already proven themselves responsible. By not allowing the discouraged child to progressively accept new responsibilities, the teacher transmits the expectation "You can't do it anyway." The power of expectations cannot be ignored, since expectations can enhance or discourage the child's self-image and development.

8. Teachers should be aware of the basic principles of human motivation—why a child will do a certain task, for example. The American education system has twisted motivation from the need to belong to the need to please. This is why bad grades are useless with the child who is not concerned with pleasing or who has given up on belonging. Homework, too, is useless as punishment, because it can be interpreted by the child not as punishment but as a logical extension of school.

9. Teachers should learn to anticipate the children's actions and reactions. Strange as it may seem, a good rule of thumb is for teachers to react in a way that is exactly the opposite of their first impulse—for example, ignoring the attention seekers instead of nagging them.

10. Teachers often talk more than is necessary, perhaps on the assumption that talking to a child will change the child. The counselor can help the teacher see that letting the children bear the consequences of their actions is more effective than giving them lengthy admonitions. Act more and talk less!

11. Establishing a classroom council will promote cooperation among

the children by making the entire class, instead of the teacher, responsible for the atmosphere and tone of the classroom. Dreikurs (1957) and Glasser (1969) have made similar suggestions to increase the mutual responsibilities of teacher and child.

Often, the major contribution that counselors can make to teachers and students is something that has very little to do with imparting specific knowledge. Becoming a stimulus for professional growth in the willing teacher is the highest goal the counselor can seek. Teacher education often makes little or no attempt to train teachers to deal effectively with behavior and motivation, when, in fact, this is the cornerstone of any child's growth and success. Encouragement and emotional support, as well as positive expectations, are preferable to diagnoses, solutions, and evaluation from the counselor.

WORKING WITH TEACHERS IN GROUPS

Rationale

The Adlerian holistic approach stresses the social significance and consequences of behavior. If the counselor does not provide an opportunity for teachers to interact in a socially significant climate—in groups, rather than in the limited one-to-one consultation—a potent, positive, problem-solving, and educational opportunity is lost. It is a unique in-service training opportunity.

Traditional in-service experiences neglect the therapeutic forces that the group can provide. Working with teachers in groups can be the counselor's most important contribution to the school staff. Group work makes efficient use of time, allows education as well as problem solving to occur, and removes one of the biggest possible barriers to an effective teacher/counselor relationship. Counselors are no longer the experts who "don't know what the classroom is really like" but become, instead, members of a group of peers with whom they can share their feelings as well as their skills.[1]

The rationale for the group setting is that most problems experienced by teachers originate in the group setting of the classroom. By working with teachers in a group, the counselor can see exactly how the teacher's life style functions in the group setting—dominating, accepting, passive, demanding, and so on. The group allows each teacher to function as an integral part of a group. This process will give the participants insight into the group dynamics that are at work in their classroom every day. The counselor's leadership skills will shape the group experience so that each member will benefit from the experience.

Teacher educational opportunities seldom, if ever, are as valuable as this type of experience. The school schedule is not conducive to teacher group

---

[1]The group setting described in this section is a C-group, so called because, as discussed in detail in Chapter 12, its main functions begin with the letter C.

interactions. Indeed, by design, the teacher is a lone adult throughout the school day, except for faculty meetings and the respite of the teachers lounge.

A number of unique therapeutic forces can occur only in the group setting. The group can provide an unusual atmosphere of acceptance, so that each teacher may receive constructive empathy from his or her peers. In sharing their experiences, teachers learn that their problems are not unique and that there is a universal quality in classroom situations. The group is a place where teachers can ventilate and express frustrations, concerns, and ideas about their classroom and be heard. The group also provides the counselor and the individual teacher with a wealth of resources—the other teachers in the group. Each member of the group can become a supportive and therapeutic agent for the other members of the group, be they experienced or inexperienced teachers.

Organization

The staff must be educated to the goals, purposes, and potential benefits of the teacher group. This implies that the counselor's first contact is with the administration. If the administration perceives the teacher group as a limited, self-serving experience, the counselor must point out the benefits that will accrue for the students, as well as for the teachers. Another valid point is that teacher groups can effectively provide the kind of training that the current emphasis on in-service educational experiences seems to demand. When compared to the results of the one-day, one-shot teacher workshop, the cumulative effects of the ongoing group can be far greater. The administration must also be exposed to the holistic basis on which the teacher group will function.

Counselors must pay careful attention to the process and procedures they use to introduce the concept of group to the staff. Their goal should be to make the staff aware of the purpose and function of the group. In addition, counselors must be prepared to dispel some of the faulty beliefs that teachers may initially have about the group. The group process is not psychotherapy. It is not intended to be a remedial group for those teachers who feel that they have been designated as "inadequate" by the counselor or in some administrative evaluation.

It may be useful for the counselor to "mini-demonstrate" during a faculty meeting just what a teacher group will be like. This gives the staff an opportunity to vicariously experience a group while becoming aware of the value of the process. Counselors should make clear that the teacher group is not a sensitivity-training group, an encounter group, or any other group with which the teachers, in the absence of information, may associate it.

The group should meet once a week, for at least one hour. Teachers make a commitment to stay with the group for at least six to eight sessions, at which time the group as a whole may evaluate the group's needs and possible reorganization. The group can meet with effectiveness in a variety of places and times. It can meet during the lunch hour, or immediately before or after school. Once the administration and staff see the effectiveness of the group, changes in scheduling, covering for classes, and other arrangements will take place. It is important that counselors don't let imaginary barriers of time and space discourage their efforts to start a group.

The group should begin by establishing a few general rules about group membership. No one should be allowed to join the group once it has begun. New groups can be formed when the interest is aroused and other teachers express a desire for the same experience. This allows the ongoing group to remain exactly that and avoids the repetition of past groundwork and history. A physically comfortable and private area should be provided for the group. Often this is the counselor's office. The group should be arranged in a circular fashion so that each member can see all of the others and no member is "at the head of the table," especially the leader.

It is important that the group be heterogeneous. The group should be composed of experienced as well as inexperienced teachers, so that the diversity of classroom experiences and teacher training can be shared. On the other hand, the group should be composed of teachers from approximately the same grade level. Great discrepancy in the age level of the students being discussed can become a major handicap.

Group size must be limited, so that each member has an opportunity to share in each session. For this reason, the group should be restricted to five teachers plus the counselor (leader). Membership in a group is always voluntary and not by the recommendation of other teachers or administrators. The counselor should have a brief interview with each volunteer before the first meeting. Teachers qualify for participation by two criteria: (1) having a concern they wish to share with the group and (2) wanting to help others with their concerns. It is the commitment to these different types of sharing that qualifies the potential member.

Content

The first meeting of the group may be structured so that the leader allows all members to share something about themselves and, in turn, listen to the others. The leader might take this opportunity to point out any similarities in the concerns or ideas expressed by members of the group. The group therapeutic forces can be utilized immediately to generate cohesion and commitment in the group. The leader must exercise control of the group and offer a direction by providing the necessary psychological foundations as well as therapeutic forces. Introducing the Adlerian socioteleological concepts of behavior promotes the group's problem-solving skills by providing a useful common basis on which the group can approach the problems discussed.

Anecdote sharing is a technique that is used to present situations to the group in a systematic way. The format is the same as the one used in individual consultation. Once the teachers have identified the feelings they experienced during the incident, tentative hypotheses can be formulated. While it is important for teachers to recognize the individual differences in their approaches to classroom management and communication, each group member must accept the common elements in their classrooms—purposive misbehavior, discouragement, and practical alternatives to ineffective methods.

Focus

Even though the leader will have clarified the purposes of the group and the role expectations for group members, the first few sessions are likely to produce a certain degree of confusion and anxiety. This is a new experience for most of the teachers, and there will be many attempts to clarify roles and test new behaviors. No longer "a single tall tree in a forest," the teacher is now a coequal with several other teachers and the counselor.

The leader should be aware of several procedures that can make the group experience more effective (see Chapter 9). A primary challenge for the leader is to see that each member of the group has an opportunity to describe his or her unique situation, so the others can offer feedback. For the typical C-group, this means that one teacher will be on center stage for no more than 15 minutes each session and that no less than three teachers will actively present their challenge or problem.

Thus the counselor must utilize techniques that will both set the stage for and conclude a teacher's statements. When a particular problem appears to be very complex, the leader might seek clarification of a specific aspect of the situation. For example,

> *Leader:* It seems that a lot of the kids are giving you different challenges. Is there any particular kid we could concentrate on, so that everyone here can respond to your situation?

The leader must not feel that he or she is the only one responsible for reacting to each teacher's contribution. For example, a teacher may share a concern that is not relevant to the group. The leader can verbally or nonverbally solicit the attention and input of another teacher in the group. If the participants feel that a topic is relevant and the counselor does not, the counselor must then clarify the purpose and content of the group before continuing, lest the time be spent purposelessly.

The C-Group in Action

The following is an excerpt from a typical C-group. It is the third session of this group, composed of second- and third-grade teachers and the school counselor.

Leader: Okay, who'd like to begin this week? Do we have any feedback on how things went this past week and on some of the strategies we developed?

Carla: That idea of ignoring Lisa's crazy behavior and trying, instead, to encourage some specific, good behaviors seems to be working! She doesn't make a big deal of going to the pencil sharpener anymore. However, she isn't too interested in doing "good" stuff.

Craig: Was this the girl that didn't do anything unless she got some attention?

Carla: Yes, we said it was attention-getting misbehavior and that I should ignore the problem behaviors and pay attention to the good things she was doing. It's not easy to find some, though!

Betty: Maybe you'll have to encourage some of the positive things Lisa does. I had an attention getter like this, and he wasn't too interested in cooperating until I came up with some ideas that he liked.

Leader: So, there were things he did over which you really had no control—in which he had all the power?

Betty: Yeah, I got really angry about it one day.

Michael: Then it seems that it was a power struggle rather than just attention-getting behavior.

Betty: Ricky still likes to do certain things, as a matter of fact. Today we had a hard time figuring out where his lunch pail was.

Leader: It seems that Betty has something going on now, and your situation has improved, Carla. Can we move over to Betty for a few minutes?

Betty: I'm sure interested to see whether Ricky's goal is power or attention; I'm not too sure that I see all of the differences between the two.

Leader: Well, could you tell us about the lunch-pail incident?

Betty: As we were going to lunch today, Ricky complained loudly that he couldn't find his lunch pail. I had to hold up the entire class—I can't leave them by themselves—and look for Ricky's lunch pail.

Michael: It sounds like you were pretty annoyed by this.

Betty: Yes, he knew we had to wait for him. And then he remembered that he didn't bring his lunch, after all, and he didn't have the money to buy one. (Laughter)

Craig: He really had you cornered!

Betty: Yes, I was pretty angry, because I felt like it was a game, and I lost—not my temper—but the power struggle.

Leader: What would be the alternative to Betty's dealings with Ricky?

Carla: It would be to withdraw from a power struggle. But how do you avoid dealing with him and his lunch?

Betty: And this isn't the only time I get challenged by Ricky to see who's in control.

Leader: Okay, but let's return to the lunch situation. How would you withdraw from the situation?

Betty: Leave the classroom and let him deal with his problem?

Craig: Can you leave a kid alone? And what if he really didn't have money?

Michael: It's still his problem, and I think that probably he won't keep it up if there isn't any attention or prestige in holding up the class.

Betty: I can see the need to withdraw, but I'm not sure I can leave him alone. What would he do? (Pause)

Craig: I think it would be worth trying just to find out!

Betty: If this situation does come up again, I'll do exactly that and see what happens. I have a feeling that it will come up again, because Ricky was quite pleased with the results today.

Leader: He really got to you, didn't he?

Betty: Yes. Sometimes I do get into power struggles with the kids, but I feel pretty responsible about the classroom atmosphere, and disruptions really get to me.

Craig: The kids probably know it. They can tell if there are ways to control you.

This C-group has developed an understanding of the purposive nature of behavior and has presented a formula for identifying emotions that correspond to certain goals of misbehavior. Betty felt annoyed—even angry—at Ricky's disrupting the lunch line. By sharing the anecdote with the group, Betty has made it possible for the others to help her identify Ricky's probable goal, power. The alternative is to withdraw from any "power contest," and Betty has made a commitment to use such alternative response—to let Ricky be the owner of his own lunch problem. The final exchange between Craig and Betty demonstrates and acknowledges the purposiveness of behavior and the life styles that promote certain behaviors.

The counselor must monitor the progress of the group during and after each session. As a session progresses, the leader must make certain that each member of the group becomes a "sharer" as well as a spectator. Inherent tendencies to be withdrawn and shy or verbal and dominating must be recognized and counteracted by the leader. Encouragement must be used to allow members to contribute and to recognize the value of their contributions. When a problem is presented, or an opinion or idea is needed, counselors can turn to a member, instead of responding themselves.

The leader must also recognize a need to terminate discussions that tend to wander from the purpose of the group. The C-group is a highly specific and focused experience, almost assuring statements that the counselor must respond to. To change the focus of the group, the counselor must be willing to confront and redirect the topic being discussed. This often entails picking up a feeling of discomfort with the chosen topic on the part of the group and finding the reasons behind the feeling. The leader will often have to make the first few interventions but may also encourage nonverbally and verbally the members of the group to contribute their feeling and ideas and to express their concerns.

The leader must exercise control of the group without becoming involved in a power struggle with the members.

Evaluation

The leader may wish to use a systematic list for identifying, reviewing, and evaluating the leadership skills that are employed during C-group sessions. The following 14 skills are utilized by the leader of a C-group.

- Structuring
- Using introductory exercises as needed
- Universalizing
- Linking
- Confronting
- Blocking
- Encouraging—recognizing assets and giving positive feedback
- Facilitating nonverbal clues
- Facilitating I-messages
- Paraphrasing
- Providing feedback
- Offering tentative hypotheses
- Setting tasks and obtaining commitment from members
- Capping and summarizing

Group leaders should be aware of how frequently they use each skill in the group and have specific examples of each skill. Leaders will also find that some of their interventions and activities in the group lie outside these skills. In such cases, the leader should identify the purpose of those interventions and activities.

REFERENCES

Dinkmeyer, D., & Carlson, J. *Counseling: Facilitating human potential and change processes.* Columbus, Ohio: Merrill, 1973.

Dinkmeyer, D., & Dreikurs, R. *Encouraging children to learn: The encouragment process.* Englewood Cliffs, N.J.: Prentice-Hall, 1963.

Dreikurs, R. *Psychology in the classroom.* New York: Harper & Row, 1957.

Dreikurs, R., & Grey, L. *Logical consequences.* New York: Meredith, 1968.

Glasser, W. *Schools without failure.* New York: Harper & Row, 1969.

CHAPTER 12

PARENT EDUCATION

The family exerts the most significant influence on the development of an individual. Parents, in particular, are responsible for the atmosphere in which a child is raised. As we pointed out earlier, the child's position in the family constellation will also influence his or her growth, and interaction with siblings will develop certain beliefs about peers and others. When the family structure and atmosphere are troubled and unhealthy, a child's growth is necessarily affected.

> Parents exert a tremendous influence on the child. They are the earliest and often the only models a child has and it is from them that beliefs, attitudes, and techniques are chosen. It is the parents' behavior that generally establishes the atmosphere of the home, i.e., whether it is peaceful or warlike, cheerful or depressing, marked by warmth, closeness, and mutual involvement, or cold, distant, and detached [Shulman, 1962, p. 34].

It has long been apparent to Adlerians that training is necessary if mothers, fathers, and others in child-rearing roles are to do a good job as parents. The biological heredity we all possess does not guarantee us the necessary skills. Often our past experiences are the sole source of information from which we can fashion our unique approach to raising children. If parents and other parental figures are unsuccessful in their own experience, their children may be discouraged or, at least, have no viable model for dealing with the multiple challenges of parenting.

In our society, the "average parent" and the "typical home" are becoming increasingly rare. The nuclear family is becoming only one of a growing number of life styles. An indication of the large number of children being raised in single-parent homes is the growth experienced in recent years by the national organization Parents Without Partners. Grandparents and other relatives must often assume the parenting roles with a child whose parents have jobs that allow little time at home. Therefore, it is almost impossible to draw a meaningful picture of the "average" home and parent.

Because of this diversity, the traditional parenting roles can no longer be successful. Many parents grew up in comparatively autocratic family situations, in which the questioning of parental authority was not tolerated. The basic shift toward equality that has occurred in our society has not spared the family—on the contrary. If you have any doubts as to who is in charge today, just watch a parent try to subdue a rebellious 4-year-old who seems to have mistaken the supermarket for a racetrack.

Women and children, once submissive members of minorities, have achieved a status that is equal to that of the head of the household. The autocrat's approach of "Do as I say," which implies a superior/inferior relationship, is no longer appropriate or effective. Today's children are unwilling to be less than equal. When told to "jump," instead of asking "How high?" today's child will ask "Why?" Aside from the contemporary scene, which makes the autocratic parent especially ineffective, there is an inherent flaw in the traditional autocratic methods. That flaw is the failure to produce responsible children.

Parents need to learn new techniques and approaches. They need to acquire new skills they can use to create a more equalitarian and democratic relationship with their children. By "equalitarian" we mean a relationship based on cooperation and mutual respect. The movement toward equality can be beneficial for both parent and child only if the parent has developed the necessary skills of listening, communicating, motivating, encouraging, and letting the child assume responsibility for his or her actions.

This shift toward a more equalitarian relationship has produced confusion and discouragement in many parents who are devoid of real skills in parenting. They have habits, catchall phrases, and often threats but no substance or understanding that will work in the daily challenges and confrontations with their children. It is curious that we recognize and license the skills required to be a barber, a cabdriver, or any of a number of jobs, and, yet, most of us would think it outrageous if we were to similarly limit parenting to those who are skilled. What is not just curious but tragic is the fact that the process of acquiring the essential skills of parenting is something haphazard and left to chance.

RATIONALE

The above considerations should make it quite clear that parent education is badly needed. Its essential goal is to improve the relationship between parent and child by making available more alternatives and by promoting greater understanding and acceptance. Parent education brings about an openness to new ideas and techniques that can be of crucial importance in resolving present problems and in avoiding future ones.

The parent-education group represents not only a unique experience but also a unique approach that does not call for the prescription of "cures" or the onus of therapy. Instead, it allows parents to utilize powerful and often ignored forces in traditional learning settings. It does not consist of lectures, programmed learning, or other individual forms of learning. Parent education is essentially interaction among group members, because its goal is to improve interaction between parent and child.

With such a pervasive need for parent education, the question is not whether parent education should be available but where and when it should be provided. It is often the counselor's responsibility, regardless of the setting. Traditional counselors may not be aware of the need until they recognize the conditions existing in a certain milieu or system that can be improved by parent education.

School counselors who deal only with the child in the school setting or on an individual basis neglect to take into consideration the influence that the parents share with educators. Marriage counseling often centers on disagreements about child-rearing techniques. The very differences in childhood experiences on the part of the spouses may ensure a divergence of opinions if parent education is not available to bridge the gap. The increasing number of single parents is symbolic of the different circumstances in which children are raised today. Parents cannot *directly* influence the quality of their child's school day or television viewing. As a matter of fact, they may run a poor third to these powerful elements in their children's lives (by age 17, the average child will have experienced three hours of television for every two hours of school). However, parents can not only influence but effectively determine the quality of their own relationship with their children.

Public and private agencies provide parent education for target groups or as an additional service for their clients. Community colleges allow parents to schedule their group sessions in the evening or at other convenient times. Adlerian family-education centers (see Chapters 13 and 14) also offer parent education.

In parent education, the counselor's sphere of influence extends beyond the group, because the sessions also have an influence on the participants' spouses, children, and children's teachers. The number of those who are influenced directly or indirectly by a parent study group that meets for an hour or two each week can easily reach 50 or more.

BASIC ADLERIAN THEORY FOR PARENT EDUCATION

One of the goals of parent education is to teach, in simple and understandable terms, a theory of human behavior that can be practically applied in the home. In Adlerian parent education, this theory is in all respects similar to that used in consultation with teachers (see Chapter 11). A child's misbehavior is best understood when its goal and the emotions behind it are identified. Once the purpose of the behavior is identified, parents can develop alternative courses of action, which, in turn, will encourage alternative behaviors in the child.

It is important that this basic theory be discussed and understood as soon as possible in the parent-education group. Often the first several sessions will focus on the purpose of misbehavior. The topics covered in the next sessions include: emotions as a purposeful tool, I-messages, alternatives to punishment, and encouragement. The objective of ensuing meetings is to focus on specific techniques and skills.

Adlerians are not the only ones concerned with parent education. Behavior modification and transactional analysis, for example, have originated several books and study methods in this area. Parent Effectiveness Training (PET) depends on a network of helpers to introduce the program in specific areas of the country. Adlerians, however, have a special commitment to meet the need for parent education.

Most Adlerian parent groups use one of several books that are considered especially useful for the education of parents. *Children: The Challenge,* by Dreikurs and Soltz (1964), which is the mainstay of many Adlerian parent study groups and societies, offers unique insights into the psychology of children. Also widely used are *Raising a Responsible Child*, by Dinkmeyer and McKay (1973), and *The Practical Parent*, by Corsini and Painter (1975). *Systematic Training for Effective Parenting* (STEP), by Dinkmeyer and McKay (1976), presents Adlerian parent-education materials in an unusually effective group format.

THE FOUR GOALS OF MISBEHAVIOR

Adlerian parent education—an extension of the Adlerian theory of human development—teaches a pragmatic, systematic theory of child behavior. The first step in parent education is an understanding of the four goals of children's misbehavior. As we mentioned in Chapter 2, Dreikurs (1957) classified all child misbehavior into four categories, each corresponding to the goal of the misbehavior: attention, power, revenge, and display of inadequacy.

The goal of the child's misbehavior is not apparent to most uneducated parents. They often see their children's actions as confusing and annoying and, in extreme cases, as a cause of much frustration and bewilderment. When parents don't understand the purposive nature of behavior in general and of misbehavior in particular, they may resort to extremely damaging measures, such as physical or psychological abuse.

Although parents may at first react to the concept of the four goals with a certain degree of confusion or even skepticism, they eventually learn to identify the goals by using two techniques: their own feelings in response to the misbehavior and the child's response to the parent's chosen behavior. This approach allows the parents to use themselves as accurate indicators of the child's behavior rather than rely solely on the child.

Let's now examine each goal in detail.

Attention

Each of the four goals of misbehavior reflects a degree of discouragement in the child. The first goal, attention, has many positive aspects and is particularly appealing to children as they explore and discover the world around them. "Are you noticing me? Am I still here?" express the purpose of the child's attention-seeking behavior.

> Monica, a 3-year-old, adores her mother and follows her around the house whenever possible. At times she comes up to her mother and unties one of her shoelaces or tugs at her slacks. Although annoyed, the mother generally acknowledges Monica's behavior with a friendly "Hey!" or with a slightly less friendly "Stop it!" depending on how annoying the attention-getting behavior is. Monica is pleased that her mother recognizes her efforts to attract her attention, and she stops such efforts whenever she realizes that her mother doesn't enjoy what she is doing.

In the above example, the mother is *annoyed* by the child's behavior and probably confused by her daughter's seemingly pointless efforts to annoy her. Monica's response to her mother's annoyance is to temporarily stop the behavior for the simple reason that her goal—attention—has been achieved.

Once parents recognize their children's ability to make their own decisions based on their own subjective needs, misbehavior makes as much sense to parents as it does to their children. This is true even in the more "unacceptable" behaviors of power and revenge.

Power

The second goal, power, is sought by children who exaggerate their need to be in control. The power-seeking child is guided by the faulty belief "I can count in this world only if I am in control of everybody else."

Parental reaction to this type of misbehavior is often anger and a feeling of "Who is in charge here, you or me? (It's me, of course, but I wish you would accept that!)." The autocratic parent, a model many have experienced as children or employed in their own parenting, often becomes blinded by power-oriented misbehavior, since such behavior usurps the parent's autocratic rule and challenges his or her authority.

If the parent chooses to struggle with the child to determine who, in fact, is more powerful, a battle may be won while the war is being lost. The child

INCREASED SOCIAL INTEREST ◄──────► DIMINISHED SOCIAL INTEREST

MINOR DISCOURAGEMENT ↓ DEEP DISCOURAGEMENT

USEFUL		USELESS		Child's Action and Attitude / The Message
Active Constructive	*Passive Constructive*	*Active Destructive*	*Passive Destructive*	
"Success" Cute remarks Seeks praise and recognition Performs for attention Stunts Overambition Impression of excellence (may seem to be an "ideal" student, but goal is self-elevation, not learning)	"Charm" Excess pleasantness and charm "Model" child Bright sayings, often not original Little initiative Exaggerated conscientiousness "Southern belle." (are often the "teacher's pets"	"Nuisance" Show-off Clown Restless Talks out of turn "The brat" Makes minor mischief "Walking question mark" (questions not for information but for notoriety) Speech impediments Self-indulgence	"Laziness" Clumsiness, ineptness Lack of ability Lack of stamina Untidiness Fearfulness Bashfulness Anxiety Frivolity Performance and reading difficulties	"Nuisance" Show-off Clown Lazy Puts others in his service, keeps teacher busy. I only count when I am being noticed or served.
A criterion of Social-Emotional Maturing is "Social Interest" Respects the rights of others Is tolerant of others Is interested in others Co-operates with others Encourages others Is courageous Has a true sense of his own worth Has a feeling of belonging Has socially acceptable goals Puts forth genuine effort Meets the needs of the situation Is willing to share rather than "How much can I get?" Thinks of "we" rather than just "I"		"Rebel" Argues and contradicts Openly disobedient Refuses to do work Defies authority Continues forbidden acts Aggressive May be truant	"Stubborn" Extreme laziness Stubbornness Disobedience (passive) Forgetting	"Stubborn" Argues Temper tantrums Tells lies Disobedient Does opposite to instructions Does little or no work Says "If you don't let me do what I want you don't love me." I only count when I am dominating.
		"Vicious" Violent Brutal Steals (Leader of juvenile delinquent gangs)	"Violent passivity" Sullen Defiant	"Vicious" Steals Sullen Defiant Will hurt animals, peers and adults Kicks, bites, scratches Sore loser Potential delinquent I can't be liked and I only count if I can hurt others.
		"Hopeless" Stupidity Indolence Inaptitude (Pseudo feeble-minded) (Inferiority complex)	"Feels hopeless" Stupid actions Inferiority complex Gives up Rarely participates Says "leave me alone, you can't do anything with me." I can't do anything right so I don't ever try. I am no good and incapable.	

Table 12–1. Identifying the goals of children's misbehavior.

Teacher's or Parent's Reaction	The Child's Probable Goal and His "Faulty Logic"	Teacher's or Parent's Corrective Procedures	Teacher's or Parent's Interpretations of Child's Goal to Him (All questions must be asked in a friendly non-judgmental way and NOT at times of conflict.)
To be kept busy by child. To help, remind, scold, coax, and give child extra service. Is delighted by constructive AGM child. Is annoyed. "He occupies too much of my time." "I wish he would leave me alone."	GOAL I. (AGM) ATTENTION-GETTING Child seeks proof of his acceptance and approval. He puts others in his service, seeks help. "Only when people pay attention to me do I feel I have a place."	Give attention when child is not making a bid for it. Ignore the misbehaving child. Be firm. Realize that punishing, rewarding, coaxing, scolding, and giving service are attention.	"Could it be that you want me to notice you?" "Could it be that you want me to do special things for you?" ". . . keep me busy with you?"
Feels leadership of the class is threatened. Feels defeated. "Who is running this class? He or I?" "I won't let him get away with this."	GOAL II. POWER Wants to be the boss. "I only count if you do what I want." "If you don't let me do what I want you don't love me."	Withdraw from the conflict. "Take your sail out of his wind." Recognize and admit that the child has power. Appeal for child's help, enlist his cooperation, give him responsibility.	"Could it be that you want to show me that you can do what you want and no one can stop you?" "Could it be that you want to be the boss?" ". . . get me to do what you want?"
Dislikes the child. Feels deeply hurt. Is outraged by child. Wants to get even. "How can he be so mean?"	GOAL III. REVENGE Tries to hurt as he feels hurt by others. "My only hope is to get even with them."	Avoid punishment. Win the child. Try to convince him that he is liked. Do not become hurt. Enlist a "buddy" for him. Use group encouragement.	"Could it be that you want to hurt me and/or the children?" "Could it be that you want to get even?"
Feels helpless. Doesn't know what to do. "I can't do anything with him!" "I give up!"	GOAL IV. DISPLAY OF INADEQUACY Tries to be left alone. Feels helpless. "I don't want anyone to know how stupid I am."	Avoid discouragement yourself. Don't give up. Show faith in child. Lots of encouragement. Use constructive approach.	"Could it be that you want to be left alone?" ". . . you feel stupid and don't want people to know?"

From "The 'C' Group: Integrating Knowledge and Experience to Change Behavior—An Adlerian Approach to Consultation," by D. Dinkmeyer, *The Counseling Psychologist*, 1971, *3*(1), 63–72. Reprinted by permission.

who loses a power struggle over bedtime, playtime, and other parent/child issues may become even more convinced of the importance of power. Mother or Father showed, by struggling for power, that it is indeed important to be more powerful than the child. So power becomes in the eyes of the child even more valid and attractive.

Revenge

The goal of revenge is the result of a child's feeling hurt, betrayed, or otherwise treated unfairly. Children seeking revenge are trying to get even with the person responsible for the "injustice" they have suffered. Since it is unlikely that a child will be able to retaliate directly—for example, by taking his mother over his knees and spanking her, just as she spanked him —he will try to get even in other ways.

A child is aware of certain misbehaviors that are particularly irritating to his parents and may choose to use one of them, such as abusive language, in revenge. The parent, unaware of the goal of the child's behavior, is likely to be utterly confused by what appears as the child's senseless need to hurt and will often return the revenge in kind, thus perpetuating the cycle.

Display of Inadequacy

If all four goals of misbehavior are expressions of the child's discouragement, the fourth goal manifests an extreme form of discouragement.

> Billy is the youngest of three brothers. On weekends, his father often takes the children to the basketball court, shooting and scrimmaging with the boys. Billy hasn't mastered yet the art of dribbling the ball. Whenever he gets the ball, he quickly passes it away. Soon the weekend comes when Billy doesn't want to go to the court: "It's too hot out. Besides, I'm no good anyway." He has competed but, discouraged at his lack of progress, has decided to give up the pursuit altogether.

Any of the four goals may be used by the child, depending on how he or she chooses to interpret the situation. Misbehavior does not necessarily progress through all four goals, beginning with attention and ending with display of inadequacy. However, they are increasingly discouraged behaviors.

The child's misbehavior will stop when the parent chooses to respond to the situation in a different way. Billy's father, for example, must recognize his son's goal and extreme discouragement with his basketball abilities. While Billy may not necessarily be aware of his own goal, he is aware of its consequences. If he succeeds in convincing his family that he is inadequate, he will be excused from the embarrassment of being the "worst" basketball player—when, in fact, he is only the youngest. The father's corrective strategy for his son's behavior would include encouragement of positive efforts, modification of the games so that Billy can compete on an equal level, and so forth.

PARENT GROUPS UTILIZING BOOKS

A specific nine-session format has been developed for the book group using *Raising a Responsible Child,* by Dinkmeyer and McKay (1973). A typical format for a session will include five basic topics: discussion of the activity and homework from the previous session, discussion of the current reading assignment, a practice exercise, summarization, and reading and other homework assignments for the following session. The leader may rely on prepared questions or allow a discussion of the specific technique presented in that session—for example, natural and logical consequences. Often the leader's most difficult task is to focus the direction of the group's discussion.

Leadership also involves moving the members of the group from a discussion of theory into the practical application of the theory to their own relationships. The practice exercise allows the participants to experience a specific concept or skill, such as reflective listening. Some of the material presented in parent education relates to basic communication skills as they apply to parent/child communication.

Since the group implies a work commitment from each member, the leader must exercise discretion and skill in making sure that each member has the opportunity to share his or her new experiences. Also, the leader may develop a group expectation that reading and trying new skills are necessary activities and that involvement outside the group session is also part of the process. In book-study groups, obtaining commitment can often be a difficult task.

Parent groups utilizing books have functioned successfully across the continent for many years. Their advantage lies in the availability of a single source for reading and referral. The drawback is that this type of group demands inherently motivated participants.

PARENT C-GROUPS AND STEP PROGRAMS

C-Groups

Parent C-groups are an adaptation of teacher C-groups and have similar goals—going beyond the study of principles into the sharing of experiences. An awareness of how we function and of how our attitudes, beliefs, and feelings affect our relationship with our children is an essential element of the C-group. The *C* stands for the many forces that occur in the group, all beginning with the letter *C*.

- *Consultation,* which is provided and received by all the group members.
- *Collaboration* on the concerns of the group members, who work together as equals.
- *Cooperation* among members, so that encouragement can be offered and received.

- *Clarification* of the concepts under discussion, as well as of the members' belief systems and feelings.
- *Confrontation* of the purposes, attitudes, beliefs, and feelings that interfere with the successful modification of the parent/child relationship. If change is to occur, confrontation of old, useless beliefs must take place. A norm of confrontation—not to prove who is right but to share discrepancies and observations—is established by the group leader at the beginning of the group.
- *Confidentiality,* which assures the members' confidence that their concerns will be shared only by the group.
- *Commitment* to the tasks confronting each member, which go beyond reading the assignment and discussing it at the next meeting of the group.
- *Change*—the purpose of involvement in the group—which is assessed by each member in specific terms, from the point of view of both rate and targets.

STEP Programs

The group experience provided by STEP programs is based on the sharing of a parents' handbook that all members receive and study, on large group-discussion charts, and on the utilization of taped exercises. Discussion-guide cards also structure the expectations of sharing, genuineness, and listening. A large leader's manual covers the format for each of the nine sessions that make up the program. The manual also contains additional information on necessary leader skills dealing with problem members and tape scripts. Flexibility can be exercised by the leader, who has the option of sticking to a prepared format or linking together various activities that may be appropriate to the experience of a particular group.

GETTING GROUPS STARTED

The organizers of group programs for parents are often faced with the problem of having more prospective participants than can be accommodated in a single group. When this happens, a waiting list is prepared, or the possibility of creating more than one group is investigated. Groups should not exceed 10 or 12 participants (excluding the leader), in order not to deprive the members of the advantages of the small group. It is important that the participants have children of approximately the same age level, so that the basis of their experiences and challenges is somewhat similar.

STEP programs provide an introductory brochure and an 8-minute tape that outlines the focus of the program and some of the topics to be covered. When proposing a book group or a C-group, the leader will often wish to demonstrate one of the more enticing topics in the program, such as the differences between punishment and logical consequences or the purposes of misbehavior. Parents experience a small part of the program and find that the acknowledging of their need for education is not a sign of weakness but, instead, a sign of intelligent commitment to growth.

This point is especially important and deserves the leader's full attention. In the absence of pat "explanations," parents must deal with the many possible reasons for getting or not getting involved in an education program. Often a parent is stuck with the rationalization "It worked for my parents, so it'll work for me" or some other defensive posture and, yet, realizes that such posture does *not* work. In such cases, the leader must help the person appreciate the basic shift from autocracy to democracy that has taken place and that has left many parents without effective strategies for dealing with their children. It is not that the parents of today lack ability; they lack skills and viable models. It is up to the leader to point out this essential difference, and its implications, to parents in need of help.

GROUP-LEADERSHIP SKILLS

Parent-group leaders must use certain skills to help the group experiences be truly constructive. These skills are similar to those required in other group settings. Yet, because of the universal quality of parenthood, the parents' group experience is unique and calls for unique skills on the part of the leader. The focus is on learning and on the universalizing quality of being a parent.

Structuring. Structuring allows the group to know exactly what will be expected of each member. Meeting times and places, length of sessions, purposes and goals—all will be used to structure the group. Structuring is done during the group's first sessions. As the group progresses, the leader feels free to restructure it as needed. A leader must be constantly aware of what is going on in the group, so that he or she can determine whether the current situation is in the best interest of the group's stated goals and purposes.

Universalizing. Universalizing allows members to become aware that their experiences are similar to those of others. As we said earlier, parenting is one of the most universal experiences and provides many opportunities for the members of a parent group to realize how much they have in common. It is up to the leader to tap this great well of common experiences and to bring the similarities to the surface for everybody's benefit. When one of the members shares a problem with the group, the leader can elicit reactions from the others by asking "Has anyone had a similar difficulty?" or some other open-ended question that invites the participants to share experiences of their own. Often a parent will spontaneously react in agreement, verbally or nonverbally, and the leader may then encourage additional response from that member.

Linking. As you may recall from our discussion in Chapter 9, linking is the process of identifying common elements in the group members' comments. A leader often finds that an idea keeps coming up time and time again—a "theme" of the members' experiences. With parent groups, this may be "Bedtime is usually pretty difficult" or "Sometimes, spanking is really the only way to get the message across." It is important that the leader use these themes in positive ways to link the members during the early stages of the group. Linking and universalizing promote cohesiveness, a feeling of togetherness, and a sense of purpose. Once a theme is expressed and detected, the leader can articulate the common element by making comments such as "I sense that both Tom and Elaine feel concerned about their middle child." The leader can then continue with a brief discussion of the problems common to most middle children and of possible new ways of dealing with such problems.

Feedback. Feedback allows members to hear how they are being perceived by others. Effective feedback refutes the widespread notion that honest feelings and ideas cannot be shared with others. As you know, feedback does not demand change; it simply tells a person how he or she comes across to others. When feedback is received, the person must then decide whether to accept or reject what has been offered. In order to make feedback a tool of growth, the members of the group must be willing to accept the elements of risk inherent in feedback, such as the possibility of rejection or attack, no matter how seldom the risk becomes reality.

Tentative hypotheses. The skill to make tentative hypotheses must also be developed by the members of the group. Questions like "What purpose did the misbehavior serve?" "What did the child do?" "Could it be that the goal was power?" "How did you feel when that happened?" promote the understanding of behavior and the ability to apply such understanding and to explore hunches about misbehavior. The tentative diagnosis also allows the parent to try alternative behaviors.

Focusing on the positive. It may be difficult for parents to see the positive side of their children while they are immersed in a power struggle or other conflict. Yet the parents' ability to focus on the positive and to encourage skills and assets in their child will often help to change the child's behavior. The leader can model encouraging behavior by recognizing the changes and improvements the parents report. Often parents won't see improvement unless others in the group help them realize the changes that have taken place.

Commitment. Leaders must keep group members aware of their commitment to the group. This may be accomplished by reading a particular chapter in the book that the group is using and by practicing a certain skill that has been discussed during the session, such as I-messages or logical consequences. It is important that the person make a commitment to do, not just to try, the new behavior. Attempts based on low expectations will actually inhibit growth in the person. A leader can ask for specific commitments at the end of the session and, at the start of the next session, ask the members to briefly share their experiences with their new behaviors. Commitment may consist of simply agreeing to send one encouraging I-message every day or to spend five minutes with each child every night before bedtime.

Summarizing. The summarization that takes place at the end of the session deals with feelings and ideas as they occurred at any time during the session. It may deal with the content of the meeting or with the commitment each member has made for the upcoming week and may be started by asking each participant to complete the sentence "I learned . . ." This procedure allows the members to share what they have gained during the session and gives the leader the opportunity to correct or clarify any confusion or doubt.

Encouragement. Encouragement is a skill that parents may find especially difficult and confusing. It is often mistaken for praise—a more widespread form of communication in our culture. The essential difference between the two is that praise generally focuses on external things, while encouragement recognizes inherent abilities and positive expectations.

GROUP STAGES

During its life, the parent group will usually experience three stages, each of which requires certain skills on the part of the leader.

1. As the group begins, the leader may be seen as an expert, know-it-all, or problem solver. Participants may have high expectations about improved atmosphere and better relationships with their children, and they may hold the leader accountable for the success or failure of their expectations. Often these expectations are inappropriate and unrealistic and must, therefore, be changed. "Fix the parent" is a more appropriate focus for the group than "fix the child." The leader needs to create exercises or experiences by which members get to know one another. An additional task that the leader must perform in the initial stage is that of aligning the members' goals. Summarization and the expectations the leader expresses for the group can make goals clearer and more attractive.

2. When parents realize that, before their children can change, *they* must change, the group enters a stage of lessened enthusiasm. The members question not only the new ideas that are being presented but the very philosophy of the group's approach. Some of them stand firm in beliefs that the leader·sees as inhibiting change. The leader cannot demand absolute compliance and complete acceptance of the model and ideas presented; yet, one member's discouragement cannot be allowed to spread to other members. Loss of enthusiasm, fear of failure, or embarrassment about current beliefs

may all lead parents to question the value of change. By recognizing the tentative nature of the group's atmosphere, the leader can move on to situations that foster change and positive growth. Parents may unintentionally use their high expectations to discourage progress. Then, the leader must help members set realistic goals and recognize effort.

3. The final stage of group experience is characterized by improved relationships among family members, new skills utilized by the parents, and new ideas about common situations. Change must be accompanied by a willingness to assume responsibility for one's own behavior. All these elements, characteristic of the final stage, are strengthened by the member-to-member communication and encouragement that increase as the group progresses.

GROUP-LEADERSHIP PROBLEMS

Individual members of a parent group may interfere with the purpose and progress of the group. Generally, this is due to *resistance* to the group's direction. A member may be aware or unaware of the intent of the interference, which often surfaces in the form of a "game." The common denominator of these games is manipulative behavior and is expressed in any of the following beliefs and attitudes.

"Try and make me!" places the leader and the parent in opposite corners and challenges the leader to get the parent to comply with the leader's goals. It may take the form of active disapproval of the ideas presented in the group or the form of a direct challenge to the leader to prove his or her firmness. The group leader will always try to communicate respect for the parent's differing opinion but will also stress that the purpose of the group is to study the new ideas and not to make sure that each member accepts all of the ideas being discussed.

"I'll try it" creates an expectancy of failure and/or an inability to commit oneself to the idea. Firm and consistent plans are needed if expectations are to be realized. The leader can avoid this attitude by obtaining a commitment at the end of each session and by encouraging all progress reported at the next session.

"Talkers" may not realize that their stories, opinions, and generally overbearing verbal interventions are actually disrupting the group's progress. In other words, they may not be aware of the game they are playing. Talkers will focus on themselves only and fail to recognize the value of listening to others. Confrontation of the derailing behavior generally occurs in a firm but friendly way, such as "How does your comment tie into the topic of this week—the family meeting?"

"Intellectualizers" would rather discuss the merits of an idea than

explore how the idea applies to their home. Their point of view is often different from that of the group. The leader will recognize the person's point of view but will then move on with the broader goals of the group.

"Yes, but" statements allow people to play on both sides of the net. They seem to accept an idea and, at the same time, offer evidence as to why they are an exception to the rule. A leader might help these members understand the duality of their statements by commenting "I hear *yes*, but doesn't *but* mean *no*? I guess you'll have to make a choice!"

"Prove it" and other monopolizing behaviors demand full attention from leader and members. This game is played when a person believes "I count only when others notice me." A "prover" may ask for facts, research studies, or other evidence that will "sell" that person on the merits of an idea. A leader must not let the group get bogged down in these challenges and, instead, place attention on ideas that are more relevant to the group as a whole.

All games challenge the leader's ability to keep the group on target. Group education is a unique and often unfamiliar experience; leaders must set a tone and offer reasonable positive expectations of change and progress. Parents will express certain beliefs and emit certain behaviors that demonstrate their concept of parent groups. Whatever their concepts, a leader must keep in mind the paramount importance of the movement of the group.

Games may occur because parent education asks parents to change so that their children, in turn, will change certain behaviors. Parenting skills are developed when new behaviors and attitudes are experienced by the parents. The degree of risk can be reduced by setting realistic goals and expectations in the group and by encouraging all efforts.

REFERENCES

Corsini, R., & Painter, G. *The practical parent: The ABC's of child discipline.* New York: Harper & Row, 1975.

Dinkmeyer, D., & McKay, G. *Raising a responsible child.* New York: Simon & Schuster, 1973.

Dinkmeyer, D., & McKay, G. *Systematic training for effective parenting (STEP).* Circle Pines, Minn.: American Guidance Service, 1976.

Dreikurs, R. *Psychology in the classroom.* New York: Harper, 1957.

Dreikurs, R., & Soltz, V. *Children: The challenge.* New York: Hawthorn, 1964.

Shulman, B. The family constellation in personality diagnosis. *Journal of Individual Psychology,* 1962, *18*, 35–47.

CHAPTER 13

FAMILY THERAPY

Family therapy—that is, therapy dealing with the nuclear-family unit as the client—is a product of therapy developments that have occurred during the past two decades.

Adlerians have worked with family dynamics ever since Adler's demonstrations in the child-guidance clinics of Vienna. The Adlerian theory of the role that the family constellation plays in the development of the personality is decidedly different from any psychological approach that emphasizes the triangle of the two parents and the child and that tends to ignore the relationships between the siblings. Furthermore, since Adlerians see all problems as social problems, they assign greater importance to the relationships between people than to what is going on within the individual (interpersonal versus intrapersonal approach).

NATURE AND AIMS

When one or more members of the family are having problems, the whole family unit is affected in one way or another.

A couple with two sons, ages 10 and 14, are experiencing severe marital problems. The mother has developed profound depression with marked suicidal tendencies necessitating hospitalization. Before she is ready for discharge, the father, too, requires hospitalization for his severe psychosomatic disorders. When the entire family is seen together, it becomes apparent that these disruptions have been and still are a major source of concern for the children. The 10-year-old boy is very worried that his parents will get divorced. The 14-year-old boy is keeping his feelings to himself; he has become more and more socially withdrawn and shows a tendency toward obesity.

In its most traditional form, family therapy is based on the assumption that chronic family conflict involves, in one way or another, all the members of a family and is responsible for the problems of one or more individuals within the family group. Therefore, family therapy should include all the members of a family. Because of the Adlerian holistic approach, the object of treatment is a particular group of people who are currently forming an indivisible unit—a unique whole—called the family.

Although family therapy may result in changes in the personal life style of the various family members, such change is not the primary goal. Adlerian family therapy is aimed at teaching a group of people how to better deal with one another and how to live together as social equals. This aim is accomplished by sharing with the family group the principles of democratic conflict resolution, by reorienting the family members away from destructive modes of communication, and, most importantly, by teaching all members of the family to be agents of encouragement.

THE FAMILY THERAPIST

Although family therapists may come from a variety of disciplines, the complexity of family therapy necessitates that therapists be fully qualified professionals in their field, with considerable additional training in working with the family as a unit. If the therapy involves more than one therapist, at least one of them must have these qualifications.

We (the authors) decry the current tendency on the part of some counselors to present themselves as family therapists, merely because they sit down with the entire family. Family therapy is perhaps the most demanding of all the educational therapies, requiring broad life experiences on the part of the therapist as well as specialized training. Although not essential, it is helpful, for example, if the family therapist has also had the experience of being a parent.

Family therapists must walk a very tight rope. Empathy and concern are essential elements of the therapeutic process, but so is the capacity to maintain enough psychological distance to be effective and avoid being pulled into a destructive family situation. A family in trouble tends to divide into factions. The therapist or therapists often feel a pressure toward identifying or siding with one or the other faction. When there are two therapists, one therapist can, for a short time, be more understanding of one family member or one subgroup within the family, *if* the other therapist is able to remain somewhat aloof. But this kind of balance cannot persist for any length of time. For example, if one therapist becomes too understanding of the plight of an adolescent seeking independence from the family, the parents may consciously or unconsciously torpedo the therapy in every possible way in order to maintain (or reestablish) the old balance and prevent the adolescent's move toward autonomy.

STRUCTURE

Once family therapy has been agreed upon as the treatment of choice, initial sessions should, if at all possible, include all members of the family. After the entire family has been seen together as a unit, in subsequent sessions a decision may be reached to exclude certain members—for example, the very young.

Families often raise the question as to whether sessions could be held in the family home. While certain kinds of information can be obtained only with a "house call," in general therapists are strategically in a much better position working on their own turf, so to speak. If the father in the family, for example, is sitting in *his* own chair, drinking sherry and smoking a cigar, while the therapists are situated in less comfortable positions—often in a place from which it is difficult for them to see or hear all family members—the effectiveness of therapy is significantly reduced by both psychological and physical factors. The ideal location for family therapy is a room large enough to seat all members, preferably in equal-sized chairs, in a circle, without any distraction of smoking, refreshments, and so forth. This can, of course, present some complicated logistic problems.

Family members often ask early in the course of therapy about prognosis, a question that most of the time also refers to the duration of therapy. We believe that giving a prognosis is mischief. If we give a good prognosis, some family members may feel constrained to prove that we are wrong. If we give a bad prognosis, the prognosis is often interpreted as an indication that we don't think we can be helpful. And, if we don't think we can be helpful we probably can't. As to duration, we usually ask the family to agree to meet five or six times and then reevaluate the situation at the end of that period. Sometimes more definite agreements are useful.

> A woman was quite doubtful whether she wanted to stay married to her husband, because she felt that she was always being manipulated by him. From time to time, he would show some temporary improvement, but his wife didn't feel that she could trust his long-range commitment to their marriage. The husband acknowledged that she was right as far as the past was concerned. However, he seemed to realize that he was likely to lose his wife and children if he didn't change his ways and wanted to do something about it.
>
> Family therapy was recommended, and the couple reached an

agreement to hold off on any decision about their marriage until they had been in therapy for six months. This agreement provided a very important sense of stability for the children, who otherwise might have felt a great deal of concern as to whether their parents were going to stay married or not. This concern might also have kept them from being as deeply involved in family therapy as they were capable of being.

Since family therapy is in fact a specialized form of group therapy, the knowledge that has been gained about optimal duration of sessions for groups is applicable to families as well. Sessions of less than one and a half hours are generally not as effective. Sessions that last beyond two or two and a half hours invite disruption on the part of some family members and fatigue on the part of the therapists. Ideally, family-therapy sessions should be held weekly to give the members of the family time to process what has gone on during the session and to carry out the specific recommendations they have received from the therapists. At least in the early stages, meeting with the family less often than every other week is apt to break up the continuity of therapy and make each new session almost a separate experience.

MULTIPLE THERAPY

Probably in no other form of therapy is the concept of multiple therapy (that is, therapy conducted by more than one therapist) so important as in family therapy. If the family is any larger than the parents and one child, it is virtually impossible for a single therapist to be both an active participant and an acute observer of all the verbal and nonverbal communication that goes on.

Ideally, cotherapists should represent both sexes, but that is a point of limited importance. What is truly important is whether the cotherapists strike the family as people who communicate well and clearly and who show mutual respect. This does not mean that it is inappropriate for the cotherapists to disagree. In fact, such an experience provides an opportunity to demonstrate to the family that people can disagree without disastrous consequences and can resolve their disagreements peacefully and cooperatively.

Pitfalls to Watch For

Preconceptions. For the most part, it is desirable that the cotherapists discuss the various issues concerning the therapeutic process in the presence of the family. This allows the family members to take advantage of and learn from the therapists' discussions. As with any other form of group therapy, it is important that the therapists do not begin the session with any preconceptions of what should happen. It is impertinent for the therapists to try to decide in advance what is most important to the family at the moment and how it should be best approached.

Scapegoating. Many families "elect" one of their members to be the scapegoat, or symptom bearer, for the family's troubles. For example, often a child is identified as "the problem." It is one way for the other family members to avoid looking at themselves and facing the part they play in the problems they have.

> Betty, 14 years old, had been a problem to her parents "from the day she was born." Now she was failing in school, experimenting with drugs, and associating with unsuitable companions. She was indignant that her mother wouldn't permit her to go to another city and visit her 19-year-old boyfriend, who was in prison. Her younger sister, Sally, was sweetness and light and had goodness oozing from every pore. Father and Mother insisted that theirs was the best marriage ever. During family-therapy sessions, all members converged on Betty, repeatedly implying in one way or another that the family would be just fine if it weren't for Betty's bad behavior. Sally was seemingly genuinely concerned about her sister but, at the same time, judgmental. The therapists were unable to get parents and sister "off Betty's case," since these people, totally unwilling to look at the role they played in the family problems, insisted on scapegoating Betty.
>
> After hospitalization and several more family sessions, Betty disappeared and no one heard from her again. If the therapists had known in advance the seriousness of Betty's situation and the unwillingness of the family to stop scapegoating her, they might have arranged for Betty to be placed in a foster home or in a group home.

Avoidance of the here and now. Another reason for scapegoating—or, for that matter, for any other kind of fault finding or standing in judgment—is the common need to avoid the here and now. By recounting in detail the "facts" of the past, including all of the injustices each of them has suffered, the family members avoid dealing with themselves and one another in the present. Other families avoid the present by being future oriented. Yet in other families, some members have become highly skilled at minding the business of other members while neglecting their own problems. Here is an example.

> At the first family-therapy session, Mother began by saying that Joan, 13, was not going to talk. Joan actually sat behind her vivacious little sister, Karen. When Joan was asked a question, Karen would answer for her. When Karen talked about herself and described how she felt, her father listened with obvious impatience, literally jumping up and down on his chair, until he could give an edited version of what Karen had said, explaining how Karen really felt and why she felt that way. Then, when Father expressed his disapproval of Mother's behavior at the country club, he was interrupted half-way through by her. His wife insisted that she knew what had really happened and that he wasn't speaking for himself but, rather, was repeating his mother's comments about her daughter-in-law. At home, the story was the same—each person interfer-

ing all the time with the others and injecting himself or herself in the business of other family members. There were constant criticism, bickering, and marked defensiveness on the part of all the family members.

When therapists are faced with a family like the one in the example above, they have to be firm, insisting that each person speak for himself or herself. Another situation often encountered in family therapy is the attempt by one or more family members to lead the discussion away from those present and talk instead of family members who are not present. Also, as we mentioned earlier, family members are often adept at taking sides, and they will try to involve the therapist in the family feud. Many children in troubled families have become highly skilled at the divide-and-conquer process with their own parents and will try out this technique with therapists, too.

Pity. It is essential that the therapists recognize and avoid the pitfall of pity. Feeling sorry for a person is a very discouraging, demeaning way to treat another human being.

Johnny, 5 years old and the smallest in his kindergarten class, had not had a particularly good year. His teacher recommended that he repeat kindergarten. In a family-therapy session, it became apparent that Mother felt terribly sorry for Johnny, believing that his whole future life would be blighted by his present failure in school. In pursuing this subject further, the therapist discovered that Mother, too, had been held back while in school, that she had found this a source of constant discouragement, and that she was now taking Johnny's "failure" as a personal failure. When she learned to stop feeling sorry for Johnny, she discovered that her son had thought the whole situation through and had come to the conclusion that he would be better off if he could spend another year in kindergarten.

GOALS OF THERAPY

The overall goal of family therapy can be simply stated as the therapists working themselves out of their job by teaching the family to communicate accurately, honestly, and openly, with each member speaking for himself/herself about his/her own ideas and feelings. This overall goal is the outcome of the successful accomplishment of several specific goals. One of them is to teach the family members to resolve their own conflicts by relying on the principles of (1) manifesting mutual respect, (2) pinpointing the issue, (3) reaching a new agreement, and (4) participating responsibly in decision making.

As we said earlier, it is important for the parents to learn to recognize the mistaken goals of their children's misbehavior. However, the process of learning is not an easy one and may be more efficiently carried out in a family-education center or in a parent study group. Another goal of family therapy is to help the members of the family learn to be responsible for their own behavior and to become cooperative and contributing parts of the family group. In order to have a family that operates in a democratic fashion, parents often have to make major adjustments in their roles. Sometimes such adjustments cannot be made in family sessions but require individual sessions, group therapy for one or both parents, or marital therapy. Family therapists should not assume that all problems can be best handled by dealing with the entire family as a group.

Family therapy is used when the degree of conflict or the duration of the problems is such that more intense work is necessary than could be done, for example, in the family-education center. However, family therapy can be enhanced if the family attends, at the same time, a family-education center, or if the parents participate in a parent study group. Family therapy is also enhanced when the parents read material that can help them carry out their tasks more successfully. Such material would include, for example, *The Practical Parent,* by Corsini and Painter (1975), *Raising a Responsible Child,* by Dinkmeyer and McKay (1973), or *Children: The Challenge,* by Dreikurs and Soltz (1964). Private family therapy is more often used in situations involving delicate personal problems, such as incest.

Resistance

We speak of resistance when there is a difference between the goals of the family and those set forth by the therapist or a difference between the goals of different members or groups within the family. When resistance is encountered, it must be dealt with immediately.

One of the most effective ways to overcome resistance and get things moving again is to add another ingredient to the therapeutic process. This ingredient can be an additional therapist or other family members who are not locked into the nuclear-family system or into the new system that has developed in therapy and that includes the therapists.

If there is disagreement concerning goals and if the addition of new elements to the therapeutic process doesn't help, termination of therapy may be contemplated and discussed. Termination must always be an option that is openly discussed. Therefore, it is essential that the therapist not be so identified with the counseling process that termination becomes a personal issue.

The Role of Absent Members

With some complicated family systems—for example, with blended families[1]—often there are absent members who, although never physi-

---

[1]A blended family is a family in which both partners bring children from a previous marriage into the new marriage.

cally incorporated in the family-therapy sessions, cannot be ignored as significant influences.

> A woman lost her husband through death and married a widower. With her children and his children under the same roof, a complicated family system developed. He studiously avoided talking about his first wife, while she, even after several years, felt herself a stranger in another woman's home. If this family had undergone therapy, the man's first wife would have had to have been discussed because of her continuing influence on the various members of the family.

> In another family, one child with extremely severe behavior problems required institutionalization. The father maintained close contact with his son. The mother, instead, feared the boy and was unwilling to discuss the possibility of his return into the family. The other children were pulled first in one direction and then in the other, thus showing how deeply this absent member was still affecting the everyday life of the family.

In family therapy, we usually think of two generations—parents and children. However, in some instances, three or even four generations have been successfully incorporated in family therapy.

> In one family, the paternal grandfather had been living with his son and daughter-in-law from the day of their marriage. The wife resented every moment of his presence, which she considered a heavy burden. According to her husband, she consistently lined up the children against their grandfather. Successful therapy for this family obviously would have required consideration of the role of the grandfather.

FAMILY-EDUCATION CENTERS

In the family-education centers, counseling is conducted in public. Volunteer (demonstration) families are interviewed by the co-counselors in front of an audience who participates in the counseling process. As in private therapy, specific behaviors are identified and precise recommendations are offered.

Goals and Organization

The purpose of a family-education center is threefold: (1) to disseminate basic mental-health principles to a large audience (actually, this is a form of community education); (2) to provide a resource for troubled families; and (3) to train parents, teachers, and other people to work more effectively with children. Family-education centers may be housed in hospitals, churches, schools, or other public buildings.

Funding sources are varied, but in many centers much of the work is done by volunteers. The staff of a family-education center includes the director or codirectors, who are professionals in the mental-health field and who have had extensive additional training and experience with the Adlerian model. In some communities, however, lay people have been trained to direct family-education centers under professional supervision. Other staff usually includes a coordinator, an intake worker, a recorder, and the director and staff members of the activity center.

The focus of the family-education center is twofold: (1) the counseling center, where the volunteer families are interviewed with the participation of an audience, and (2) the activity center, where children and adolescents can be engaged in a variety of educational activities if they choose not to be in the audience of the counseling center. The members of the staff of the activity center are specifically trained to observe children and to present their observations for the benefit of the parents and counselors in the counseling center.

In most family-education centers, admission is free. Although the audience members are encouraged to participate in the counseling process by offering suggestions and encouragement, participants can be as involved or uninvolved as they choose. The volunteer families that are counseled function as coeducators. They actually help the co-counselors teach Adlerian principles to the larger group through the interview process. The volunteer families will have been in the audience for several weeks before becoming a demonstration family. Also, they (usually) will have learned basic Adlerian principles of child rearing. The co-counselors vigorously ensure that, no matter how great the participation of the audience may be, the family is in no way put on the spot.

A counseling session with a family often ends with the audience participating in an encouragement session. The members of the audience are invited to give their honest reaction to the family regarding the family's strengths and assets they appreciate. They feed back the positive things they see about the family relationship and about the individuals within the family. Volunteer families are usually asked to return for follow-up sessions during which they describe their successes and failures with the techniques and principles they have learned. The interview in the center is enhanced by reports from the activity center, from the children's school(s), from the family physician, and from any other professional who is working with the family.

Adolescents are invited to attend the education center to be interviewed, even if their parents are unwilling to participate. When parents are present, adolescents and parents are usually interviewed together. If young children are involved, the co-counselors generally talk with the parents first. Some tentative agreement is reached about one or two family problems that can reasonably be tackled through specific recommendations during the coming week. Then the children are interviewed separately and briefly and informed of their parents' concern. Counselors, after validating the impression of the children's goals, will tell the children what recommendations have been given to their parents. The children are then dismissed to go back to the activity center while the activity-center staff member reports his or her observations.

As the counseling proceeds and the parents become aware of the goals of their children's misbehavior, they learn how to deal with it—what to do and what *not* to do. In other words, they learn what kinds of responses will reinforce the children's mistaken beliefs and what they should do to avoid them. They learn methods that allow for a reduction of conflict and for more cooperation and harmony. For instance, when power conflicts are obvious, parents learn to sidestep conflict often by removing themselves physically. If a child is displaying a temper tantrum, the parents may follow the recommendation to retire to the bathroom until the child's tantrum subsides. The counselors also teach the fallacies of reward and punishment and how to use, instead, the principles of natural and logical consequences.

After parents have learned to get out of the power struggles with their children, the use of natural and logical consequences is introduced. As family conflict diminishes, regularly scheduled family-council meetings are recommended as a laboratory for democratic decision making, problem solving, and conflict resolution. With family-council meetings, parents learn to teach responsibility by sharing responsibility, and children learn more self-reliance and greater self-esteem. An important result is that both parents and children learn to encourage one another.

A Practical Example

Here is an example of a session at a family-education center.

The Jones family, which consists of father, mother, and two daughters, aged 8 and 10, sit together on the stage. Behind them is a blackboard showing their names, ages, and how many years the parents have been married. The co-counselors sit on either side of the family, and one counselor writes information on the blackboard as it becomes available. Such information concerns, for example, how the family conducts family-council meetings (see Chapter 14), what is discussed at these meetings, who is the facilitator, what the focus of the week is, how decisions are made, and how often these meetings take place. The audience is presented with the dynamics of the family and sees the family members as they are. There are candidness and openness, and the audience, rather than just observing the family, actually shares the educational experience with them. This is accomplished by the co-counselors turning to the audience for encouragement, questions, and support.

"What do you appreciate about the Joneses?" the counselor asks.

"They are friendly people."

"They check things out with each other. They are considerate of each other."

"They care about one another."
"They look at their family life as experimental and changing."
"They have much going for them"

Roles and Principles

The family-education center is an example of primary mental-health care. Three groups can be discerned in the center: (1) the counselors and the family being interviewed, (2) the audience, and (3) the larger community that is reached indirectly through the people attending the center. Thus the counselors are able to reach many more people than they could by talking with individual families. This preventive aspect and the aspect of community outreach and community education have particularly interested a number of hospitals as a way of enlarging their circle of care.

Besides being a community resource, the family-education center is also a referral agent for other community agencies. For example, a number of juvenile-court systems have utilized family-education centers as one resource in a comprehensive treatment program for families in which one of the children was a juvenile delinquent.

All the Adlerian approaches to the family are based on the assumption that parenthood is a very important profession for which very few people are adequately prepared. Another cornerstone of the Adlerian view is the need for a new tradition in child rearing, since most parents are the products of autocratic child rearing. When the parents choose to relate differently to their children, they often have a tendency to swing in the opposite direction and be permissive. Adlerians believe in mutual respect. If parents are overpowering their children, then they are not respecting the children. If parents are doormats for their children, then they are not respecting themselves. The Adlerian model for child rearing—a democratic model based on principles of cooperation, responsibility, respect for order, mutual respect, and social equality—is the guiding principle of the family-education center.

In North America today, the family exists in many forms. It has been estimated that, in the near future, nearly one out of five children will be born to unwed adolescent mothers. The mythical "extended" family is rarely seen, and the ongoing, monogamous nuclear family can be considered almost an alternate life style. About 50% of the mothers with children between the ages of 6 and 16 are in the working force. Nearly one-half of the children growing up in our society will spend a significant amount of time in a one-parent family. There are literally dozens of alternate life styles under experimentation—triads, communes, and tribes, just to name a few. Therefore, family theory and practice in 1978 must (almost) be tailor-made for the particular family in question. The Adlerian "model of man" is universal enough to cut across all types of relationships. All parents, regardless of how they go about trying to achieve intimacy and overcome loneliness, can learn more effective ways of dealing with their children.

REFERENCES

Corsini, R., & Painter, G. *The practical parent: The ABC's of child discipline*. New York: Harper & Row, 1975.

Dinkmeyer, D., & McKay, G. *Raising a responsible child*. New York: Simon & Schuster, 1973.

Dreikurs, R., & Soltz, V. *Children: The challenge*. New York: Hawthorn, 1964.

CHAPTER 14

MARRIAGE COUNSELING

In marriage counseling, the relationship is the client. It is, therefore, essential, that both parties in the relationship participate in the counseling process. In the authors' experience, counseling one marriage partner is counseling for divorce.

The marriage relationship must be worked at constantly and nurtured like a tender plant. Because of the changes that are occurring in the traditional patterns of sex-role behaviors in our society, this may be truer today than it was in the past. The changing roles of men and women and the concomitant reduction of sex-role expectations are the source of a number of special kinds of problems experienced by many couples today.

The shift toward equality between the marriage partners began in the United States during the Great Depression, when high unemployment among men made it necessary for the woman to become the breadwinner in the family. The shift became even more pronounced during World War II, as thousands of women moved into the labor force and discovered that they no longer had to be second-class citizens controlled by their husbands.

Just as husbands lost their control over their wives, parents lost their control over their children. As we saw earlier, authoritarianism gave way to increasingly equalitarian relationships between parents and children. The old ways of relating in a marriage and in a family were gone forever. Couples were faced with the necessity of trying to live together in a relationship of equality for which they had no background or training. In the 1960s, the changing nature of the marital relationship was accentuated first by the civil-rights movement and then by the women's movement.

These changes are still going on, and the problems that they generate for the marriage partners, as well as for the relationship, are still unresolved. The element of change is a potential source of conflict in any intimate relationship. Partners change but rarely in tandem. Consequently, the problems of differential growth in intimate relationships are quite special. Birth control now gives both parties, but particularly the woman, much greater freedom. By rejecting their subservient role of the past, women have also rejected the concept that their own growth and development as persons—rather than just as wives —have no validity or, at best, are of secondary importance when compared to the success of the marriage. Many men today still don't know how to function in a relationship other than as the "superior male." These men are baffled at their wives' demands for an equalitarian relationship, self-actualization, and sexual satisfaction.

THE INITIAL CONTACT

As we said earlier, it is essential that both marriage partners participate in the counseling process. Therefore, when husband or wife gets in touch with the marriage counselor, the counselor will always try to see both parties together. In the first interview, the focus is on establishing an effective counseling relationship and on developing a working contract.

Establishing the Counseling Relationship

The establishing of an effective relationship may require varying amounts of time and effort. For people who have never had a trusting relationship with anyone, establishing such a relationship may take considerable time. In some cases, it is easier for one partner to become involved in the counseling relationship than for the other. But, in general, establishing a relationship is easiest when the counselor can demonstrate to both partners that he or she understands their problems. To do so, the Adlerian counselor uses a number of shortcuts that permit the partners to see that some aspects of their personalities or some characteristics of their relationship make sense to him or her.

One of the most reliable methods involves pinpointing each partner's number-one priority (the use of this technique in marriage counseling is presented in more detail later in the chapter). When a wife with a priority of pleasing becomes aware of such priority, she also realizes the price she pays for it—self-neglect, reduced personal growth, and a grossly exaggerated significance of rejection. She sees, often for the first time, that she takes her husband's rather innocuous behavior as personal rejection, and she understands why. If the husband's number-one priority is control, he may, for the first time, understand how he brings about distance from others. This new awareness and the concomitant feelings of being understood and accepted make an effective therapeutic relationship much more likely.

> *Counselor:* I can't entirely explain it, but I find myself feeling somewhat annoyed with you, John.
>
> *John:* Is it something I'm doing?
>
> *Counselor:* No, not really *doing*. I think it has something to do with your number-one priority. I'd guess that your priority is comfort. If that is so, the more you strive for comfort, the less productive you're likely to become. The price people pay for a number-one priority of comfort is reduced productivity. I suppose my feeling annoyed has to do with my puritan work ethic.
>
> *John:* You're perfectly right. I set goals for myself, but I never seem to accomplish as much as I want to.
>
> *Counselor* (to wife): Do you find it difficult to pin John down—to get him to deal with issues?
>
> *Beverly:* I certainly do. How can you tell?
>
> *Counselor:* Many people with a number-one priority of comfort behave like artful dodgers. The worst thing for them is to feel trapped. I think John has become very competent at avoiding conflict with you, which is a way of avoiding stress for himself.
>
> *Beverly:* Well, I certainly appreciate that someone else understands what a big problem that is for me.

> *Counselor:* I think that your number-one priority is pleasing.
>
> *Julie:* You're probably right. If I'm not pretty sure that what I'm about to do will be accepted, I'm likely to pull back.
>
> *Counselor:* And, if Bob fails to give you approval, that's a personal rejection.

Developing a Working Contract

The establishment of a working contract requires, first of all, a clear indication on the part of the counselor that there is hope for the marriage. It is the Adlerian position that, as long as people are alive, they have a potential for growth. It is also the Adlerian position that any couple can, if their relationship is one of mutual respect and cooperation, work their difficulties out, regardless of how complicated and profound their problems may be.

After asking each partner to explain briefly why they are seeking counseling, we ask, early in the interview, whether they want to stay married. If the answer is affirmative, we propose personal life-style formulations before we look at the present problems in the relationship. If one or both partners are doubtful, we might still propose that they hold off any decision making until we have completed the life-style formulation.

Even if both parties agree that they don't want to stay married, we still offer to formulate their life styles. If they agree, the partners may learn something from the dissolution of their marriage that may reduce the likelihood of their repeating the same process over again with another partner. If one partner wants to stay married and the other does not, we again suggest life-style formulations, asking the partner who doesn't want to remain married to hold off on any action until we have completed that aspect of the counseling process. There are times, of course, when a couple will come in for counseling as a final gesture to show that they have done everything they can do, but, in fact, they have already made up their minds not to remain married.

We prefer to establish a definite contract that has an end point as well as a clearly defined initial arrangement. Such arrangement usually entails five or six hours of counseling—enough time to complete the formulation of the life style for each partner. At the end of that period, it is appropriate to renegotiate the contract. Sometimes the partners will feel that, for the moment, that's as far as they want to go. In other instances, the partners feel that they would like to spend some time working on their relationship alone and then come back later. Others, after completing the life-style formulation, want to continue working with the counselor on the relationship. If, at the end of the life-style formulation, it becomes clear that one partner needs ongoing individual therapy, an agreement is reached to resume the marriage counseling with both parties at a later date.

The Absent Spouse

Sometimes a person will come in alone, complaining about the marriage and protesting vigorously that his or her partner will not join in marriage counseling. Our strategy in such cases is to ask immediately for permission to get in touch with the reluctant spouse, which is often done by telephone on the spot. In our experience, almost invariably the other spouse agrees to come in and frequently is very cooperative.

After hearing about the absent spouse, we are often amazed to see how different he/she turns out to be from the description we had been given. We know, of course, that what we are hearing is a biased account and that, if the partner we are interviewing is angry and intolerant, we will hear mostly about his/her spouse's bad points. This is often accompanied by the person's blindness about his/her own defects. It is most important, in order to win the cooperation of a reluctant spouse, to point out that only he/she can speak for himself/herself and that we would truly like to hear what he/she has to say. Speaking to only one spouse about a marriage relationship is like seeing two actors on the stage but hearing only one of them deliver his/her lines.

> A man was referred to us by his family physician. His complaint was premature ejaculation. He claimed that his problem was a medical problem and that his wife had nothing to do with it. He also repeatedly refused to let us get in touch with his wife. A life-style formulation was completed, and, as a trusting relationship was established, we were finally able, with his permission, to get in touch with his wife and invite her to join us.

When she came in (willingly), she told, to her husband's surprise, quite a different story. He had never mentioned, for example, that he had left home several times, threatening divorce. Also, it became obvious in the course of the session that he didn't know the depth of her affection and her commitment to their marriage. A personal life style of the wife was completed in her husband's presence. Marriage counseling was initiated. Special attention was paid to the symptom of premature ejaculation, which we saw as a problem that originated from the marital relationship and that, therefore, had to be solved through the spouses' joint efforts. After a relatively short period of counseling, the couple had resolved their differences enough to want to keep working at their marriage.

Individual and Family Counseling

Individual counseling is sometimes indicated as part of the marriage-counseling process. However, those problems of the individual that are essentially unrelated to the marital relationship must be kept separate from those that are indeed related to it. Even though one partner may seem to need more intensive individual work, it is important to stay away from the view that he or she is "the problem" in the marriage. Examples of problems that may be better dealt with individually rather than jointly include unresolved grief over the loss of a parent, difficulty in relating to persons of the same sex, problems related to discovering and mobilizing one's own strengths (which may require vocational or academic counseling), psychosomatic complaints, and problems related to chronic medical conditions.

In family counseling, it often becomes apparent that the problems of the family are essentially problems between the spouses and that the entire family will not run smoothly until husband and wife have worked out their differences. At that point, the family counselor will often recommend marriage counseling, which sometimes can be done concurrently with family-counseling sessions. At other times, the counseling of the family is temporarily discontinued until marriage counseling has been completed.

USE OF THE LIFE STYLE IN MARRIAGE COUNSELING

Assessment

Life-style assessments are conducted in the presence of both partners whenever possible. As we pointed out in Chapter 6, the recreation of a style of living (Adler, 1958) is based on a fairly specific method of data collection (see life-style forms in Appendix A). The family-constellation is diagrammed. It includes brief descriptions of each member of the family of origin, with particular attention to all the parental figures who were influential in the formative years, as well as deceased siblings and other children who were close enough to the person to be considered like siblings. When this inquiry is carried out in the presence of the partner, he/she may learn for the first time some very significant elements in the partner's childhood. The nonparticipating partner is asked to withhold comments at this stage. The reason is that we're trying to get into the subjective world of the person whose life style is being formulated and the partner cannot contribute to our understanding, since he/she wasn't there. But, at the same time, the partner is urged to make guesses to himself/herself, checking out his/her own psychological sensitivity to and knowledge of his/her partner's personality structure. Of course, sometimes the partner knows the spouse's parents and/or siblings and, in that case, can occasionally clear up confusing material for the counselor. It is important, however, that the counselor pay attention to the person whose life style is being formulated and not be unduly influenced by whatever the other partner may have to say.

It's worth repeating that the formulation of the life style is meant to provide us with an understanding of the individual's subjectivity, and, therefore, there are no "right answers." We are merely looking for overall patterns and trying to get some idea of this individual's place in the family. Brief inquiries are made into physical, sexual, and social development and educational and occupational experience. Here, too, the partner often learns significant new things about his/her spouse, which perhaps had never been discussed before. In the area of sexual development, for example, a spouse may learn "secrets" that can be very upsetting.

Bess: Well, I want you to know that we were up all night after our last session.

Harold: Yes, it was a very difficult time, and I don't know whether we have everything worked out yet.

Counselor: What came up that was so disturbing? The information about Harold's early sex life?

Bess: That's it. I was so sure that I had married an inexperienced man—a man that was, well, pure. And, then, to find that he had had all that sexual experience in the service . . .

Harold: It wasn't that much. Only a few one-night stands. I never saw any reason to mention it.

The next part of the data collection is not specifically related to the formulation of the life style but is, instead, a way of learning how each partner evaluates himself/herself and the spouse in the various life-task areas. For this purpose, Adler's three life tasks of love, friendship, and work have been broken down into subdivisions, as follows: worker, friend, lover, spouse, relating to the other sex, getting along with oneself, search for meaning, relating to members of the same sex, parent and player (see life-style forms in Appendix A). The person is presented with a scale of 1 to 5 (1 being the highest rating) and asked to rate himself/herself, for example, as a worker. The question we ask is "How responsibly are you attending to the task of work at this point in your life?'' After the person has asked himself/herself and has predicted how his/her partner will rate him/her, the partner is asked to give his/her rating of the person, using the same procedure. This is a way of bringing the spouse back into the counseling process, after he/she has been involved only passively for some time. This "taking a temperature of the marriage" often pinpoints trouble areas in the relationship or areas that need to be more fully explored. The counselor gets some idea of how well the partners know themselves and each other and is provided a base reading that can be referred to later on to evaluate the success of the therapy.

Next, early-childhood recollections and dreams are recorded verbatim. Both reveal subjective themes and melodies in a person's self-view and show how a person finds his/her place in life. Both partners are also asked to recall a song, a fairy tale, a nursery rhyme, a poem, a character from the Bible, a biblical story, a television show, a radio show, and a movie that made a special impression on them when they were children and to describe what impressed them about each item.

The counselor summarizes the data that have been collected and interprets the early-childhood recollections and dreams. After the counselor has listed the primary themes that have emerged (the individual convictions and guidelines about who one is, what life is, what one's expectations are, and what ethical considerations one operates with), both partners and the counselor cooperate in listing the strengths of the person who is having his/her life style formulated. Almost invariably, by the time the formulation of the personal life style has been completed, the individual's number-one priority has clearly emerged.

Summarizing the Data

In our experience, the best way of summarizing the data is by dictating a summary of the material into a dictaphone or tape recorder. Some individuals seem to find a special value in hearing their own words repeated back to them in the process of dictating the summary. For example, one man described his parents' marital relationship as "tragic." When this comment was dictated in the summary, the man first disavowed the statement and then was amazed to discover that those were his own words, recorded verbatim by the counselor. He reconsidered and, as is often the case, discovered that his spontaneous comment was more accurate than any one that he might have carefully thought out. It is as if the words were now depersonalized and the individual could "look at them" and "see them" in a different light.

When formulations are completed and typed, each partner receives a copy. At the session following the summary, the clients are asked to read their summary aloud. The counselor pays particular attention to word slips and to what the reader emphasizes and omits; there is always an opportunity to stop and clarify.

Meshing of the Life Styles

"Meshing of the life styles" refers to the process of learning about the relationship as the life styles of both partners become known. "We fell in love" people often say when asked why they decided to get married. The acknowledgment that one chooses the direction of one's love in accordance with one's fundamental purposes makes it possible to accept the fact that one also decides whether or not to fall in love. Similarly, "we are not in love" is often given as a reason for separation or divorce.

Married people can discover that love is a byproduct of a cooperative relationship. Mates are chosen on the basis of much more knowledge than we are aware of at the conscious level. We tend to choose someone who will treat us as we expect to be treated. We accept someone as an intimate other not on the basis of common sense but on the basis of our private logic—as a person who offers us "an opportunity to realize our personal patterns, who responds to our outlook and conception of life, who permits us to continue or to revive plans which we have carried since childhood. We even play a very important part in evoking and stimulating in the other precisely the behavior which we expect and need" (Dreikurs, 1946, pp. 68–69).

Couples who have lived together for some time discover that the very attributes that attracted them in the first place may later create dissonance. A quiet man who was attracted to a gregarious woman may complain later that "she never wants to leave the party." A passive woman who was attracted to an aggressive man may later complain that he wants to make all the decisions.

As we look at the two life styles together, we always find some areas of agreement. For example, both husband and wife may have as part of their personality styles what Adler called the "masculine protest"—that is, a tendency to think that this is a man's world and that men have a better deal, are more important, have more power, and perhaps are more dangerous than women. In the case of the husband, this attitude would result in beliefs such as "I must be a real man"; with the wife, in beliefs such as "I'm only a woman." Another couple may agree, instead, that life must be exciting and dramatic. We may also find sharp differences in how the partners view life and in what expectations they have of other people. Naturally, if people were psychologically identical twins, they wouldn't get married in the first place. Ultimately, the goal of marriage counseling is for the couple to realize how much tolerance there is for individual differences within the relationship.

Often the process of comparing the life styles and pointing out the differences clarifies for the first time why the partners see life so differently. The differences can add great richness to the relationship, or they can be a source of conflict.

Ruth and Jim consulted a counselor primarily because of Ruth's paranoid psychosis. She was constantly plagued with delusions and hallucinations. For example, she got "special messages" on television and billboards, and she believed that her husband was plotting to kill her and their children. The counselor chose to relieve her symptoms with antipsychotic medication and to work with both spouses together. It became clear that Jim was a computer-type person who depended on "pure logic." Whenever he and Ruth got into a discussion and he had the upper hand because of his "logic," Ruth would flip into her psychotic mode, thus becoming totally unreachable. As the counselor and both partners came to understand this process, the counselor could actually point it out as it was happening during the counseling session. The counselor was also able to make the spouses understand that Ruth's sensitive, empathic, artistic, "right-hemisphere" approach to life was what had appealed to Jim in the first place and that Jim's logical, decision-making, and problem-solving attitude had been a great source of security for Ruth. But, in time, his "left-hemisphere" approach to life had become a problem, especially when it was related to intimate conflicts. Successful counseling centered on helping each spouse to appreciate the other, including the way the other experienced life, and to see how both approaches had value to the relationship..

Ongoing Use of Life-Style Material

Ongoing use of life-style material is part of marriage counseling if the couple chooses to continue to work together after the formulation of the life style. Each recurrent question in the relationship is examined in light of the personal life style of each partner. The counselor needs to have a summary of each life style in front of him/her at all times so he/she can refer back to that material as various questions come up. The counselor would often ask "Now that you understand your wife's (husband's) life style, how do you explain to yourself why she (he) does what she (he) does?"

Many of the partners' questions and observations are just different ways of asking "Why can't he (or she) be more like me?" Formulation of the life style helps to answer that question and shows rather precisely the ways in which the partner is not like the other and is not likely to become like the other. Furthermore, it helps to back up the counselor's repeated admonishments that one cannot control another person—something that is often attempted in one way or another in marriage. The life style is neither good nor bad; it just is. Within a given life style, there is a wide range of possibilities, but a goal in marriage counseling is to help each partner accept himself/herself as he/she is at the moment and become just as accepting of the other one.

Reorientation of the Life Style

Reorientation of the life style may be considered a necessity, a luxury, or anything in between. In most cases, it is not necessary for either spouse to make basic life-style changes, since most life styles are broad enough to allow a wide variety of behavioral possibilities. For example, a person with a "very" life style tends to see things in extremes: something is either all black or all white; a job is either done perfectly or not good at all. People with such a personality tend to think in superlatives; hence the term *very*. She is not merely a good cook; she is a *very, very* good cook. If the person has a relatively broad life style, counseling may be limited to helping him/her become aware of the choices that are available within, say, the "very" life style.

Certain aspects of the life style, however, may be so limiting that the counselor or the client concludes that counseling should be aimed at changing the life style. The following example illustrates this point. It should be noted that this is not, strictly speaking, an example of marriage counseling but, rather, of premarital counseling, since the woman's goal was to find out whether she could adjust her attitude toward men enough to find a mate.

Sylvia had an unfaltering hatred of men. She had grown up in a male-dominated family that numbered four boys and only one girl (Sylvia). When she grew up, she ended up working in an all-male office. The result was that Sylvia had devoted her life to outdoing men, both as a child and as an adult, and had never known anything but prejudice and dislike toward men.

When she came for counseling, the first hurdle was to develop a trusting relationship with the male co-counselor. Since she was being interviewed in a marriage-education center, on many occasions men in the audience had a chance to show her that they empathized with her and that men can be sensitive, tender, and gentle. Therefore, she was forced to reconsider her basic premise that "all men are bastards."

Eventually, she had readjusted her bias enough to enter a relationship with a young man. But, consistently with her life style, she chose a man who was likely to fulfill her negative expectations—which he did. However, at this point she was able to resume counseling, reevaluate what had happened, and see rather clearly what had brought her to choose a man who would be most likely to let her down.

If one person elects to work at changing his or her life style, this goal may be pursued in individual, group, or marital therapy. It may also be dealt with in a marriage-education center, although, as in family-education centers, the basic goal there is not therapy or a change of the life style. As counselors, we must continually guard against the conviction that one partner must *help* the counselor change the other partner. It is much more important for both partners to learn to accept themselves and their spouse as they are at the moment. Whether or not to strive toward basic changes in the life style ultimately becomes a matter of choice for the individual. If each marriage partner learns to understand and accept the other with all his/her strengths and weaknesses, life-style changes may not be so important.

The forms of intervention in marriage counseling then can focus on a variety of goals—change of behavior, change of feelings, change of environment, or change of attitudes, which is basically aimed at changing the life style. None of these is exclusive of or unrelated to the others. Some people can make rather marked changes in behavior without any particular change in insight. Some people can learn to deal with their emotions by understanding the purpose of the emotion—that is, by understanding the goal they are pursuing. If and when they decide to change their goal, the emotions take care of themselves. Naturally no one can consciously change his or her feelings. It is much more important for the person to get to the point where he or she can say "I'm a pretty good person, and, if I feel the way I feel, I must have some reason for it."

Mini-Life-Styles

Mini-life-styles are utilized particularly in marriage-education centers or in other types of brief counseling. A mini-life-style involves merely a superficial look at the family constellation and atmosphere and the interpretation of two or three early recollections. This is done in order to elucidate a few of the basic themes but is not in any way a complete life-style formulation, which usually requires at the very least one hour and often two or three, depending on the complexity of the childhood family and the manner in which the individual produces data. Here is an example of the use of mini-life-styles.

> Sarah and Mike, a young married couple, work in the same office. She is the only woman employee there. From her comments, it is pretty clear that she has a difficult relationship with her fellow employees because of her lack of acceptance of male behavior. She is critical, for example, of their constant discussions of professional athletics and of their swapping of "dirty" jokes. Mike, as a fellow employee, is not spared her criticism. Since all her colleagues are men, Sarah wonders whether there might be something in her life style that would cast light on her current situation.
>
> A brief diagram of Sarah's family constellation shows that her *Gegenspieler*[1] was her older brother and that she revered her father. From one of her early recollections it appears that she was stunned at the sudden revelation of a flaw in a man's character. Another early recollection clearly shows that she was very impressed with how good and important men must be. With the help of the counselor, Sarah comes to see how these conflicting views of men can present problems in her daily work. The mini-life-style also helps Mike, who, until now, has not been able to understand his wife's problems on the job.

[1]The *Gegenspieler* is the child, often closest in the constellation, against whom the person plays in the childhood drama.

Other Shortcuts

Other shortcuts include techniques such as "two points on a line" and the "hidden reason." The first of these techniques involves finding a line that connects two apparently contradictory attributes of a person. This makes it possible to locate innumerable other characteristics along the same line.

> A woman described herself as the most pleasing of her siblings but also the one with the worst temper. The counselor found that the connecting line between these two characteristics was the woman's need to be the best. The other characteristics the counselor located along this line were that she operated with very high-flown ambition and that, as long as she received from others the approbation she thought she deserved, she could be delightful but, when things didn't go her way, she could be a bitch. She was like the little girl with the curl in the middle of her forehead: when she was good, she was very very good, and when she was bad, she was horrid. When these lines were quoted to the woman, she was amazed to remember that her father had said the same thing about her when she was little. So, here was a person who wanted to be the best, and, if she couldn't be the best at being good, she would try to be the best at being bad.

The "hidden reason" is a technique meant to uncover the rationalization process that we go through when we decide to do or not to do something. We begin this thinking process fairly consciously, but then the process sinks below the level of consciousness, and we are no longer aware of it. And when we are asked why we behaved in a certain way, our answer will be either a new rationalization or an honest "I don't know."

Searching for the hidden reason is best done in a group setting. Group members are asked to put themselves in the client's shoes and imagine what he/she might say to himself/herself—for example, "I'm always late because . . ." After a number of guesses have been made, the client is asked "Who came close?" and whether someone has hit on the client's private logic. At that point, the person will understand and recognize his/her hidden reason, just as the child recognizes his/her short-term goal when presented with the four goals. Sometimes the involuntary "recognition spasm" is so strong that it cannot be disguised. In marriage counseling, often the use of the hidden-reason technique allows both partners to understand their behavior and the behavior of their spouse.

CONFLICT RESOLUTION

Since Individual Psychology is an interpersonal psychology, all conflicts are seen as interpersonal. Problems that develop in a marriage are seen by Adlerian counselors as problems in the relationship. As we said earlier, many marital difficulties are due to the spouses' attempts to experience an equalitarian relationship, without having the necessary background that would enable them to treat each other (and others) as equals. Most human relationships are characterized by some degree of superiority/inferiority. Adler, as early as 1931, saw the fallacy of this approach and pointed out that equality is the only standard for a successful marriage. Whenever one partner tries to elevate himself or herself above the other, the relationship becomes shaky and temporary, because the partner in the inferior position will always attempt to reverse the situation.

Intramarital fighting not only doesn't lead to a solution of the problem but lays the groundwork for the next conflict. Only with courage and self-confidence can people face the difficulties of cooperation. Dreikurs (1946) stated that two misconceptions exist with regard to human cooperation: "One is the belief that resentment can lead to improvement or that it is even a prerequisite for actions directed toward improvement. . . . The husband will gladly adjust himself to his wife's desires if he feels fully accepted by her. But he may drive in the opposite direction if he senses her resentment and rejection" (pp. 103–104). Another misconception about cooperation is expressed in the statement that "when interests clash, nothing can be done except to fight or yield."

Dreikurs' Four Principles

The Adlerian marriage counselor deals with all marital problems by using Dreikurs' four principles of conflict resolution: (1) showing mutual respect, (2) pinpointing the issue, (3) reaching a new agreement, and (4) participating in decision making. Every marriage conflict involves a violation of one or more of these principles.

Showing mutual respect is neither fighting nor giving in; it is neither overpowering nor capitulating. It is, instead, acknowledging that the resolution of conflict rests with understanding and respecting each other's point of view, not with winning or losing.

Pinpointing the issue takes into consideration the fact that behind most marital complaints there is a social issue. For example, a couple may complain about sex, in-laws, work, money, or children. Behind the complaint will be some threat to personal status, prestige, or superiority and some concern with who is winning or who is going to decide or who is right. The partners are specifically taught the technique of pinpointing the issue so they can learn to resolve conflicts on their own, without requiring the help of professionals.

The resolution of conflict is based on the understanding that, when the partners are fighting, they are doing so because they have reached an "agreement" to fight. Therefore, if conflict is to be resolved, a new agreement must be reached. Reaching a new agreement ultimately comes down to each party's stating "This I'm willing to do, with no strings attached." The attempt to reach a new agreement is best made for a limited period of time. At the end of that time, a reevaluation will take place to determine whether the new agreement works or not.

Husband and wife must participate in decisions that affect them both. Such participation is not limited to the decision-making process but includes assuming responsibility for the decision. The violation of this principle (unfortunately, quite frequent) reflects a lack of respect for one's partner and is bound to be deeply resented.

> A husband came home and announced to his wife, rather emphatically and enthusiastically, that he had made arrangements for them to spend a weekend at a resort motel and had also made reservations for dinner at a fine restaurant. He was quite surprised and disappointed when his wife didn't show the enthusiasm he had expected. What he didn't realize was that, by acting without consulting her, he had shown little respect for his wife and violated the principle of participation in decision making.

THE NUMBER-ONE PRIORITY

Often people's number-one priority becomes particularly clear at a time of great stress or conflict. A couple who seek counseling for their marital problems may be revealing their number-one priorities so clearly that the counselor has no problem identifying them and sharing his/her insight with the partners. In our experience, this is one of the most effective ways of demonstrating to the couple that they are understood, thus laying the foundations of a strong working relationship.

> *Loraine*: Al tries to control me constantly through criticism.
>
> *Counselor*: Could it also be that, with your number-one priority of superiority and your emphasis on justice and fairness, you compound the problem by criticizing him for his criticalness?
>
> *Loraine*: I think I see your point.
>
> *Counselor*: Would both of you agree to refrain from criticizing each other for one week and try, instead, to say something encouraging to each other every day?
>
> *Al*: I'm willing to do that. But how do I know that what I say is encouraging?
>
> *Counselor*: There are no guarantees, but encouragement means giving honest recognition for whatever you appreciate about your wife. Naturally, if she doesn't believe that about herself, she may not find it encouraging. How about trying it right now? What do you appreciate about Loraine?
>
> *Al*: She is very bright and has a good sense of humor.
>
> *Counselor*: And what do you appreciate about Al, Loraine?
>
> *Loraine*: He is honest and reliable.

The Number-One Priority: Choice of Partner

"The number-one priority: choice of partner" is a relatively new addition to Adlerian theory and practice. It appears that people choose marriage partners on the basis of their own number-one priority; that is, people choose partners with whom they can be themselves and pursue their number-one priority. For example, the man with a number-one priority of control is likely to choose a wife who, he believes, will permit him to exert his leadership and organizational ability. If his wife has a number-one priority of superiority, she may have chosen him because, at some level of awareness, she felt that she could be better than her husband.

Problems in marriage relationships develop when the individual moves toward the "only if" absurdity (which is an extreme form of the number-one priority), such as "Only if I am comfortable, do I really belong." The more an individual moves toward the "only if" absurdity, the higher the price he/she pays. As marriage partners learn about their own and their partner's number-one priorities, they become aware of some of their partner's vulnerabilities. One of the tasks of the counselor is to teach each partner to be an effective agent of encouragement instead of attacking vulnerabilities.

Married couples seldom have the same number-one priority. The most common pairings are control/superiority and comfort/pleasing. If the counselor is skilled at pinpointing the number-one priority very early in the initial interview, he/she has reached a valuable insight into the life style of the partners, which will help the clients feel understood and facilitate a good counseling rapport.

CHILDREN

When children are involved in the marital conflict, the whole situation becomes much more complex. It is crucial that the counselor convince the spouses of the devastating effects of using the children to get at each other.

A couple who had been in a conflict situation for many years also disagreed on how to deal with their very troublesome "hyperactive" child. The youngster was eventually removed from the home and put in residential treatment. In her deep discouragement, the mother reached the conclusion that she couldn't tolerate the child in the household again. The father never accepted the separation from his son but never tried to work the conflict out.

By the time the couple sought marriage counseling, the child's treatment was seriously handicapped by the fact that, since he couldn't return to his home, long-range planning was almost impossible. After the husband announced that his son was ready to come home and the wife refused to accept the child back, the husband decided that he would move out and take care of his son. This led to a most serious marital crisis, which culminated in divorce.

Children of course, know when there is disagreement between their parents, and there is no point in trying to hide it from them. The children can be told very simply that their parents are having some difficulties and that they are working on them. But, beyond that, in most cases it is not advisable to draw the children into the marriage-counseling process. Occasionally, with adolescent or adult children, we have found it advisable to include the young persons in some of the sessions, if the children are deeply enmeshed in their parents' relationship. If a couple are planning divorce, we remind them that they will continue to be the parents of their children. We also try to help them see that there is an advantage to dissolving the marriage peacefully and cooperatively, thus maintaining some type of friendly relationship, if for no other reason than to make it easier for the children to deal with the disruption of the family.

Often, when a couple begin to think about the children and the effects of marital conflict on their growth and development, they can be led to more cooperation and less battling. In other words, as the partners begin to realize how selfish they are and to what extreme they are concentrating on what each is getting out of the relationship to the exclusion of anyone else's interest and well-being, they can be led back toward a state of higher social interest and more courage. On the other hand, we never recommend that couples stay together "for the good of the children." If a relationship is built on phony premises, the children will always sense it and suffer from it. A destructive marital relationship is hardly a decent model for the children as they are growing up, if they are expected to know later in life what an adult marital relationship is like.

OTHER PARTIES

In our experience, it is very unusual for a marriage relationship to survive the prolonged existence of another party in the life of one of the spouses or both. In our society today, people are trying in so many different ways to overcome loneliness and achieve intimacy that long-lasting monogamous marriage has almost become one item in the large list of alternate life styles. We believe that, ultimately, monogamy will be seen once again as the most viable form of a lasting relationship between a man and a woman. We also think that people will choose a monogamous relationship not because of pressure from the church, the family, or the state but because of the advantages of such a relationship for both parties.

Each individual must choose his or her own definition of monogamy and agree on that definition with his or her partner. A monogamous relationship, for example, might mean a long-term deep commitment on the part of both parties and, yet, still allow significant relationships with members of the opposite sex, from time to time, for both partners. Our marriage-counseling experience, however, has taught us that the existence of another man or another woman is often merely a symptom, not a cause, of the degeneration of the marriage relationship. Frequently, an affair is revealed to the partner in an effort to get him or her off dead center. We said "revealed," but we wish to add that there are very seldom any secrets in a marriage; the other partner usually "knows" at some level of awareness about the extramarital affair. We also wish to say that quite often the other man or the other woman is not nearly as important as either spouse believes.

GOALS AND RESISTANCE

The counseling goals must be continually kept in mind. In marriage counseling, we are always faced with the issue of limited versus ideal goals, which is another way of saying that counselor and clients must try to answer the question "How much counseling (or therapy) is enough?" For one individual, a relatively minor change in attitude about one aspect of life may be sufficient. For one couple, a recommitment to working at the marriage and an increased tolerance of each other may be all that is needed. The counselor often can see that, ideally, a couple would benefit from extensive counseling including basic reorientation of the life styles. But, ultimately, the couple must decide for themselves what their goals in counseling will be.

Resistance develops when there is a lack of alignment between the goals of the couple and those of the counselor or between the goals of the two partners. Whenever resistance is detected, it is important to stop immediately the counseling process and attempt to negotiate a new set of goals that are acceptable to all parties. There are times when the negotiation leads to the agreement that goal alignment is not possible and that termination is indicated. No matter what the outcome may be, the process here is essentially that of working toward consensus. By "consensus" we mean not that everybody agrees 100% but that everybody feels that they can live with a particular decision, preferably for a limited period of time. So, for example, a married couple may decide to suspend any major decisions and to work on their relationship for two months, with the intent of reevaluating and renegotiating the agreement at the end of that time. If the counselor feels comfortable with working within such parameters, a consensus is reached, even though the counselor might like to see the couple commit themselves for a longer period of time.

MULTIPLE THERAPY

As we indicated in Chapter 13, multiple therapy (or counseling) is therapy (or counseling) conducted by more than one therapist (or counselor). The advantage of this approach is more evident in marriage and family counseling than in any other area. One counselor can be effective in working with a couple, but two counselors add many additional dimensions to the counseling process, particularly if they represent both sexes. The ideal situation probably is when the counselors themselves are married to each other and the two couples can sit together in "four-track therapy." When the counselor is a male, the wife may feel ganged up on by two males and is often tremendously relieved to have a female counselor introduced into the process.

> *Ted*: I think that Mary and I should meet each week and have an evaluation—particularly of how we are using our time.
> *Mary* (in tears): That's not what I'm talking about at all.
> *Male co-counselor*: I think Ted's idea has merit. It might be incorporated in a family-council meeting.
> *Female co-counselor*: What Mary is looking for is some appreciation. I suspect that the term *evaluation* sounds like she's going to be graded.
> *Mary*: That's just it. And, if I don't pass, Ted will have one more way to control me.

However, wives do not always identify with female counselors and husbands with male counselors. Frequently, the male counselor finds that, for some reason or other, he can understand the woman's point of view better, and vice versa. If the counselors are married to each other, their credibility with the couple is raised considerably, particularly if they are able to be open about the rough spots that they have maneuvered in their own relationship.

> *Female co-counselor*: I get so mad at Larry I could bite him. But, when I have a chance to be heard for a whole half hour in a marriage conference, I often find that I calm down considerably.
> *Male co-counselor* (to female co-counselor): But you still always want some kind of resolution.
> *Female co-counselor* (to male co-counselor): Yes, that's true, and you seem to be able to function much better when things are left hanging.
> *Clients together*: That's just the way it is with us.

Whenever marriage counseling is faltering, the addition of another therapist to the ongoing counseling process or simply for consultation is extremely helpful. Co-counseling and multiple therapy can be excellent methods for training counselors and therapists, and it is quite possible to have three or more counselors working with a couple at one time.

Most couples are pleased to have more than one counselor. They often feel that they are getting their money's worth, so to speak, and that, the more counselors present, the more points of view that are introduced into the counseling process. When a new counselor joins the process, the "temperature of the marriage" is often taken again to give the new counselor some idea of the quality of the relationship and of the trouble spots that are existing now, as compared to those that existed at the beginning of counseling. Sometimes this reevaluation opens up new directions in the counseling process.

> A couple had initially rated themselves 3 as lovers, and there was no

discrepancy between the partners' ratings. Once the process was repeated a few months later, both partners had gained considerably in their self-esteem and were much more assertive about what they wanted in their relationship. At this time, they still rated themselves 3 as lovers, but, since they were rating themselves so much better in other areas, they were now able to bring up and deal with the problems they were experiencing in the area of sexuality. Therefore, the counseling focused for several sessions on the issue of sexuality. The spouses were asked to read McCary's *Human Sexuality* (1978) independently and to underline, with pencils of different colors, the things that impressed them. By doing so, both partners discovered that there were areas of sexuality that they didn't know much about. They were also advised to attend a weekend sexual-awareness reassessment session at the University of Minnesota. During this session, they were bombarded with multimedia presentations on all levels and participated in numerous group discussions. Finally, they were recommended various techniques of the Masters and Johnson's type and asked to pay special attention to those that emphasized the importance of giving pleasure to the other partner.

With their increased sophistication, it became clear that the issue behind their conflict in the area of sexuality was often one of control. The partners were asked to conduct an experiment. During the first week, the wife was to make all the decisions concerning expressions of affection, tenderness, and sexuality. The following week, the husband was to be in charge. The partners agreed to the experiment and also to cooperate with each other to the best of their ability. She learned to be assertive and that it was OK to be the initiator. He learned that he didn't require immediate gratification every time he felt sexually aroused. Both partners learned to greatly enhance their own pleasure and the pleasure of the other. As a result of the process, they learned to deal more effectively not only with sexuality but also with parenthood, and their relationship with their teenage children improved considerably.

MARRIAGE-EDUCATION CENTERS

Marriage-education centers are patterned after family-education centers. They are inspired by the same models and operate in the same manner. Therefore, you will find much of the discussion contained in this section quite familiar.

The three purposes of marriage-education centers are (1) to communicate to a large audience basic mental-health principles that lead to more joyful and cooperative living, (2) to provide a resource for troubled couples, and (3) to train other counselors to work more effectively with couples. Volunteer couples are interviewed in a public group setting and function as coeducators with the co-counselors. As the partners are interviewed, the co-counselors have the opportunity to teach the larger group about the democratic principles that are being violated in that particular relationship and about methods of conflict resolution. The situation provides a unique setting for teaching principles of harmonious living as well as a unique source of encouragement to couples in the audience. By participating in the interview process, the members of the audience realize that they are not alone and that other couples have problems similar to their own.

The co-counselors then give the clients specific recommendations and ask them to return to the center in a week or two to report on their successes and failures. Each interview with a couple is ended with an encouragement session. The members of the audience are urged to give honest, sincere feedback about the strengths they see in the relationship and about everything else they appreciate in the couple.

Marriage-education centers may be housed in hospitals, churches, schools, or other public buildings. Funding sources are varied, but in many centers much of the work is done by volunteers. The staff of a marriage-education center includes a director and a codirector, who are professionals in the mental-health field and who have had extensive additional training and experience with the Adlerian model. In some communities, however, lay people have been trained to direct marriage-education centers under professional supervision. Other staff usually include the coordinator, an intake worker, a recorder, and the staff of the activity center for children and adolescents. Admission is free in most centers. Participants can simply observe, or they may ask questions, or they may volunteer to be the demonstration couple.

Although we speak of marriage-education center, the volunteer couples are not necessarily married. They may be contemplating marriage or living together in a variety of alternate life styles, including homosexual relationships. In other words, they are two adults attempting to overcome loneliness and achieve intimacy.

Every effort is made by the co-counselors to see to it that the volunteer couples are not analyzed, diagnosed, or in any way put on the spot. Since for many persons one's own marriage is still somewhat of a taboo subject, we are constantly amazed at the freedom with which people will attack virtually any subject, given the trust, support, and encouragement that are generated in the marriage-education center not only by the counselors but by the other participants as well.

Like the family-education center, the marriage-education center is an example of primary preventive mental-health care. The counselors are able to reach many more people than they could by talking with individual couples. This preventive aspect and the aspect of community outreach and community education have particularly interested a number of hospitals. Often, the marriage-education center becomes a referral agent to other community agencies. For example, in the course of two or three weeks, we referred one young man to a local hospital for treatment of his depression, a young woman to another hospital for treatment of her schizophrenia, and another woman for residential treatment of her alcoholism.

SPECIFIC TECHNIQUES

In marriage counseling, marriage therapy, and marriage education, we teach couples specific techniques that enhance communication and cooperation.

Listening

When this technique is used, one partner agrees to sit down and listen to the other partner until he or she has finished, without any interruption or nonverbal static. Then, the listening partner has the option to respond (but does not have to), and the partner who spoke first will become the listener. This process is particularly helpful when one partner is very upset and the other one is not, yet he or she needs to understand what is bothering the other.

Paraphrasing

In this process, one of the partners makes a statement. The other one is to refrain from answering until he or she has paraphrased to his or her satisfaction whatever the other one has said. This technique is difficult to follow for those partners who, while the other one talks, are busily composing their own responses instead of listening. Before they are ready to practice it at home, they must receive a great deal of guidance from the counselors.

Feedback

If one partner comes home tired, angry, or discouraged, the other partner is often all too willing to give feedback. With this technique, we teach the couple to ask the discouraged partner "Would you like to get my reaction?" or "Would you like to hear my suggestions?" and be willing to take "No" for an answer. Sometimes the discouraged partner will say "No, not now." Sometimes he or she will say "Yes, I would like to hear your ideas, but at a later time." Through this technique, couples learn that feedback is accepted much more gracefully when it is offered courteously and tentatively.

Marriage Conferences

The marriage conference is one of the most satisfactory ways of dealing with intense conflict situations. This technique, which was first described by Corsini (1967), is taught to couples being interviewed in marriage-education centers. Often members of the audience try the technique, too.

The partners are asked to make a series of appointments to meet with each other for one hour at a time and in a place where they are unlikely to be interrupted. The appointments should be at least two or three days apart. With couples who are experiencing significant conflict, we usually recommend at least three appointments. The marriage conference is a self-help process that can be carried out by couples in their own time and at their own convenience. It is quite normal for couples who are using the marriage conference for the first time to report disappointment with the experience, unless they follow the directions carefully. Innovating is not advised until the couple have had some experience with the technique.

At the time of the first appointment and as a result of a previous agreement, one partner has the floor for the first half hour while the other partner listens silently and refrains from interrupting, making faces, or in any other way interfering with what the other one is saying. Generally, we recommend that the partners conduct the conferences without looking at each other and avoid television, radio, note taking, smoking, eating, drinking, or any other distraction. During his/her half hour, the person who has the floor is free to say whatever he/she chooses and has also the option to remain silent. It is his/her half hour to use as he/she chooses. At the end of exactly one half hour, the process is reversed, and the first partner becomes the listener. At the end of the second half hour, the conference is completed. As a result of a previous agreement, the partners do not discuss until the next marriage conference any controversial items that came up during the conference. Noncontroversial items or any other subject can, of course, be discussed in between conferences. At the time of the second conference, the process is repeated, except that the partners reverse the order in which they speak and listen.

After experimenting with marriage conferences, a number of couples choose to continue having them as a regularly scheduled event in their lives. Other couples choose to conduct couple council meetings, which then grow into family council meetings as children become part of the relationship.

> Kathy and George are both extremely busy professionals with complicated schedules. Devoting 15 minutes a week to a couple council, which they refer to as a ''board meeting,'' has probably saved them from divorce. They sit down every Sunday and work out the schedule for the week, transportation, who's going to do what work, financial matters, and so forth—in other words, all the regular business of living together and operating a household.

Listing Expectations

Another helpful technique is to ask couples to independently write out their expectations for themselves, for their partner, and for the relationship. When they bring their lists back, the counselor reads each list aloud, checking with the other partner to find out whether the items on the list are understandable and whether they are considered reasonable. Sometimes the partners are asked to live for a month according to these expectations. Often items from the list provide springboards for further discussion.

> Sue and Jerry had never seriously considered having children. As Sue approached the conclusion of her academic career, she started feeling more and more strongly about having a baby. The fact that she was over 30 and most of her friends had children contributed to her feelings. While Sue was in school, Jerry had settled into a very comfortable life style, and the thought of disrupting it with a child's presence didn't particularly appeal to him. Sue and Jerry's difficulty was compounded by their respective families' putting subtle and not-so-subtle pressure on them. When they wrote out their lists of hopes and expectations, it was obvious that, while Sue and Jerry were far apart with regard to the issue of having children, they were in almost complete agreement about everything else. Since neither felt ready to make a final decision in one direction or the other, they decided to discontinue their day-to-day discussion of the issue and bring it up, instead, every three months. This decision was also motivated by the fact that they were expecting many changes in their lives, with Sue becoming a full-time professional and Jerry considering going back to school at least part time.

Homework

We regularly prescribe homework, and the partners agree to commit themselves to doing the prescribed activity. The kinds of homework prescribed are limited only by the imagination of the counselors and of the audience (when the counseling takes place in a center). For a couple who haven't been away from their children for many months and resent the situation, the assignment may be to hire a babysitter and spend a weekend at a resort motel. For a couple who complain about sex but whose underlying problem seems to be one of control, the homework may require each spouse to take full responsibility and make all decisions in the area of sex and affection for alternate weeks.

Paradoxical Intention

One of the most powerful techniques in marriage counseling is the use of the paradoxical intention. The partners are asked to go home and do whatever they have been doing all along but to do it on schedule. For example, a couple who have been fighting all the time may be urged to carry on a 10-minute fight each evening, using the very same procedures they have always followed. But they have to do it every night and for 10 minutes.

Many couples can't believe that such a recommendation will do them any good. All they know is that they have come asking for help and are being told by the helper to go home and do exactly what they had been doing before. But, if they are serious about improving their relationship, they usually make a strong effort to follow our instructions. The paradoxical recommendation is always put in the form of an experiment: "See what you can learn." Whether or not the couple follow the recommendation, they learn that they can choose when to fight and when not to fight. Frequently, couples have a great deal of difficulty carrying out the recommendation without laughing, and the absurdity of their fight becomes apparent to them.

> A man found himself attracted to a younger woman who worked with his wife. This attraction was particularly devastating to his wife because at the time she was suffering from a serious illness. Although the couple wanted to remain married, the husband found himself fantasizing a great deal about the other woman. A "paradoxical recommendation" was made to the husband: he was supposed to sit for 20 minutes after dinner each evening and fantasize about the younger woman. This recommendation was made in the presence and with the agreement of his wife. One week later, the man announced that his fantasizing had clarified the situation for him. He now realized that he wasn't really in love with this other woman and that he had been looking to her as a source of encouragement during a period of deep concern related to his wife's illness.

> A couple reported that they had problems because of the husband's premature ejaculation. We asked them to have intercourse twice a day and without foreplay. We emphasized that the husband was supposed to ejaculate as quickly as possible. The reason for our recommendation was that a symptom cannot be maintained unless one fights against it. Under the right circumstances, the symptom of premature ejaculation often disappears. In fact, it is not unusual for a couple to report the opposite experience—that is, the man having difficulty ejaculating or even reaching an orgasm.

Separation

Many couples keep the threat of separation dangling between them. In that situation, we occasionally recommend that they separate. We do so when we suspect that a separation will help the couple realize how much they love and miss each other. We also recommend separation when the fighting in between counseling sessions is so extreme that the partners don't seem to have time or energy for any kind of conflict resolution or problem solving. Generally, however, separation is not a frequently recommended process. When it occurs, it is much more likely to have been decided upon by the couple than to have been recommended by the counselors.

OTHER HELPFUL PROCESSES

Parent Education

Parent education often results in better relationships between the spouses. The principles that are taught in family-education centers and parent study groups, although specifically designed to improve adult/child interactions, are also effective in promoting equalitarian marital relationships. Consequently, as a couple learn these principles for dealing with their children, they also learn to apply them in their own relationship. Couples who have been devoting a great deal of time to fighting with their children often find themselves with free time once they have learned to deal with their children more efficiently. Although sometimes this gives them more time to fight with each other, often the marriage relationship is enhanced as the spouses learn to put things in perspective and to consider their marriage relationship first and their apparent parental obligations second. Many couples report that their marriage has improved considerably after family counseling, even though nothing specific was recommended with regard to the marriage.

Marriage Study Groups

The marriage study group is an outgrowth of marriage-education centers and of the emphasis on the benefits of study groups. A group of couples meet weekly for eight to ten weeks to study a book, such as Dreikurs' *The Challenge of Marriage* (1946). Study groups are led by lay people and depend on the ability of the participating couples to learn the useful principles and put them into practice on their own. When couples find this difficult, marriage therapy or marriage counseling may be indicated.

Couple Group Therapy

As pioneers in group therapy, it is not surprising that Adlerians have adapted the group process to marriage counseling. A group of five or six married couples are seen for two hours a week, usually for a limited period of time—for example ten weeks. Couples benefit from the group by identifying with and getting ideas from peers. They discover that they are not alone and that their problems are not unique. Ideally, such couples will have had some private sessions, including formulation of their life styles. Couple group therapy may take place in conjunction with attendance at a marriage-education center.

TECHNICAL QUESTIONS

Counselor's Directiveness

The question of how directive counselors should be is one that we face all the time. Although the answer rests in great part on the personality of the counselors, it seems that in marriage counseling more direction is indicated and that counselors can often take the initiative rather than sit back and wait for the clients to develop their own insights.

The counselor can organize and verbalize back to the couple those points that he or she believes the partners have learned. This procedure helps the couple get a deeper understanding of the issue and enables them to better retain and recall the relevant points. Also, the partners can be given recommendations that, although based on broad principles, are very specific.

Marriage counseling is basically an educational process—a process in which the partners are taught principles that they can then apply on their own. Once the spouses have learned these principles, they can also learn to become their own counselors and to deal with many difficult situations on their own.

Frequency and Length of Counseling

The frequency of counseling sessions is often dictated by factors that are extraneous to the counseling process itself, such as financial considerations and available time. However, the optimal frequency would seem to be once a week. This gives the couple enough time to work on things between sessions and yet keeps up the intensity of the counseling experience. After 8 to 12 weekly sessions, most couples can be seen less frequently, often coming back at monthly or quarterly intervals for checkups.

The length of each session in marriage counseling can probably be the same as in individual counseling—most commonly the 50-minute hour. In cases of four-track therapy, we have experimented with two-hour sessions, and with very good results. Since it is often difficult to get the therapists and the couple together, it helps to have a longer block of time, particularly if the couple are traveling long distances. With a two-hour block of time, we are able to get into the relationship more deeply and still have enough time to bring about resolution. We have also experimented with more intensive kinds of therapy—for example, meeting with couples six or eight hours a day for three days in a row. Although some of these couples had profound and complex problems, the process could be brought to completion by the end of the third day.

As we said earlier, marriage counseling can be combined with individual and/or group counseling. Generally, if one partner is receiving individual counseling, the marital relationship should not be part of that counseling process, and the counselor should be quite insistent about dealing with relationship problems only when both partners are present. When one partner seems to need a group experience, certain hazards should be kept in mind—for example, the likelihood of the partners' differential growth and the possibility that the other partner may feel left out and worry about what is going on in the group. When these kinds of problems are present, participation in a couple group may be a better solution.

Marital History

In our experience, a complete marital history is seldom necessary. We obtain sufficient information by discussing the current situation and by doing the personal life-style assessments. However, when we are puzzled and do not understand the dynamics of the relationship, it may be important to go back and ask the couple to describe in considerable detail their courtship, the early days of their marriage, and the various phases of their marriage relationship.

We look for recurring patterns, and often we see that the very things that attracted the partners to each other in the first place are those that, in their current fights, are brought up most often and objected to most strongly.

> Mark appreciated Clara's sociability and witty conversation, but now, when they fight, he claims that she talks too much. Clara appreciated Mark's strong, quiet, and logical manner, but now, when they fight, she complains that he wants to make all the decisions.

Sexual Problems

The sex act represents the ultimate test of a couple's willingness to cooperate and contribute to the welfare of each other. Therefore, it is not surprising that most "sexual" problems turn out to be relationship problems. We seldom find it useful to accept the couple's diagnosis that they have a sexual problem, thus dealing only with the symptom. Many couples report that, as their relationship improves, their sexual life improves also. If a couple have ever had a good sexual relationship, the chances are that they can have it again. If a couple have never had a good sexual relationship, it is more likely that we are dealing with sexual problems per se.

It is amazing how many couples are sexually ignorant. Therefore, we often recommend that they read *Human Sexuality* by McCary (1978) and that they underline, with pencils of different colors, the portions that they consider important. Thus the couple can learn together through reading. They can also learn through various desensitization procedures, such as the multimedia sexual-awareness weekend for couples, patterned after the Sexual Awareness Reassessment Program at the University of Minnesota. Similar but less sophisticated experience can be achieved by having the couple see some of the more artistic "pornographic" movies or use other sexually arousing materials of high quality. We find it very helpful for couples to read resources like *Our Bodies, Ourselves* by the Boston Women's Health Book Collective (1976), which may help women to understand themselves better and men to understand women better.

A complete sexual history is sometimes indicated to help clarify a confusing situation. In this case, the partners are asked to describe their early experiences with sex, both before and after they met, and provide a fairly detailed history of their sex life up to the present. An important process—but one that can be conducted only by counselors who are very comfortable about their own sexuality—is to have the couple describe their love making in great detail, from the very beginning to the very end of the experience. This often makes it possible for the counselor to identify the trouble spots and for the couple to learn a great deal about themselves and each other. We strongly recommend that such histories be obtained with both partners present. There are times, however, when one partner is unwilling to discuss in the presence of the other certain aspects or portions of his/her past sexual history. Naturally, we must be sensitive to such situations. We will then hear him/her out in private, although we tend to recommend that partners be as open with each other in this area as they can possibly be.

Another technique is to ask each partner, in the presence of the other, to close his/her eyes and fantasize aloud an ideal sexual experience with the partner. The sharing of fantasies tells both people things about themselves and each other that often they have been unable to verbalize and opens the door for further sharing of fantasies on their own.

Although it is very uncommon for sexual problems to have a physical basis, there are times when we do recommend a complete physical checkup. We do so, for example, if a couple haven't had a complete physical examination quite recently or if either partner suggests in any way that he/she believes that their sexual problems could have a physical basis. Although such physical examinations seldom add anything new to the picture, they often alleviate the partners' anxiety.

ADDITIONAL STRATEGIES IN MARRIAGE COUNSELING

Psychodrama

Psychodrama refers to a group of techniques in which the client acts out various situations from his or her life in an attempt to gain insight into and a better understanding of the situation. An example may help to illustrate.

> Shirley, age 24 and married, thinks that she is in love with another man. She reports great torment in trying to decide what she should do. We ask her to sit half on one chair and half on another. We talk with her about how it feels to be sitting on two chairs, and we ask her to predict how long she will be able to remain in that position. We also ask whether she has some idea about which "chair" she is leaning toward. Then we ask Shirley. "Do you think the chances that in one year you'll still be living with Al are larger or smaller than 50%?" She says "It's still 50-50." Had she said that the chances were greater than 50%, we would have told her that, on the basis of her own admission (at least at this moment), she really had decided to stay with Al. We would have also pointed out that the main issue then was how big a production she was going to make out of her decision.

In another psychodramatic technique, the partners change chairs, playing each other's role and experiencing each other. We use auxiliary egos, doubling, mirroring, and any of the other standard psychodramatic techniques as well as spontaneous variations that we create on the spot.

Absurdification

This technique consists in taking what the partners say and carrying it to its ridiculous extreme. It is particularly useful with people who are prone to thinking in terms of either/or and in superlatives. Once the person has become aware of the absurdity of his/her extreme stance, we use every opportunity to confront him/her with it. For example, "Is it possible that everything in your life is in terms of *always*? Do you know anybody else who *always* suffers as nobly as you do? You must be a saint in disguise."

Bibliotherapy

As we said before, we frequently recommend that partners read books together, sometimes underlining with pencils of different colors the parts of the book that have particular significance for them. Some of the most frequently recommended books include *The Future of Marriage,* by Bernard (1972); *Our Bodies, Ourselves,* by the Boston Women's Health Book Collective (1976); *The Challenge of Marriage,* by Dreikurs (1946); *The Mirages of Marriage,* by Lederer and Jackson (1968); *This Will Drive You Sane,* by Little (1978); *We Can Have Better Marriages If We Really Want Them,* by Mace and Mace (1974); *The Marriage Premise,* by O'Neill (1977); *Open Marriage,* by O'Neill and O'Neill (1972); *Shifting Gears,* by O'Neill and O'Neill (1974); *Becoming Partners,* by Rogers (1972); *On Personal Power,* by Rogers (1977); and *The Together Experience,* by Sperry (1978).

It should be noted that bibliotherapy is not limited to books that deal specifically with marriage. Many poems, novels, and plays, for example, describe very accurately the very situation in which a couple may find themselves.

Prescribing What the Partners Already Know

One of the first questions we ask the partners is "Can you think of something you could do in the coming week that would make a difference in your relationship?" Almost all partners do know things they can do and that, for whatever reason, choose not to do. Generally, the only recommendation we offer in the initial interview is that each partner do those few things that he or she has mentioned. Also, we tell them to do them for a limited period of time, preferably until the next appointment. We don't want them to have the feeling that they are committing themselves for life.

I'm Stuck With

We often ask couples to hold hands, to look in each other's eyes, and to tell each other, step by step, what they find difficult to live with both in the partner and in the relationship. One partner does this until he/she is finished, and then the other partner repeats the same process.

Diagnosis and Prognosis

Sometimes couples ask for a diagnosis. We have developed a unitary diagnostic system that simplifies this process. The diagnosis is always the same: chronic human imperfection. When the question of prognosis comes up, we simply say that we don't know. We are not prophets, we don't have a crystal ball, and we can't read minds.

Redefinition

A very important technique is that of redefinition. If Ralph keeps referring to Janet as stubborn, we redefine the characteristic as persistence and identify in considerable detail all the advantages that Janet brings to the marriage because of her persistence.

At all times, and not just when we employ this technique, we try to help the partners communicate clearly. Such attempts include using the right words, being specific and direct, and avoiding all that can obfuscate the message.

Guessing

This technique has two advantages. If we counselors guess correctly, the person or couple feel understood. If, instead, we make a mistake, we have the opportunity to demonstrate our courage to be imperfect, which is what we are trying to teach to the couple. And, the more we guess, the more we sharpen our own psychological sensitivity.

Placing Responsibility

Another related feature of our approach to marriage counseling is our willingness to go into each session with no script whatsoever. We put the responsibility directly on the couple by asking them right away "What would you like to work on today?" If they wish to report on our previous recommendation, we will ask them to tell us what we recommended, rather than try to rely on our own memory or on our notes. Then we continue with "What did you do?" and "What did you learn?"

Storytelling and Humor

Over the years, we have accumulated many stories, some of them quite humorous, that help us make a point. Our therapy sessions are often sprinkled with these stories, and we find that, when we all laugh together, therapy is well under way. "A man who learns to laugh at himself will always be amused," as someone wisely said.

We insist that each partner speak for himself or herself and are unwilling to accept statements such as "*We* had a really fine week." or "Yes, *our* relationship is better than ever.'' We would much rather hear the partner say "From my point of view, I had a good week and it seemed to me that Dorothy was having a good week too. Is that true, Dorothy?'' and Dorothy: "Yes, I had a good week. I discovered that I could put into practice a number of principles that I learned in the last session.''

GROUP TECHNIQUES

In the marriage-education center, because of the complexity of the group, many techniques are used, some of which develop directly from the group.

Feedback

> *Counselor*: You have heard Helen and George describe the situation when they were on vacation. What kind of feedback would you like to give them?

> *Counselor*: Esther said that at times she feels so discouraged that she wonders whether life is worth living and that she has even thought of suicide. How many of you have thought of suicide from time to time?

Of course, feedback can be successful only if very clear ground rules are laid down: we do not permit any analysis, any diagnosis, or direct confrontation, and all comments must come through the co-counselors.

> *Counselor*: It appears that Betty knows very well how to get into a fight with Frank. What kind of suggestions would you have for her if she chose to stay out of the fight?
> *Audience*: She could go to the bathroom.
> She could tell Frank that she loves him too much to fight with him.
> She could tell Frank she hasn't time for a fight today but she would be willing to work him into her schedule sometime tomorrow evening.
> She could tell Frank that, if he keeps on pestering her, she's going to kiss him.

Encouragement cannot be overemphasized. We have never had anybody get an overdose of encouragement, and we consistently do everything we can, and stimulate the audience to do everything they can, to help increase the self-esteem of the people being counseled.

Empathy

> *Counselor*: Helen has described a very sad and poignant situation and feels she's the only one that has ever experienced anything like it. Would all of you who have known through your own personal

experience what it's like to be in her boots come up on the stage and stand around her?

Information

Counselor: It is clear from talking with Peter that his wife is an alcoholic. How many of you have wrestled with chemical dependency in the family? What are the various resources available in our community?

Clarification

Counselor: It seems, Sue, that you still don't understand what I've been saying. Let me ask the audience if there are members who would be willing to try to restate it in such a way that it would make sense to you.

Taking Pressure off the Couple

When the going gets heavy, a very useful technique is for the co-counselors to stop and have a conversation or turn to the audience and deliver a short lecture or have a discussion with the audience while one or both partners have a chance to compose themselves. Tissues are always available, often supplied by somebody in the front row.

Desensitization

Norman has never been able to tell his wife of 26 years what he thinks and feels about sex and what would please him. In fact, he can't imagine talking about sex with anyone. A lively discussion about human sexuality is stimulated with the help of the audience. Norman listens to what is being said, and, as the discussion proceeds, he finds it increasingly easy to actually begin to use some of the terminology himself.

Support

A particularly touching experience often takes place in a marriage-education center when, after the formal counseling has ended, the people who have felt empathy for one or both partners gather around them, giving them support and encouragement.

Role Definition

The roles of male and female are certainly in a state of flux in our society today. This issue represents a very common topic in our marriage-education centers. In *The Future of Marriage*, Jessie Bernard (1972) talks about the feasibility of a shared-role pattern and points out how important this would be for the couple's children. She predicts a future of options, with some couples wanting to relate to each other in a 19th-century manner and, at the other extreme, free-wheeling relationships allowing both partners a maximum of individuality and independence and relying on emotional commitment and responsibility (pp. 302-303). In other words, Bernard feels that, in the future, marriages will be as different from "conventional" marriages as today's marriages are different from those of our ancestors. No one kind of marriage will be required of everyone, but the increased number of options will also make greater demands on the partners.

Because of this state of flux, marriage counselors need to be keenly aware of the changing forms of marriage and other adult intimate relationships. They will be most effective if they don't present a limited concept of marriage or try to impose their values on the couple they are working with.

Dreikurs has written extensively about the state of the institution called marriage. Many in the past have questioned its chance of survival in light of the changing sexual roles and attitudes in our society. Indeed, the divorce rate in this country would seem to lend credence to the argument that marriage may no longer be a functional life style. Adlerian marriage therapists take a more optimistic view. They believe that any marital problem can be worked out as long as there is a relationship of mutual respect and cooperation.

Living in such a cooperative, equalitarian relationship can be a very satisfying life style. "It means partnership and sharing what may come, for better or worse" Dreikurs (1946) writes. There can be little doubt that a marital union to which both partners give themselves totally, spiritually, as well as physically, is still one of human beings' highest aspirations.

REFERENCES

Adler, A. *What life should mean to you*. New York: Capricorn, 1958.

Bernard, J. *The future of marriage*. New York: World Publishing, 1972.

Boston Women's Health Book Collective. *Our bodies, ourselves* (2nd ed.). New York: Simon & Schuster, 1976.

Corsini, R. J. Let's invent a first-aid kit for marriage problems. *Consultant*, September 1967, 40.

Dreikurs, R. *The challenge of marriage*. New York: Hawthorn, 1946.

Lederer, W. I., & Jackson, D. D. *The mirages of marriage*. New York: Norton, 1968.

Little, B. L. *This will drive you sane*. Minneapolis: Compcare Publications, 1978.

Mace, D., & Mace, V. *We can have better marriages if we really want them*. Nashville, Tenn.: Abingdon, 1974.

McCary, J. L. *Human sexuality* (3rd ed.). New York: Van Nostrand, 1978.

O'Neill, N. *The marriage premise*. New York: Evans, 1977.

O'Neill, N., & O'Neill, G. *Open marriage*. New York: Evans, 1972.

O'Neill, N., & O'Neill, G. *Shifting gears*. New York: Evans, 1974.

Rogers, C. R. *Becoming partners*. New York: Delacorte, 1972.

Rogers, C. R. *On personal power*. New York: Delacorte, 1977.

Sperry, L. *The together experience*. San Diego: Data Books, 1978.

APPENDIX A

GUIDE FOR INITIAL INTERVIEW ESTABLISHING
THE LIFE STYLE

Name _____ Date _____

1. Reason for coming:

2.- History of this concern:

3. Current life tasks (how things are going in these areas); rate from 1 to 5 (a rating of
   1 means that things are going very well; a rating of 5, that they are very
   dissatisfying):

   Occupation _____

   Friendship _____

   Opposite sex _____

   Self _____

   Meaning _____

   Leisure _____

   Parenting _____

4. Father's age ___ Occupation _____ Mother's age ___ Occupation _____

   Personality, type of person: Personality, type of person:

   Ambitions for children: Ambitions for children:

   Relationship to children: Relationship to children:

   Way you are similar/different   Way you are similar/different
   from father: from mother:

5. Nature of parents' relationship:

265

6. Other family information:

7. Additional parental figures:

8. Description of siblings; list siblings from oldest to youngest:

    Which is most different from you? _____ How?

    Which is most like you? _____ How?

    What kind of child were you?

    Were there unusual talents, achievements, or ambitions?

    Any sickness or accidents?

    Childhood fears?

 9. Physical and sexual development:

10. Social development:

11. School and work experience:

12. Sibling ratings; list highest and lowest sibling for each attribute. If you are at neither extreme, indicate your position in relationship to siblings:

    Intelligence

    Grades and general standards
    of achievement

    Hardest worker; industrious

    Responsible

    Methodical; neat

    Athletic

    Appearance

    Mischievious

    Rebellious: openly, covertly

    Critical of self

    Charming; trying to please

    Sociable; friendships

    Withdrawn

    Sense of humor

    Demanded and got own way

    Temper and stubbornness

    Sensitive; easily hurt

    Idealistic

    Materialistic

Conforming

Standards of right/wrong; morals

Critical of others

Excitement seeker

Most spoiled

Most punished

13. Early recollections. How far back can you remember? (Obtain recollections of *specific incidents*, as detailed as possible, including the client's reaction at the time.)

14.

Number-one priority	How the other may feel	The price you pay for your priority	What you want to avoid with your priority
Comfort	irritated or annoyed	reduced productivity	stress
Pleasing	accepting	stunted growth	rejection
Control	challenged	social distance and/or reduced spontaneity	unexpected humiliation
Superiority	inadequate	overburden or overresponsibility	meaninglessness

15. Summary:

Mistaken self-defeating perceptions:

Assets:

STYLE OF LIVING RE-CREATION

Name _____   Date _____

Diagram of Family Constellation

Include brief descriptions of each member, including other parental figures, sibling most different, most similar. Indicate groupings, allies and competitors--most like father, mother--parents' relationship.

Unusual talents or achievements?

Childhood ambitions?

Serious illness, operation or injury?

Childhood fears?

Childhood habits?

<u>ATTRIBUTES</u> (Use initials. Include only sibs up to 5-6
years older or younger)

SUB-GROUPS:

Intelligence _____		Pleasing _____	
Grades _____		Cheerful _____	
Industrious _____		Sociable _____	
Standards of achievement _____		Sense of humor _____	
Athletic _____		Considerate _____	
Looks _____		Bossy _____	
Feminine _____		Demanded way _____	
Masculine _____		Got way _____	
Mischievous _____		Temper _____	
Openly rebellious _____		Sulked _____	
Covertly rebellious _____		Stubborn _____	
Punished _____		Shy _____	
Rewarded _____		Sensitive and easily hurt _____	
Standards of right-wrong _____		Idealistic _____	
Critical of others _____		Materialistic _____	
Critical of self _____		Neat _____	
Easy going _____		Responsible _____	
Charm _____		Withdrawn _____	
		Excitement seeker _____	

269

Physical development:

Sexual development:

Social development:

School and work experience:

CURRENT LIFE-TASK RATINGS 1-5 (1 high)

WORKER											
FRIEND											
LOVER											
SPOUSE											
OTHER SEX											
SELF											
MEANING											
PLAYER											
PARENT											
RUNG											

EARLY RECOLLECTIONS AND CHILDHOOD DREAMS

271

Radio:

T.V.:

Movie:

Song:

Fairy tale:

Nursery rhyme:

Poem:

Bible character:

Bible story:

Summary of Family Constellation:

Summary of Early Recollections:

Mistaken or Self-defeating Attitudes, Convictions, Guidelines:

Resources:

Number-One Priority:

274

LIFE-STYLE ASSESSMENT

Instructions:

You will be presented life-style information segment by segment. After each portion is presented to you, you are to react to the statements on the answer sheet according to the directions provided below.

This exercise will enable you to compare your evaluation of collected information regarding life style to experts in the field. As you accumulate more information, you may change your judgment regarding some of the statements you have made. That is expected to happen and is very common. *Base each judgment on all the information available up to that particular point.* Do not look ahead, but you are encouraged to look back to the previous information if it is helpful to you to do so.

How to mark the answer sheet:

   I. First decide if the statement should be marked
      A. true
      B. false
      C. no basis for judging either way
  II. Then decide how certain you are of your answer and select, by circling
      A. *1* for statements you are *very* sure of
      B. *2* for statements you are *reasonably sure of*
      C. *3* for statements you are *somewhat* sure of but which could easily be marked otherwise

Examples:

	True	False	No evidence
1. Alice is a power-oriented person.	1 2 3	1 ② 3	1 2 3
2. Alice is a person who is a getter in life.	① 2 3	1 2 3	1 2 3

In #1 the respondent felt the statement was false and was moderately sure of his belief.
In #2 he felt the statement was true and was very sure of his answer.

Reprinted by permission of Dr. Thomas Edgar.

INFORMATION FROM THE INITIAL INTERVIEW

Appearance:

Jane is attractive and neat. She is a tall woman. Her clothing is expensive and stylish.

Occupation:

Assistant to the director of a national television series. Her salary is good according to her report.

Marital status:

Single. No steady or serious relationship with a man at the present time. She has never been married, although she has been engaged to marry three times in the past five years.

Present stated problem:

Jane expressed a feeling of general boredom with life. Specifically, Jane feels her work is not satisfying and that her work is not appreciated by her boss. Her social life is unsatisfactory. She would like a permanent, long-term relationship with a male, but none have appeared who even come close to being the person she is seeking for such a relationship. Jane cries easily as she discusses her unhappiness with life in general.

She does not feel accepted by her coworkers.

THE LIFE-STYLE INVENTORY

Name___Jane X_____

Date_____

1. Bill +4½	2. Jane 30
Very good to her. Took care of her. Bought her things. Got along well. Kind. Not scholarly. Athletic. Lots of boyfriends. Tall and skinny.	Always had lots of girlfriends. Cute. Happy. Outgoing. Lessons--singing and dancing. Never shy. Good in school; teachers liked her. Not good in sports. No boyfriends.
3.	4.
5.	6.

Most different from respondent: How? He's much more introverted and quiet. More conservative. Not as good a student as she is.

Most like respondent: How? Same sense of humor. Same tastes, e.g., music (except for wife). Always very close.

Groupings (age, sex, etc.):

Which played together? Yes-- he teased her a lot and drove her crazy.

Which fought each other? He'd hit her once in a while--a punching bag.

Sickness, surgery, or accident? No.

Unusual talents or achievements?

Respondent's childhood fears? The dark. Little people lived under her bed but wouldn't bother her.

Respondent's childhood ambitions? Theater--a star.

Most	Most
Intelligence - equal	Cheerful
Grades - Jane	Sociable - Jane
Industrious - Jane	Sense of humor - equal
Standards of achievement - Jane	Considerate - equal
Athletic - Bill	Bossy - Jane
Daring - Bill	Demanded way - Jane
Looks - Bill	Got way - Bill
Feminine	Temper - equal
Masculine	Fighter - both
Obedient - Jane	Chip on shoulder - neither
Made mischief - Bill	Sulked - neither
Openly rebellious - Bill	Stubborn - neither
Covertly rebellious - neither	Shy - neither
Punished - never punished	Sensitive and easily hurt - Jane
Standards of right-wrong - Bill	Idealistic - Jane
Critical of others - Jane	Materialistic - neither
Critical of self - Jane	Methodical, neat - neither
Easy-going - both	Responsible - Bill
Charm - Jane	Withdrawn - neither
Excitement seeker - neither	Spoiled - neither
	Overprotected - Jane

FATHER Age 54 Occupation: owns store

Never hit me. Always even-tempered.
Made me laugh. Got along well with
him. Loves to sing and dance--
interested in opera and things she
likes, too. Generous. Anything he
could do for family. Never admits
he's wrong. Narrow-minded about
certain things. Somewhat protective
of her. Worried.

Favorite? Nobody. Why?

Ambitions for children? Bill--
loose standards for him but
college expected; for me,
none.

Relationship to children?
very close.

Sibling most like father?
Bill in business.

In what ways? Jane: home
personality.

May

MOTHER Age 49 Occupation:housewife

Always got along well. Loved her and
felt close to her. Temper on her.
Wake up Sunday morning in rotten mood
and then apologize. She was around
and would let them have it. Couldn't
stand for being fresh or pouting, but
could have what they wanted. Got a
kick out of raising a daughter. Very
sensitive; not much confidence in
self. Nice person; good-hearted.
Got feelings hurt easily.

Favorite? Nobody. Why?
Wanted a daughter, if
anybody.

Ambitions for children?
College.

Relationship to children?
Do things for them. Be
giving.

Sibling most like mother?
Both.

In what ways? Get feelings
hurt easily. Very sensi-
tive.

NATURE OF PARENTS' RELATIONSHIP

Very good marriage; but Mother feels inferior and Father feels confident. Similar interests. Always together. A few fights over stupid
little things. Father makes major decisions. She raised kids. Father
controls the money.

PHYSICAL DEVELOPMENT

13 at menses; school and Mother prepared her. Getting dressed to go out and called Mother "God damn it; why now?" Took it lightly. Father went and got Kotex from drugstore, and she went out. It was just a thing that happened. It was time. It was a nuisance at the moment and always has been. No difficulties. 13 at first bra (didn't need it). Doesn't remember getting first time. Feels like she could lose 5 lbs. now.

SCHOOL INFORMATION

B.A. in radio and T.V. from Iowa State. Always a good student except in math and science. Partied and still got good grades. Good in writing and reading.

SOCIAL INFORMATION

Always had lots of friends. One friend, Beth, and they were friends from grammar school through high school. Very close. Best of friends, but always competitive. Real cute and never trusted her with men/boys. Jane always felt Beth was doing things better than she did them. Very selfish, spoiled, and self-centered.

SEXUAL INFORMATION

Dated one boyfriend in high school. Necking and petting (but not really into it). Intercourse first time at 21 years. Went with one boy in college who didn't turn her on (Peter), then did it at 21 (2 years later). Not good. Terrible. But John did turn her on, and she had a good time. Six or seven men since then, but Eric the most and the best.

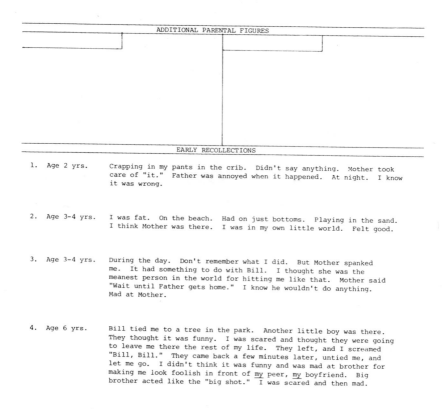

ADDITIONAL PARENTAL FIGURES

EARLY RECOLLECTIONS

1. Age 2 yrs.   Crapping in my pants in the crib. Didn't say anything. Mother took
                 care of "it." Father was annoyed when it happened. At night. I know
                 it was wrong.

2. Age 3-4 yrs. I was fat. On the beach. Had on just bottoms. Playing in the sand.
                 I think Mother was there. I was in my own little world. Felt good.

3. Age 3-4 yrs. During the day. Don't remember what I did. But Mother spanked
                 me. It had something to do with Bill. I thought she was the
                 meanest person in the world for hitting me like that. Mother said
                 "Wait until Father gets home." I know he wouldn't do anything.
                 Mad at Mother.

4. Age 6 yrs.   Bill tied me to a tree in the park. Another little boy was there.
                 They thought it was funny. I was scared and thought they were going
                 to leave me there the rest of my life. They left, and I screamed
                 "Bill, Bill." They came back a few minutes later, untied me, and
                 let me go. I didn't think it was funny and was mad at brother for
                 making me look foolish in front of my peer, my boyfriend. Big
                 brother acted like the "big shot." I was scared and then mad.

5. Age 5 yrs.   Fighting with two girls at recess. Just one at first, and then the
                    other decided to help. One held my arms back, and I bit the stomach
                    of the girl in front of me. She deserved it. Girl had mark on
                    stomach for years. I felt bad afterwards.

6. Age 6 yrs.   First grade. Teacher would send two people to thank another class
                    for play given. Teacher asked for relatives to raise their hands.
                    I raised mine and teacher said "Do you have a relative?" (She
                    knew the family.) I said "Yes, a sister you couldn't know about.
                    Her name is Emma." Teacher said "O.K." and let me go. I got
                    nervous that I couldn't carry it off and realized it didn't make
                    sense. Later, I was embarrassed and didn't feel right. I didn't
                    feel guilty. Knew I wouldn't do it anymore. "That's what you get
                    for lying. It doesn't make sense."

7. Age 5 yrs.   Being on top of slide in playground. Afraid to go down and afraid
                    to climb back down. 5th-grade patrol boys calling me down. Scared
                    to death. Afraid to move either way. Finally slid down and felt
                    relieved that I was off the slide and could go down. Embarrassed
                    at all the attention.

8. Age 9-10 yrs.   Girlfriend Jane and I crawled under barbed wire at Ravinia. Went
                    on empty stage and sang and danced and had wonderful time. Scared
                    we'd get caught. Feeling real good. Imagining orchestra and
                    audience.

		True	False	No Evidence
1.	Jane may provoke others to abuse her so she can feel morally superior.	1 2 3	1 2 3	1 2 3
2.	She finds others to be unfair.	1 2 3	1 2 3	1 2 3
3.	Jane, psychologically, is an only child.	1 2 3	1 2 3	1 2 3
4.	Jane often feels victimized by life.	1 2 3	1 2 3	1 2 3
5.	It is better for Jane to be on the edge of the action, not in the middle of it.	1 2 3	1 2 3	1 2 3
6.	Jane, as a child, was actively engaged in competition with her brother.	1 2 3	1 2 3	1 2 3
7.	She feels that, while she is not perfect, others are worse.	1 2 3	1 2 3	1 2 3
8.	Jane expects others to exercise control over her.	1 2 3	1 2 3	1 2 3
9.	Jane will tend to criticize other people a lot.	1 2 3	1 2 3	1 2 3
10.	Jane is likely to become depressed often by the circumstances of life.	1 2 3	1 2 3	1 2 3
11.	Jane questions her own femininity and would prefer being a male, given the choice.	1 2 3	1 2 3	1 2 3
12.	One of Jane's mistaken ideas in life is: women are inferior to men.	1 2 3	1 2 3	1 2 3
13.	Jane's family valued getting along with others.	1 2 3	1 2 3	1 2 3
14.	Jane will tend to become frightened and/or furious when others try to control her.	1 2 3	1 2 3	1 2 3
15.	Jane learned from her family that what she merely wants she needs.	1 2 3	1 2 3	1 2 3
16.	Jane's parents modeled a sharing cooperative realtionship.	1 2 3	1 2 3	1 2 3
17.	People who try to prevent Jane from doing what she wants are liable to get hurt.	1 2 3	1 2 3	1 2 3
18.	Jane was given responsibilities in her family.	1 2 3	1 2 3	1 2 3

		True			False			No Evidence		
19.	Jane has a great deal of confidence in herself.	1	2	3	1	2	3	1	2	3
20.	The family valued making the best of any bad situation.	1	2	3	1	2	3	1	2	3
21.	Jane tries hard to find her way in life through conformity.	1	2	3	1	2	3	1	2	3
22.	Jane's brother dominated her, much like her father.	1	2	3	1	2	3	1	2	3
23.	Jane finds it difficult to work cooperatively with others.	1	2	3	1	2	3	1	2	3
24.	Jane, when she finds herself in a difficult situation, will often be unable to act in any way.	1	2	3	1	2	3	1	2	3
25.	Relationships are a matter of who is on top.	1	2	3	1	2	3	1	2	3

Nine Adlerian raters, all experienced in counseling and psychotherapy, were asked to complete the preceding Life-Style Assessment questionnaire. The responses are listed below. On the left are the responses based on information up to and including the family constellation. On the right are the responses based on all the information available in the Life-Style Assessment, including early recollections. The modal responses to each question are listed to give the readers using this questionnaire some standard to evaluate their own responses. (T = True; F = false; NE = No evaluation)

Question No.	Mode	Question No.	Mode
1	T2	1	T1
2	T2, T3	2	T1
3	F1	3	F1
4	T2	4	T1
5	F2	5	T2
6	T2	6	T1
7	T2	7	T1
8	T2	8	T2
9	T1	9	T1
10	T2	10	T2
11	T3	11	T3
12	T1, T2	12	T2
13	T1	13	T1
14	T2	14	T2
15	T3	15	T3
16	F2	16	F2
17	T3, F2, F3	17	T1
18	F2	18	F1
19	F1	19	F1
20	NE2, F1	20	F2
21	T2	21	T2
22	T2	22	T1, T2
23	T2	23	T1
24	T1	24	T1
25	T2	25	T2

The Life-Style Inventory

Harold H. Mosak, Ph.D.   Bernard H. Shulman, M.D.

Name _____

Date _____ 197___

1

2

3

4

5

6

SIBLING RATINGS

Most different from respondent: How?

Most like respondent: How?

Groupings (age, sex, etc.)

Which played together?   Which fought each other?

Sickness, surgery or accident?   Unusual talents or achievements?

Respondent's childhood fears?   Respondent's childhood ambitions?

Most to Least		Most to Least	
Intelligence		Cheerful	
Grades		Sociable	
Industrious		Sense of humor	
Standards of achievement		Considerate	
Athletic		Bossy	
Daring		Demanded way	
Looks		Got way	
Feminine		Temper	
Masculine		Fighter	
Obedient		Chip on shoulder	
Made Mischief		Sulked	
Openly rebellious		Stubborn	
Covertly rebellious		Shy	
Punished		Sensitive and easily hurt	
Standards of right-wrong		Idealistic	
Critical of others		Materialistic	
Critical of self		Methodical – Neat	
Easy going		Responsible	
Charm		Withdrawn	
Pleasing		Excitement seeker	

PHYSICAL DEVELOPMENT

SCHOOL INFORMATION

SOCIAL INFORMATION

SEXUAL INFORMATION

PARENTAL INFORMATION

FATHER Age	Occupation	
		Favorite? . Why?
		Ambitions for children?
		Relationship to children?
		Sibling most like father? In what ways?

MOTHER Age	Occupation	
		Favorite? Why?
		Ambitions for children?
		Relationship to children?
		Sibling most like mother? In what ways?

NATURE OF PARENTS' RELATIONSHIP

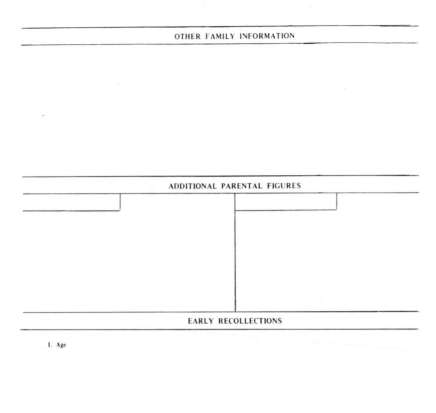

ADDITIONAL PARENTAL FIGURES

EARLY RECOLLECTIONS

1. Age

2. Age

3. Age

4. Age

5. Age

6. Age

7. Age

8. Age

APPENDIX B

ADLERIAN COUNSELING AND PSYCHOTHERAPY
COMPETENCIES

	Unsatisfactory	Good	Exceptional ability
1. Can present the Adlerian theoretical foundations underlying the therapeutic process	___	___	___
2. Can explain the psychopathology of the neuroses and psychoses as set forth by Adlerian psychology—that is, purpose of symptoms, interrelationship of the neuroses, and so forth	___	___	___
3. Can describe and demonstrate the Adlerian counseling relationship	___	___	___
4. Can deal with the disturbances and defenses that interfere with the relationship, such as externalization, rebellion, inadequacy, and projection	___	___	___
5. Can explore the current situation and the way in which the person approaches the challenges of living and the life tasks	___	___	___
6. Can use the number-one priority as a clinical method to investigate one facet of the life style	___	___	___
7. Can identify and interpret the essential life-style information—that is, family constellation and family atmosphere	___	___	___
8. Can interpret and utilize early recollections in formulating the life style	___	___	___
9. Can identify here-and-now psychological movement and interpret it to the client	___	___	___
10. Can understand the commonly observed life styles, such as "getter," "driver," and "controller"	___	___	___
11. Is able to attend to the client's verbal and nonverbal behavior	___	___	___
12. Is able to align counselor/counselee goals	___	___	___
13. Can empathically understand and reflect feelings while understanding the purpose of the feelings being shared	___	___	___
14. Can paraphase and allude to a goal or purpose	___	___	___
15. Can confront clients with their subjective views, mistaken beliefs, private goals, or destructive behaviors	___	___	___

APPENDIX C

ADLERIAN INSTITUTES, SOCIETIES, AND PUBLICATIONS

International

International Association of Individual
    Psychology
% Marven O. Nelson, Ed.D.
8 Valley View Terrace
Suffern, New York 10901

International Committee for Adlerian
    Summer Schools and Institutes
% Edna Nash
302-2020 Bellview Avenue
West Vancouver, B.C. Canada V7B 1B8

United States and Canada

North American Society of Adlerian
    Psychology
159 N. Dearborn Street
Chicago, Illinois 60601
(312/346-3458)

Publications

Individual Psychology News Letter
% Paul Rom
The Bungalow
6 Vale Rise
London, NW 11, 8SD England

Journal of Individual Psychology
Guy J. Manaster, Ph.D., Editor
Department of Educational Psychology
The University of Texas at Austin
Austin, Texas 78712

Individual Psychologist
B. Udelle Friedland, Ed.D., Editor
Coppen State College
2500 W. North Ave.
Baltimore, Maryland 21216

NASAP Newsletter
North American Society of Adlerian
    Psychology
159 N. Dearborn Street
Chicago, Illinois 60601

REGION I — WEST

Training Institutes

Alfred Adler Institute of the
    Mountain States
Box 8225, Idaho State University
Pocatello, Idaho 83209
(208/236-3156)

Mountain Institute for Mankind
Gold Hill
Boulder, Colorado 80302

Western Institute for Research
    and Training in Humanics
226 Stanford Avenue
Berkeley, California 94708
(415/524-4929)

Societies

Adlerian Society of Human Relations
5009 Guide Meridian Road
Bellingham, Washington 98225
(206/734-9424)

British Columbia Association of Adlerian
    Psychology
Box 33823 STN. D
Vancouver, B.C.
Canada V6J 4L6

California Adlerian Society
% Sue Brokaw
3117 Ravenwood Court
Fullerton, California 92635

Individual Psychology Society of Edmonton
% Edmonton Catholic School District
9807-106 Street
Edmonton, Alberta
Canada T5K 1C2

Oregon Society of Individual Psychology
% Maurice Bullard
1320 N.W. 13th
Corvallis, Oregon 97330

Puget Sound Adlerian Society
% Bill Kiskaddon
4404-242nd S.W.
Mountlake Terrace, Washington 98043
(206/776-9740)

Redwood Empire Adlerian Society
% Roberta Knuth
3260 Linwood Ave.
Santa Rosa, California 95404

Sacramento Area Adlerian Psychology
    Society
P.O. Box 609
Elk Grove, California 95624

San Francisco Bay Area Society for Adlerian
    Psychology
425 Grant Ave., Apt. #28
Palo Alto, California 94306

Family-Education Organizations

Family Education Centers of Hawaii
2950 Manoa Road
Honolulu, Hawaii 96822
(808/988-6544)

Family Study Groups of Orange County
% Chris Wood
15911 Diamond Street
Westminster, California 92683
(714/898-3296)

Laramie Institute of Family Education
% William L. Edwards, Ed.D.
255 N. 30 Street
Laramie, Wyoming 82070

REGION II — MIDWEST

Training Institutes

Alfred Adler Institute of Chicago
159 N. Dearborn Street
Chicago, Illinois 60601
(312/346-3458)

Alfred Adler Institute of Fort Wayne
1812 Fort Wayne National Bank Building
Fort Wayne, Indiana 46802
(219/422-9622)

Alfred Adler Institute of Minnesota
Suite 128, 5009 Excelsior Blvd.
Minneapolis, Minnesota 55416
(612/926-6511)

Rudolf Dreikurs Institute for Social Equality
1725 Emerson Ave. South
Minneapolis, Minnesota 55403

Societies

Individual Psychology Association of
    Indiana
1812 Fort Wayne National Bank Building
Fort Wayne, Indiana 46802
(219/422-9622)

Iowa Society of Adlerian Psychology
P.O. Box 1632
Cedar Rapids, Iowa 52406

Midwest Society of Individual Psychology
P.O. Box 1205
Maryland Heights
St. Louis County, Missouri 63043

Family-Education Organizations

Adlerian Family Education Association
109 East Grant Street
Minneapolis, Minnesota 55403

Alfred Adler Institute of St. Louis
P.O. Box 28402
St. Louis, Missouri 63141

Council for Ongoing Parent Education
5960 Winnetka Drive
Cincinnati, Ohio 45236

Family Education Association of Champaign
    County
% Barbara Brown
905 Westfield Drive
Champaign, Illinois 61820
(217/352-9591)

Family Education Association of West
    Central Indiana
P.O. Box 4072
Terre Haute, Indiana 47804

Family Education Center of Vermillion
    County
702 North Logan Avenue
Danville, Illinois 61832

Fort Wayne Family Education Association
526 Stratton Rd.
Fort Wayne, Indiana 46825

Parent Education Association
Ken Marlin, Associate Director
Box 18
Columbia, Missouri 65201

Rudolf Dreikurs Unit of Family Education
    Association
% Diane Kirschenbaum, President
3605 W. Davis
Skokie, Illinois 60076

West Suburban Unit of Family Education
    Association
701 Hitchcock
Lisle, Illinois 60532

REGION III — SOUTH

Training Institutes

Adlerian Summer Workshops
% Francis X. Walton
660 Townes Road
Columbia, South Carolina 29210

Institute for Creative Community Living
% Dr. Pattye Weaver Kennedy
2243 West Alabama
Houston, Texas 77098

Societies

Alabama Society of Adlerian Psychology
% Major John F. Bradwell
564 Alder Street
Maxwell AFB, Alabama 36113

Charleston Adlerian Society
% Mike Jones
67 Legare Street
Charleston, S.C. 29401

Columbia Adlerian Society
Jane W. Lawther, President
107 Riverwood Dr., Apt. 101
Cayce, S.C. 29033

Florida Adlerian Society
2604 Darnell Circle
Tallahassee, Florida 32301

Texas Society of Adlerian Psychology
% Dayton Salisbury, S.S.J.
3535 Wheeler
Houston, Texas 77004
(713/747-9595)

Family-Education Organizations

Family Education of Tidewater, Inc.
P.O. Box 62668
Virginia Beach, Virginia 23462

Hillsborough Organization for Parent
    Education
% Jack Franklin
5020 Grace Street
Tampa, Florida 33607
(813/879-4854)

The Hub
Dekalb Resolution Center
5115 LaVista Road
Tucker, Georgia 30084

Irmo Family Education Association
% Andy Heen
1428 Nunamaker Drive
Columbia, South Carolina 29210

Educational-Services Organizations

Communication and Motivation Training
    Institute
% Don Dinkmeyer, Ph.D.
11061 N.W. 23 Court
Coral Springs, Florida 33065
(305/752-0793)

REGION IV — MIDDLE-ATLANTIC

Training Institutes

The Adler-Dreikurs Institute of Human
  Relations
Harold V. McAbee, Director
Bowie State College
Bowie, Maryland 20715

Alfred Adler Center of Cleveland
14625 Detroit Ave., Suite 203
Lakewood, Ohio 44107

Alfred Adler Institute of Dayton
122 E. Apple Street
Dayton, Ohio 45409
(513/274-6329)

Alfred Adler Institute of Toledo
% Keith Wiggins
857 Maple Lane
Waterville, Ohio 43566

Societies

Individual Psychology Association of
  Greater Washington, Inc.
Box 11
Garrett Park, Maryland 20766

Johns Hopkins Adlerian Society
Box 1380, Johns Hopkins University
Charles and 34th Streets
Baltimore, Maryland 21218

New Jersey Society of Adlerian Psychology
377 South Harrison Street
East Orange, New Jersey 07018
(201/676-2647)

Northmont Society of Individual Psychology
% Richard Curtner
976 Kenbrook Drive
Vandalia, Ohio 45377

Family-Education Organizations

Family Education Association
2507 Spencer Road
Silver Spring, Maryland 20910

Family Education Association of Greater
  Baltimore
4607 Hawksbury Road
Baltimore, Maryland 21208

Family Education Center
% C. C. Presbyterian Church
3120 Belair Drive
Bowie, Maryland 20715

Family Education Center of Delaware, Inc.
4900 Concord Pike
Wilmington, Delaware 19803

REGION V — NORTHEAST

Training Institutes

Alfred Adler Institute of New York
37 West 65th Street
New York, N.Y. 10023
(212/874-2427)

Alfred Adler Institute of Ontario
4 Finch Ave. West, Suite 10
Willowdale, Ontario
Canada M2N 2G5

Alfred Adler Institute of Rhode Island
% Woonsocket Family and Child Service
8 Court Street
Woonsocket, R.I. 02895
(401/762-5656)

Alfred Adler Mental Hygiene Clinic
37 West 5th Street
New York, N.Y. 10023

Societies

The Adlerian Psychology Association of
  Montreal
% Mrs. Liliane Bensinger, Coordinator
4939 Grosvenor Ave.
Montreal, Quebec
Canada H3W 2M2
(514/731-5675)

Individual Psychology Association of New
  York
37 West 65th Street
New York, N.Y. 10023

Family-Education Organizations

Family Education Center
100 Mansfield Ave.
Burlington, Vermont 05401

300

Greater Providence Family Education Center
P.O. Box 9012
Providence, Rhode Island 02904
(401/949-3648)

Rhode Island Family Education Centers, Inc.
Woonsocket Family Education Center
8 Court Street
Woonsocket, Rhode Island 02895
(401/762-5656)

INTERNATIONAL ASSOCIATION OF INDIVIDUAL PSYCHOLOGY

Austria

Society for Individual Psychology
% Dr. Erwin Ringel
Psychiatr. Universitats Klinik
Lazarettgasse 14
1090 Vienna

Denmark

The Danish Society of Individual
    Psychology
% Inge Born Rasmussen, M.D.
Sortedams Dosseringen 29
2200 Copehagen N

England

The Adlerian Society of Great Britain
% Neil R. Beattie, M.D.
Coniston House
36 Dobbins Lane
Wendover, Bucks.

France

French Society for Individual Psychology
% Herbert Schaffer, M.D.
28 rue des Archives
75004 Paris

Germany

German Society for Individual Psychology
% Prof. Dr. phil. Wolfgang Metzger
am untren Tor 5
Bebenhausen
D-7400 Tubingen 8

% Dr. med. Rainer Schmidt
Ludwigsalle 5
D-5100 Aachen

Greece

Greek Society of Adlerian Studies
% Mrs. Fifi Vervelidis
Semitelou Str. 6
Athens 611

Israel

International Association of Individual
    Psychology
% Achi Yotam
15 Ester Hamalka St.
Tel-Aviv

Society of Individual Psychology of Israel
% Wera Mahler, Ph.D.
185 Dizengoff St.
Tel-Aviv

Italy

The Italian Society for Individual
    Psychology
% Prof. Francesco Parenti
Piazza Irnerio 2
20146 Milano

Netherlands

Netherlands Society for Individual
    Psychology
% drs. H. W. von Sasson
A. C. Kerckhofflaan 14
Zeist

Switzerland

Swiss Society for Individual Psychology
% Erik Blumenthal
Kippenhorn 3
D-7759 Immenstaad/Bodensee

United States

International Association of Individual
    Psychology
% Dr. Bernard Shulman
2913 No. Commonwealth
Chicago, IL. 60657

INDEX